FAKETOSHI

Fraud, Lies and the Battle for Bitcoin's Soul

Volume I

Mark Hunter & Arthur van Pelt

Copyright © 2025 Mark Hunter & Arthur van Pelt

All rights reserved.

No part of this publication may be reproduced, stored in a retrieval system, or transmitted in any form or by any means – electronic, mechanical, photocopying, recording, or otherwise – without the prior written permission of the publisher or authors, except as permitted by UK copyright law.

ISBN: 9781068475511

Published by Tulip Publishing
27 Sutton Grange Close,
Harrogate,
North Yorkshire,
HG3 2UR,
United Kingdom

First Edition, 2025

Also by Mark Hunter

Ultimate Catastrophe: How MtGox Lost Half a Billion Dollars and Nearly Killed Bitcoin

About the Authors

Mark Hunter is an author and ghostwriter with twenty years of experience in the literary world. He has ghostwritten for a very eclectic range of clients, from members of the Kuwaiti royal family to self-made millionaires, and has worked as a writing workshop leader in British theatres.

Mark became interested in the cryptocurrency world in 2017 and has been writing for blockchain projects and crypto news websites ever since. In 2023, he published *Ultimate Catastrophe: How MtGox Lost Half a Billion Dollars and Nearly Killed Bitcoin*, the first book covering the 2014 collapse of Bitcoin exchange MtGox.

Mark lives in Harrogate, England, with his wife and two children.

Arthur van Pelt learned about Bitcoin in 2012 and now works as a Bitcoin consultant. Having first heard about Craig Wright in 2015, Arthur became more interested in his activities in 2019 and soon began mapping out the depth and breadth of Wright's operations to an ever-increasing audience through online channels, including Medium and X. He is now regarded as the most knowledgeable and dedicated Craig Wright debunker on the planet.

Arthur lives in the Netherlands with his two children.

Contents

Authors' Notes vi
A Word on Impartiality and Accuracy viii
Introduction xi
Chapter 1 – A Man of Conviction 17
Chapter 2 – A Matter of Time 30
Chapter 3 – Genesis 44
Chapter 4 – Building Bitcoin 54
Chapter 5 – Life on the Mining Farm 75
Chapter 6 – A Taxing Situation 89
Chapter 7 – Satoshi Bows Out 97
Chapter 8 – D.I.V.O.R.C.E 113
Chapter 9 – From Panama to Panopticrypt 129
Chapter 10 – Planting Tulips 138
Chapter 11 – The Professor Rees Affair 161
Chapter 12 – Welcome to Bitcoin 170
Chapter 13 – The $57 Million Swindle 181
Chapter 14 – A Miner Issue 192
Chapter 15 – Failure to Launch 207
Chapter 16 – The Hacker Hacked 216
Chapter 17 – The ATO Strikes Back 234
Chapter 18 – A Wicked Deed 252
Chapter 19 – Call Me Satoshi 266
Acknowledgements 275
References 276

Authors' Notes

There are a few things that need explaining with regard to Bitcoin and Craig Wright's story before we begin. These will be addressed here.

Nomenclature

Naturally, this book uses the word 'Bitcoin' throughout, but there are different meanings attached to Bitcoin depending on how it is spelt:

- 'Bitcoin' – the system, overarching concept or brand
- 'bitcoin/s' – the coins/currency transmitted on the system

There is no concrete agreement on the plural of 'bitcoin', but seeing as Satoshi Nakamoto used the term 'bitcoins' to refer to multiple coins, that is good enough for us.

All references to dollars refer to Australian (AUS) dollars unless specified otherwise.

Court cases

Craig Wright has been involved in more than a dozen court cases in his life, many of which include testimony on the topics we discuss in this book. We will cover most of these court cases chronologically at the appropriate time, but Wright's version of history on the same topic can change from case to case and, thus, over time. We have, therefore, tried to strike a balance between discussing too many elements of cases not yet covered and the desire to illustrate Wright's changing narrative over those topics. There will be occasions, therefore, when we discuss elements from later cases to reinforce a point and occasions when we intentionally leave out a change in the narrative until the coverage of that particular case. We hope the reader will understand our rationale on this front.

In 2023, several of Craig Wright's UK cases were amalgamated into one – the Identity Issue trial – which spurred off the *COPA v Wright* case. To avoid confusion, we will refer to this case and trial throughout as the *COPA v Wright* case/trial.

Quotes

Many of the quotes in this book are posts from social media platforms and online forums. The nature of these posts means that spelling and grammar will be erratic. It is standard practice to use '[sic]' to indicate when a word has been copied in its original, misspelt form, but given the sheer volume of quotes used in this book, this would be impractical.

As such, all quotes have been faithfully reproduced except where corrections are required to ensure comprehension.

A Word on Impartiality and Accuracy

As outspoken critics of Craig Wright, Arthur and I have received our fair share of insults and even death threats over the years, with our assailants taking after their hero who has threatened his enemies with financial ruin, prison and even physical harm. We are routinely accused of ignoring evidence and incidents from Wright's past in order to shape our version of events to suit a bias, but all too often, these accusations come from individuals who are unaware of many of the elements of Wright's story. While we freely admit that we are convinced that Craig Wright is not Satoshi, we have come to this conclusion based on the same facts that have also convinced multiple judges that Wright's claim is bogus. These same facts will be laid out across this series of books for readers to make up their own minds, facts that are supplemented with witness testimony, forensic document examination and more, much of which has survived courtroom cross-examination. In contrast, Wright's ever-changing Satoshi story is typically backed with either invalidated evidence or no evidence at all, and if one removes these, his account is only supported by a sole precept: the word of Craig Wright. This is particularly problematic given that these same judges have unanimously found that Wright persistently lies under oath.

Another arrow in the hide of the bias argument is that, unlike Wright's supporters who try to brush uncomfortable events and rulings under the carpet, we have gone to great lengths to state Wright's side of the story. Wherever possible, we have noted Wright's rebuttals to accusations of evidence forging and other misdemeanours, chiefly because they hold little to no weight and often further undermine his case. If we have neglected to offer a rebuttal, it is likely due to us not having found one in our research. These attempts were made harder in early 2024 when, in the wake of his catastrophic defeat to the Cryptocurrency Open Patent Alliance (COPA), Wright removed five years' worth of blog posts at a stroke. At the same time, one of Wright's core mouthpieces, the sycophantic 'news' website *CoinGeek*, removed hundreds of news articles, interviews and videos which referenced Wright's Satoshi claim. This made tracking down his historical arguments and statements all the more challenging. Another difficulty in reporting on Craig Wright is that he treats his Satoshi story with a fluidity that all but his most ardent supporters find damning, often augmenting long-standing stories with suddenly remembered events. Where possible, we have pointed out where a story has changed over time. We would strenuously deny any claim that we have deliberately neglected to feature an event, comment or piece of evidence, and further editions will address serious omissions where appropriate.

One of the most common accusations against Arthur and me is that we are being paid to denigrate Craig Wright by those with a vested interest in maintaining Bitcoin's status quo. Wright and his supporters believe that the leadership of Bitcoin was ceded to a collection of corporate monoliths who are intentionally kneecapping its performance for their own financial gain, which has led to everyone from MasterCard to Jeffrey Epstein allegedly helping to fund Wright's critics, including us. This is typical of both the belief structure that Wright has fostered and the type of people that have bought into it; as with political or religious zealots, there is nothing we can say that will assuage the negative opinions this group has of us and our motives. This is despite facts, court rulings and sheer plausibility being firmly in our favour. The irony is that many of these critics are actually in the pay of Wright's backers, either directly as commentators or through the funding of their projects on Wright's blockchain, Bitcoin Satoshi Vision (BSV). All we can say is that we do not, and have never, received a penny from any outfit for deliberately creating negative content about Craig Wright, BSV and the related ecosystem. We believe the facts speak for themselves and are confident that they, combined with our other research, stand on their own merits.

Introduction

On 20 May 2024, IT security consultant Craig Wright entered the pantheon of British legal history when he was outed as one of the most prolific evidence forgers of all time. According to The Honourable Mr Justice Mellor, judge of the Chancery Division of the UK High Court, during his battle against the COPA, Wright forged or manipulated almost every single piece of evidence presented in the case across nearly all possible mediums, representing a catalogue of malfeasance that surpassed 500 in number. In addition to this, Wright was found to have committed 'wholesale perjury' throughout his time in the witness box, leading to his case being referred to the Crown Prosecution Service (CPS) for assessment of criminal charges. This festival of fabrication had one goal toward which Wright had been working for over a decade: to prove he was Satoshi Nakamoto, the creator of Bitcoin.

Wright's obsession with being hailed as Bitcoin's creator was fuelled by two motives: to make himself one of the richest men on Earth and to prove his plentiful doubters wrong. Had he been legally recognised as Satoshi Nakamoto, Wright would have ripped the rug out from underneath the entire Bitcoin ecosystem, claiming personal ownership of every aspect of the asset. Bitcoin itself, in the form it had occupied since its launch in 2009, would have ceased to exist, with Wright's vehicle, Bitcoin Satoshi Vision (BSV), taking its place. The impact on the multi-trillion-dollar Bitcoin ecosystem would have been nothing less than catastrophic; hundreds of companies that rely on Bitcoin's status quo would have folded, while those that survived would have been forced to license the Bitcoin name and software from Wright's companies if they still wanted to utilise it, as well as pay massive damages. Wright and his backers would have been billionaires many times over as a result, a vision they had been trying to realise ever since Wright first burst onto the scene as a Satoshi candidate in 2015. There was only one problem with Wright's Satoshi claim, however: it was completely and utterly fictional.

Wright's defeat to COPA brought a decisive end to his years-long crusade, marked by grandiose promises to seize control of Bitcoin by wielding his alleged identity as its creator like a sword of Damocles. This audacious cosplay has its roots in a battle with the Australian Taxation Office (ATO), which ran between 2009 and 2016. The agency alleged that throughout this period, Wright attempted to defraud it out of almost ten million dollars in tax rebates and deductions, and, faced with penury after having these payouts withheld, Wright donned the Satoshi mask in a last-ditch attempt to exculpate himself from imminent bankruptcy and possible criminal action. Inexplicably, Wright's Hail Mary worked, and he secured funding to launch a company in the UK aimed at monetising his supposed creation.

A disastrous attempt to publicly prove his Satoshiness in 2016 led to Wright and his backers using the UK's generous libel laws and their financial muscle to try to obtain a legal ruling that Wright was Satoshi Nakamoto. However, rather than obtaining a license to print money, Wright's backers received nothing but ruinous legal bills as his multifarious lies were brutally exposed case by case, while Wright himself was handed a General Civil Restraint Order (GCRO), the most extreme restraint order it is possible to receive in Britain. COPA's lawyers accused Wright of presenting an 'elaborate false narrative supported by forgery on an industrial scale' in an attempt to prove his case, and this was no exaggeration; Bird & Bird, the internationally renowned law firm hired by COPA, could find nothing in the annals of British legal history that even came close to the colossal levels of fraud Wright perpetrated in the *COPA v Wright* case. It is no overstatement to suggest that Wright's record in this regard will likely never be matched.

To those steeped in Wright's chequered past, his ignominious end in 2024 represented a fitting – and wholly predictable – conclusion to more than a decade of staggering charlatanism. His failed ten-year battle to assume the identity of Bitcoin's pseudonymous creator is breathtaking in its scope and magnitude. In addition to the 500-plus forgeries seen in the *COPA v Wright* case alone, Wright is thought to have fabricated or manipulated at least another 500 for court cases on three continents between 2013 and 2024, during which time he attempted to defraud the legal systems of multiple countries as well as the U.S. Copyright Office as part of his plan to assume the mantle of Bitcoin's creator. For ten years, Wright managed to convince very intelligent people to ignore the mounting inconsistencies in his story and back him both morally and financially to a remarkable degree, leading them to pour hundreds of millions of dollars into his empire, all of it utterly wasted. Despite this, some inexplicably continue to stand by Wright and his Satoshi claim, often echoing his own excuses that external forces, from multinational corporations to governments, are desperate to silence him out of fear for the revolutionary nature of his technology.

Wright's talent for attracting idealistic followers and well-heeled backers lies in his knack for storytelling; like all good cult leaders and con men, he has an undeniable gift for persuasion. Since 2015, Wright has successfully sold thousands of credulous individuals on the notion that he is an oppressed genius trying to fight the established order that overthrew him in Bitcoin's earliest days following his creation of the cryptocurrency. It doesn't matter that Wright's claims are backed by either forged evidence or no evidence whatsoever; his followers still swallow what he says without question, parroting the notion that anyone who doubts him is either in the pay of Bitcoin's overlords or is scared of the damage Wright could do to the bastardised ecosystem in which Bitcoiners put their faith and their money. He and they want to kill Bitcoin and have Wright's version replace it, seeing as it represents – in their eyes – the only version of Bitcoin true to Satoshi's principles. Wright's supporters still dream that Bitcoin will one day crash to zero and BSV will replace it, making them instant millionaires. Similar to a rapture, they argue that the few staunch Wright believers will be saved while everyone else will be sent to financial purgatory. Their chances today are more remote than ever.

Between 2015 and 2024, Craig Wright was able to forge an astonishingly lucrative career by pretending he was Satoshi Nakamoto, one that allowed him to live a life of luxury without ever actually managing to prove his claim. Since he first put finger to keyboard in this regard, Wright has lied to all and sundry about his Satoshiness through interviews, conferences and countless thousands of social media posts on various platforms, augmenting this overarching lie with a plethora of grandiose claims to emphasise his suitability for the task. These include that he has a higher IQ than Albert Einstein, Stephen Hawking and Marie Curie; that he has earned over thirty postgraduate degrees, including Master's and doctoral degrees; and that he was the victim of Britain's biggest heist (over US$1 billion). He has also made multiple baseless and often vile accusations against his critics, including that Bitcoin's early developers facilitated the proliferation of child pornography. These slanderous claims, and dozens more, were exposed during Wright's ill-fated attempts to legally gag his critics, during which he was never able to back them up with evidence and typically only made them in situations where legal privilege prevented those he detracted from taking action.

If there is one thing to be said in Wright's favour, it is the dedication he has shown to his Satoshi act. From the first time he referred to himself as Bitcoin's creator in January 2014 to his shambolic performance in the witness box during the *COPA v Wright* trial exactly ten years later, Wright maintained the Satoshi façade in front of family members, five-figure audiences and judges the world over. In this respect, he can have no equal. There have been con men, of course, but their efforts typically extend no further than their own scams, some of which are absurdly simple and require little research. Craig Wright, on the other hand, played a character for a full decade, being paid handsomely to do a job under the guise that he was someone else in the hope of a trillion-dollar payday. As we will see, Wright's decision to slip on the Satoshi mask was supposed to be a private thing, known only to the men who peddled his lies for profit and afforded him a rescue package that literally kept him from falling into a life of destitution.

Wright's Satoshi claim was never supposed to get out, or at least not until he was financially secure enough to let the mask slip away. That all changed in 2015, however, when two outlets announced him to the world as a potential Satoshi candidate. This led to Wright walking a tightrope for the next eight and a half years until he finally came off in 2024. Wright may have so far avoided jail for his fraudulent activities, but he has come close, having twice been found guilty of contempt of court; in 2006, he maintained his liberty only because of judicial leniency, while in 2024, he fled to Asia following defeat to COPA before the contempt charges were levelled. Had he remained in the UK, he would have been jailed for twelve months. At the time of writing, however, the CPS is still weighing up potential perjury charges, so Wright's liberty may yet still be threatened. Also hanging over him is the more than US$145 million he owes in judgments and litigation costs from his legal entanglements, although he has shown no intention of ever paying these.

One of the hardest things about telling the Craig Wright story is knowing how to actually do it. The depths to which Wright sunk in order to try and cheat his way to his goals, which he compounded with further maleficence when his initial lies were exposed, leads to the literary equivalent of wrestling a whale; it is so big and slippery that you just don't know where to start. Focusing on one particular area means neglecting others of equal or greater intrigue, with a risk of the whole undermining its constituent parts. It is a story that contains allegations of multi-million-dollar tax fraud and thefts, computer hacking, witness tampering, unrivalled levels of forgery and perjury, Bletchley Park codebreakers, supercomputers, bonded couriers and much, much more. Many of these are worthy of a book all on their own, and yet they all represent different aspects of the activities of one man throughout one decade, all in the pursuit of riches and recognition for something he had no part in.

Arthur and I began our podcast series documenting Craig Wright's activities, *Dr Bitcoin – The Man Who Wasn't Satoshi Nakamoto*, in late 2021, hoping to chronicle his life and crimes in an easy-to-digest manner. In order to achieve this, we had to leave out some truly staggering stories from Wright's past that exemplify his shamelessness, incompetence and disregard for the rule of law. It is impossible to do justice to the entirety of Wright's chequered career in one book without it being bigger than the bookshelf on which it would sit, so we have decided to tackle it in three volumes: Volume I covers Wright's early years and his alleged tax fraud in Australia, which ended in 2015 when he moved to the UK; Volume II will cover Wright's new life in London, his disastrous attempt to prove his Satoshi candidacy in 2016, and the US$600 billion *Kleiman v Wright* lawsuit; and Volume III will tackle Wright's legal campaigns of 2019-2024, which ended in his defeat to COPA, a criminal conviction and a restraint order. Along the way, we will see him fake multi-million-dollar contracts with a porn baron and a dementia patient, claim to have been infiltrated almost a dozen times by everyone from globally renowned gangs to his own employees and proclaim to be an expert in everything from ancient philosophy to Chinese notepad manufacturing.

Given that I compared tackling Wright's story to wrestling a whale, the tale of *Moby Dick* comes to mind when considering how to start the saga. Wright's pursuit of recognition as Satoshi Nakamoto is not unlike Captain Ahab's pursuit of the white whale, with many suggesting that Wright, too, has been dragged to madness through his single-minded quest. We should end this introduction, therefore, with a quote from the famous captain, which neatly sums up Wright's approach to his ultimate goal of recognition as Bitcoin's creator:

It is the easiest thing in the world for a man to look as if he had a great secret in him.

Sharpen your harpoons, shipmates, and let's set sail.

Mark Hunter
Harrogate

August 2025

Chapter 1 – A Man of Conviction

Craig Steven Wright was born on 23 October 1970 in Chermside, a suburb of Brisbane, Australia. The Wrights were a Catholic family, with Craig growing up alongside his older sister, Lisa, and his younger sister, Danielle, with half-sisters entering his life in later years. Their neighbourhood was populated by people Wright later classed as 'absolutely poor white trash' and where 'half the people I knew were now drug dealers or bikie members'. Wright seems to have had a good relationship with Danielle, but in 2019, he likened his relationship with Lisa to 'oil, water, petrol and a match'. Lisa, in turn, has distanced herself from Craig and his activities despite the pair both working in the cryptocurrency sector.

If this relationship was combustible, then the relationship between the entire family and its patriarch, Frederick, was a forest fire. Wright says that Frederick, a Vietnam War veteran, was a changed man when he returned from the conflict, turning to drink and becoming verbally, and then physically, abusive to the children's mother, Julie Archer; abuse which soon extended to the children. Indeed, a 2020 psychological report on Wright alluded to these experiences:

> *Dr. Wright and his siblings were exposed to, and experienced, traumatizing events attributed to his biological father, and, subsequently, to one of his stepfathers.*

Wright told author Andrew O'Hagan for a piece called 'The Satoshi Affair', published in June 2016, that he was 'never admired' by his father, who made the young Wright feel that he was 'never fucking good enough'. This sentiment allegedly played a part in the date Wright chose to release the Bitcoin whitepaper in 2008, as he tweeted on its fifteenth anniversary:

My father told me I would never succeed. 31 Oct is his birthday. Now you know why I released Bitcoin that day. Happy birthday dad. FU.

Wright's decision to memorialise his abusive father over his loving mother, who Wright once called an 'amazing woman', was almost certainly a misguided attempt to capitalise on a coincidence. It also doesn't check out: the Bitcoin whitepaper was released on 31 October 2008 at 2.10 p.m. Eastern Daylight Time, which would have been 5.10 a.m. on 1 November in Sydney. Wright had already addressed this three years before the aforementioned tweet, where we encounter the first case of him rewriting history:

The Bitcoin whitepaper was not published on October 31, 2008 as many falsely suppose. For a start it was distributed are not published and in fact had been sent or distributed to a number of other people prior to this date. More importantly, it was in fact sent on November 1, 2008. It could have been sent earlier but I was still working at BDO.

Frederick and Julie divorced when Wright was five, with Julie keeping the three children. However, in line with the repressive attitudes of the Catholic religion, the foursome was ostracised by their local church and the community, making life even tougher. This ostracism left Wright with a 'chip on his shoulder', as he told O'Hagan, but the impact may have been more severe. Dr Ami Klin, the author of Wright's psychological report, opined that Wright's childhood trauma left him with a burning desire to succeed and a craving for public recognition from a young age. This has undoubtedly played out in Wright's adult life, with many assigning his pursuit of wealth and desire for dominion over the entire crypto space to this facet of his personality. As we will see, however, this drive to be perceived as rich, highly successful and supremely intelligent led to Wright taking shortcuts that have left him with a criminal conviction and owing hundreds of millions of dollars in legal settlements and bills, with the prospect of more to come. The only recognition he has received outside his curated bubble of supporters is as a serial fraudster and incompetent evidence forger.

Julie was forced to work multiple jobs in order to keep the family afloat, leading to Wright spending 'six days out of seven' with his maternal grandfather, Ronald Lynam. Ronald's son, Donald, described his father and how his interests impacted Wright in a 2020 deposition for the *Kleiman v Wright* case:

> *My father was a radio engineer and so he had a whole lot of technical paraphernalia there, which Craig found absolutely intriguing, and he spent all the time he could with [his] grandfather.*

During their many hours together, Wright got hands-on experience with radios and telecom equipment in Ronald's workshop, and it was Ronald who introduced Wright to Japanese culture, a fascination that grew with age, leading to Wright wearing samurai clothes out in public and learning karate, judo and Ninjutsu. During the *COPA v Wright* trial in 2024, Danielle vividly retold an episode from their youth where she and some friends were frightened away from a park by a man dressed as a ninja and performing related moves, which turned out to be Craig Wright. Indeed, Dr Klin told in his report how Wright 'could be observed [at the] playground alone, dressed as a ninja and playing as if he was the weirdest person in the world.' It was Donald, however, who would have the biggest impact on Wright, growing into a father figure for the youngster, who was enthralled by his uncle's position as Wing Commander in the Royal Australian Air Force (RAAF).

In 'The Satoshi Affair', which blew Wright's Satoshi claims wide open when it was published, Julie admitted that as a child, Wright had a 'long-standing habit of adding bits on to the truth, just to make it bigger'. Andrew O'Hagan, who spent seven months in Wright's orbit for the piece, recognised something of this during their time together:

> *In what he said, he often went further than he needed to; further than he ought to have done. He appeared to start with the truth, and then, slowly, he would inflate his part until the whole story suddenly looked weak.*

Justice Mellor made a similar observation in his *COPA v Wright* ruling:

> *It is sometimes said that a good lie contains a kernel of truth. In my judgment, on many and frequent occasions, Dr Wright adhered to this proposition. I sensed there was often something in his answer which was true, but the answer as a whole was a plain lie or not an answer to the question put.*

We have seen dozens of examples of this over the years, but a very vivid one relates to Wright's purported reading prowess. In 2019, Wright boasted to his followers that he had read 15,500 books up to that point, which equates to more than one book per day for every day of his life from the age of four. Not satisfied with such a Herculean task, Wright went further, claiming that he was able to remember the text on the pages of the books he had read, too. Two years later, Wright augmented this incredible claim by stating in an interview to have read 2,400 books in 2020 alone, an average of six and a half per day. When asked how this was possible, Wright told the interviewer, 'I read very fast' and that 'some books are smaller than others'. In that same interview, Wright claimed that when he wasn't reading, he was busy writing, clocking up almost three million words in the same time frame – equating to more than 8,000 per day – thanks in large part to the twenty-plus degrees he claimed to be studying simultaneously. All this was accomplished while carrying out his duties as Chief Scientist of the British blockchain company nChain. It's safe to say that Wright's critics are not convinced of this achievement.

Wright attended Everton Park State High School in North Brisbane between the ages of thirteen and fifteen, where he 'topped the state in Australian math and physics tests'. However, his mother moved him to the nearby Padua College because, in Wright's words, he 'had other problems and the school had difficulty with me'. It was here, Wright says, that he was diagnosed with Asperger's Syndrome:

> *In Padua College, when I started having problems...they saw how I was doing in math and couldn't understand, so the school psychologist had me tested and told me I had Asperger's.*

To assess this claim, we have to do some brief time-hopping. Wright made this statement during the *Kleiman v Wright* trial in 2021, five years after he and his family had discussed Wright's past with Andrew O'Hagan for 'The Satoshi Affair', conversations which included Wright's apparent neurodivergence. However, there are no mentions in O'Hagan's piece of any such diagnosis or even a hint of one. Three years later, in a June 2019 deposition for the *Kleiman v Wright* case, Wright claimed, 'I'm actually autistic, and I have what most people commonly mislabel as Asperger's, although I'm high-functioning.' If Wright thought the Padua School psychologist had misdiagnosed him, he didn't say so, once again not relating the alleged diagnosis. Nine months later, Dr Klin was asked to assess Wright for Autism Spectrum Disorder (ASD) specifically for the *Kleiman v Wright* case, where Wright would almost certainly have told him about the Padua College diagnosis. Dr Klin diagnosed Wright with ASD, but not once in his extensive report, which detailed Wright's behavioural difficulties and differences in childhood and young adulthood, did he report Wright claiming to have had a prior diagnosis of ASD or Asperger's. Only after Dr Klin's diagnosis in April 2020 did Wright come out with the Padua College story.

Wright says that he moved colleges again at sixteen, this time to the Brisbane College of Advanced Education. Here, he says he attained his first degree, a Bachelor of Applied Science in Discrete Mathematics, in 1987, claiming that he was '16 [years old] for most of it' before graduating at seventeen. However, this achievement is entirely absent in the earliest formal record of Wright's education – his military record – where he is recorded as attending Everton Park between 1983 and 1985 and Padua College between 1986 and 1987, the latter of which saw him complete his high school education only. Wright's military record does not mention the Brisbane College of Advanced Education or his alleged degree, which are also absent from the education section of his LinkedIn profile. Of all people, Craig Wright would not have passed up the opportunity to crow about this achievement were it true.

In 2025, Wright boasted about his hardship and academic prowess at this tender age:

I went to shit schools. Not one or two—eleven schools before I made it out of year 12. Year twelve, I barely blinked at. I was already in university before the rest of them knew how to write a coherent paragraph. While they were prepping for exams, I was already tearing through first-year law and reading Wittgenstein for sport.

There is no evidence of Wright attending so many schools during this period, however, while his university studies began in 1988, the same year as his contemporaries.

Wright was inducted into the Australian Air Force Cadets at fifteen, following in Don Lynam's footsteps by applying to the Australian Defence Force Academy to train as a pilot the year after, but he was rejected for unspecified reasons. Perhaps tellingly, the mandatory psychologist's report, which should have appeared in Wright's file, was replaced with a blank sheet of paper. Nevertheless, Wright maintained during the *Kleiman v Wright* trial that at this tender age he 'helped redesign a parts database for the F-111s' for the

RAAF because he 'had family there'. Wright was a busy boy in 1985: alongside his studies and his database work for the RAAF, he allegedly worked in the IT department of the Australian department store Kmart and embarked on his coding journey, as he relayed in 2023:

> *My fascination with coding and computing began when I dabbled with C and C++ around the age of eight or nine. By age 11, l had already started writing code for games. I used C and C++ because they were the languages that games were written in.*

This sequence of events is impossible, however, because C++ wasn't released to the public until Wright was fifteen. When he was challenged over this during the *COPA v Wright* trial, Wright insisted that he was talking about precursor languages, not C++ itself, but Justice Mellor ruled that Wright's explanations were 'either wholly or partially fabricated' on the matter.

Wright must have been a proficient coder as well as a time-travelling one; he claimed to have sold his first videogame just a year after first experimenting with computer languages before working for a game developer called Thermonuclear WarGames. Wright expanded on this in an interview for *CoinGeek TV* in 2021:

> *I was a code tester for Buckaroo Banzai. A horrible movie came out of it, too. There was also Kangaroo Jack – that was also horrible. I have this habit where any game I was involved in was horrible.*

This story was augmented three weeks later when Wright told his followers that in the 1980s, he had been 'on a team of a company EA games took over' and added that he was mentioned in the credits of the game. However, this is almost certainly not true: Kangaroo Jack wasn't released until 2003 and was developed by Tantalus Interactive, not Thermonuclear WarGames, while Buckaroo Banzai, released in 1983, was created by Florida-based developer Adventure International. Adventure International founder Scott Adams explained in an email to a source that the idea of his company utilising the services of a thirteen-year-old Australian boy to help code the game was improbable:

> *The name Craig Wright is not familiar to me. The Buckaroo Adventure game was done in-house by a number of my employees and I oversaw the effort at the time.*

Wright enrolled at the University of Queensland in 1988, where he studied for a joint degree in Electrical Engineering and a Bachelor of Science in Computer Science (if he was 'tearing through first-year law', therefore, he was doing it in his own time). He held down two jobs to financially support himself at this time, one of which was 'gutting chickens'. However, Wright dropped out of this course in 1992 on medical grounds, having discovered a melanoma on his back for which he underwent treatment. Wright says that the melanoma was at stage four when it was caught, telling an interviewer in 2020 that he was given three months to live if he didn't start treatment immediately. Indeed, at stage four, the cancer would have spread beyond the original site and into lymph nodes and internal organs, giving him around a 22% chance of survival, according to the website curemelanoma.org. However, Julie Archer appears to have played down the illness to Andrew O'Hagan, saying, 'This was after he got out of the air force, and when he recovered he was off to university.' Wright claims that he discovered the melanoma while with the RAAF, which clashes with his 1989 re-application, where he was accepted into a nine-year officership program to study electrical engineering, beginning his first semester in 1990 as an Officer Cadet. Wright's records show that he passed one class, Law of War, and didn't pass any engineering or maths classes, although there is the chance, as we saw with his rejected pilot's application, that these records are incomplete. Wright was again released on medical grounds seven months into his course, having completed – but apparently failed – a lone semester. In 1996, Wright claimed that this release was due to a 'conf[l]ict of interests'.

Wright says that after his release from the RAAF, he 'earned money by doing whatever I could get', including working in a petrol station, while still studying at the University of Queensland. In the mid-1990s, Wright became a member of the cypherpunk movement, the growing online community of libertarians who were using the advent of the Internet to further their battle for privacy. In fact, in 2019, Wright claimed not just to have used the fulcrum of this movement, the Cypherpunks Mailing List, on a regular basis, but to have been 'one of the first people' to do so, a claim that is easy to make but impossible to verify. The cypherpunk movement defended freedom of expression, access to information and privacy as basic rights that should be protected and promoted by technology and cryptography, something that was quickly becoming a reality rather than just a theory thanks to the introduction of the Internet into homes around the world. This group of libertarians spawned several attempts at a decentralised currency, including David Chaum's 'Digicash', Wei Dai's 'B-money' and Nick Szabo's 'Bit Gold', all of which had either failed on launch or remained simply theoretical in nature. Wright engaged in discussions on the Cypherpunks Mailing List but left after less than a month because he 'couldn't stand people like Julian Assange' and their ultra-libertarian views. However, this complaint came after Wright had embarked on one of his famous grudges, so this may be nothing more than an extension of that. Wright has also since claimed that Bitcoin's creation had nothing to do with the cypherpunk movement, a claim we'll assess soon.

Around the time he was trying, and failing, to ingratiate himself into the cypherpunk world, Wright began chatting online with Carol Lynn Black, then a nursing manager at a military hospital in Ottawa, Canada. The pair hit it off right away, despite an eighteen-year age gap, and Wright proposed to the forty-four-year-old just six weeks later. To Andrew O'Hagan, Lynn said that Wright 'always has to be the best', adding that he 'stepped on people' and 'left bodies by the wayside' in order to get what he wanted. This, she said, was down to his 'very sociopathic personality', something that Wright would come to demonstrate during their coupledom and in the years after its termination. Craig and Lynn married the same year, with Lynn moving to Australia shortly afterwards and beginning a new life as Mrs Wright. 1996 also saw Craig create his first two companies: Vin De La Terre Pty Ltd, on 9 June 1996, which morphed into DeMorgan Information Security Systems Pty Ltd (DISS) on 17 December 2001, and Ridge's Estate Pty Ltd (Ridges Estate). The two companies would link up in 2002 when Ridges Estate joined the Wrights as majority owners of DISS. This represents the first time that Craig Wright would involve a spouse in his schemes, but it certainly wouldn't be the last.

In June 2003, the Wrights entered into an agreement with an associate, Michael Ryan, to sell 5% of DISS for an investment of $50,000, but in August, the Wrights resigned, handing Ryan the rest of the shares. Shortly after, Ryan discovered that the pair had breached the terms of their resignation by approaching DISS clients and touting for work, with Craig using his DISS email address to confer legitimacy on the offers. Ryan sued, leading to the Wrights counter-suing, claiming that they had been reappointed as directors in an 8 August meeting. However, no evidence of this meeting was ever produced, and the pair were banned from calling themselves directors of DISS and contacting DISS clients. This didn't stop Craig Wright, however: in 2004, he was dragged back to court again by Ryan, who accused him of ignoring the judge's ruling and continuing to solicit business from DISS's clients. Ryan cited email records, mobile phone logs, visitor sign-in logs and invoices Wright issued to the companies in question to illustrate the lengths he had gone to in order to steal the clients.

Wright was summoned to a three-day contempt of court hearing to address the allegations, where he relied on a defence that would become a staple of his legal affairs over the next two decades: other people had access to his machines, so the damning emails and phone logs could have been manipulated or fabricated by a third party. The judge didn't buy this defence, however, and Wright was handed a twenty-eight-day prison sentence, suspended on condition that he perform 250 hours of community service. In sentencing Wright, Judge Gzell made a comment that, like Wright's defence over third-party interference, was to be echoed down the years:

> *In my view Mr Wright's deliberate flouting of his undertaking makes this a serious offence. His lack of contrition exacerbates its seriousness. There is a need to bring home to a contemnor the seriousness of his contempt. For the purposes of the Crimes...these are my reasons for my determining that a sentence of imprisonment is required in this case.*

Wright appealed the ruling, expanding on his argument that his email account had been compromised, but the appeal judge ruled that 'The fabrication of such an email by an outsider without this being immediately detected by the recipient is glaringly improbable.' It's important to note that Wright put forward no potential candidates for the 'hack', the start of another pattern that would weave itself throughout Wright's chequered legal career. Wright wasn't finished yet, however; he took his objection all the way to the New South Wales Supreme Court, where, despite his submission of 'fresh evidence of a highly technical nature' over the incriminating email, his final petition was dismissed. Wright discussed this case during the *Granath v Wright* trial in 2022, where he refuted the suggestion that his sentence counted as a criminal conviction:

> *I was given a contempt of court, but it is not a conviction. It's not a crime in Australia; it's not a criminal offence.*

This is patently untrue; contempt of court is an offence under section 24 of the Local Court Act 2007 and section 199 of the District Court Act 1973 and carries, as Wright found out, a maximum penalty of twenty-eight days in prison. Wright went further during the same line of questioning and denied that he had been handed a twenty-eight-day suspended sentence at all before completely misremembering why he had incurred the wrath of the judge:

I was rather belligerent, and, unfortunately, the judge didn't like my attitude.

This was probably true, but court records show that it was Wright's utter lack of repentance and the lies he was accused of telling about the key email that really antagonised the judge.

Wright may have avoided jail over the DISS affair, but he was hit with a bankruptcy notice of $425,000 after DISS collapsed in the wake of his legal battle. The debt was bought by Michael Ryan's lawyer, Chris McArdle, who chased Wright for the payment for almost seven years before the pair finally settled in 2013, leaving Wright virtually penniless. McArdle said at the time of Wright's 'unmasking' as Satoshi Nakamoto in late 2015 that he was shocked to hear of a connection between Wright and the secretive creator of Bitcoin, saying that Wright simply 'existed in his own fantasy world' and didn't appear capable of accomplishing such a feat.

Outside of the DISS debacle, Wright was making strides in his career. His legal issues split a year-long stint with the Australian Securities Exchange (one of the clients he tried to pinch from DISS), where he worked on information security, and four years within the IT department of accounting firm BDO Kendalls (October 2004-December 2008). Wright says he held this position while remotely studying two master's degrees – a Master of Statistics at the University of Newcastle and an International Commercial Law at Northumbria University – saying of his time studying for the former that he 'did not put down that I was Satoshi' in his application, preferring to remain 'just another postgraduate researcher and student'. Wright says that during this same fruitful spell, he also worked on further Master's degrees in Systems Development and Information Systems Security at Charles Sturt University in Australia and a PhD in Computer Science from the same institution. It seems, however, that Wright didn't complete this course, given that the defendants in the *Tulip Trading Ltd v Bitcoin Association for BSV & Ors* were confident enough to claim in an April 2023 filing that 'Dr Wright does not have a computer science degree'. Wright also claimed to have spent three years concurrently studying psychology at Charles Sturt, although the results of this vague undertaking have never knowingly been publicised. Perhaps tellingly, Andrew O'Hagan commented on Wright's lack of staying power in 'The Satoshi Affair', which raises questions over his alleged educational successes:

> ...over the following 25 years [Wright] would finish, or not finish, or finish and not do the graduation paperwork for degrees in digital forensics, nuclear physics, theology, management, network security, international commercial law and statistics.

It's not a stretch, therefore, to believe that Wright has listed qualifications he hasn't actually attained on his CV, a theory that was backed up in 2024 when Justice Mellor considered that 'it would not come as a surprise to find that he had also engaged in significant exaggeration as to his degrees and qualifications'. The matter was partially cleared up in December 2015 when Charles Sturt University confirmed Wright's qualifications (or lack of them): no PhD in any subject, no Master's in Systems Development and no psychology degrees. Wright has also in the past claimed to have a doctorate in theology, and has even published the thesis he says led to it. However, he has never named the awarding university and told *The Economist* in 2016 that it held 'no relevance' anyway. These claims *do* hold relevance, however, because, in July 2021, Wright claimed to have been 'enrolled in up to 25 university qualifications simultaneously' and to have lost count of how many degrees he had earned (*The Economist* also revealed that Wright 'got most of his degrees via distance-learning programmes and in the other cases rarely went to lectures'). Wright has been more than keen to regale his social media followers and blog readers with the number of degrees, master's and other certifications he purports to have obtained, and at the time of the publication of this book, that number stands at over twenty-five postgraduate degrees and five doctorates. As we shall see as this story progresses, there are serious question marks over the authenticity of a number of these awards, and Volume II covers serious allegations of plagiarism over more than one dissertation used to achieve these qualifications.

In the late 1990s and into the 2000s, Wright began assisting in the development of the earliest online casinos, claiming in 2021 that 'all the operations that I was associated with were legally licensed and managed, and they monitored the activities of individuals who might have been addicted to gambling'. However, this was the dawn of the online gambling age, so it's highly doubtful that all the platforms Wright worked for were fully licensed, given that many countries simply didn't have licenses for that sort of thing at the time. Indeed, long-time associate Stefan Matthews confirmed as much when telling Andrew O'Hagan about emails that Wright had been reluctant to pass to the author:

> I know what's in there...It will be chatter to do with illegal stuff that he and Dave were doing in Costa Rica – particularly around Costa Rican casinos where they got $23 million of income. And you don't get paid that amount just for doing a security review.

Wright also boasted in a July 2018 tweet, referenced in an interview, that he was 'proud to have made my first $20 million before I was 30', expanding on this during the *Kleiman v Wright* trial, where he said that the money had come from 'an IPO back in the nineties where I had an Internet company that I listed'. There is no evidence that Wright ever possessed and then lost such a sum, however, with Wright never mentioning the name of the company, for perhaps obvious reasons.

Wright claims that the legal minefield of early online gambling regulations led him to request payment into a pseudo-bank called Liberty Reserve. Liberty Reserve was a payment processing platform founded by Costa Rican entrepreneur Arthur Budovsky, who had left the U.S. following a five-year prison sentence for illegally operating GoldAge, a forerunner of Liberty Reserve. Budovsky launched Liberty Reserve and its own currency, Liberty Reserve dollars, in 2006. Liberty Reserve dollars were pegged 1:1 with the U.S. dollar and allowed anyone to move money around without identity checks, using a global network of facilitators to act as offramps into real-world bank accounts. Naturally, this became hugely popular with criminals, including child pornographers and human traffickers, who could disguise and launder their income. We will look at Wright's alleged use of Liberty Reserve and the moral implications of his claims later in this book, but the notion that he transacted on the same platform as child pornographers and hackers is interesting, given his later criticism of Bitcoin for facilitating such crimes.

2003, the year in which Wright's battle with Ryan began, saw him encounter someone who would end up playing a bigger part in his life when dead than when he was alive. Wright met computer scientist David (Dave) Kleiman when the Floridian was contracted to work on a project for the Australian government. During the same period, Wright was involved in developing various software applications related to encryption and security. At this time, Kleiman was a contributor to computer security mailing lists such as those maintained by securityfocus.com and metzdowd.com, where discussions over cryptography and other computing and privacy issues regularly took place. By this point, the aforementioned early attempts at a digital currency had come and gone, but there was still an appetite in this group for a decentralised currency developed by the people for the people with no government influence. Kleiman was a former soldier who was made paraplegic in 1995 after a motorcycle accident and relied on the use of a wheelchair as a result. His mind was unaffected, however, and at the turn of the millennium, he, like Wright, was working in the nascent online gambling industry. Kleiman's job was to investigate fraud and other issues related to casino transactions, and it's possible that he may have rubbed shoulders with one of the pioneering individuals in the space, Calvin Ayre, who would come to play an even greater role in Wright's life than Kleiman.

Calvin Ayre wouldn't enter Wright's life for another fifteen years, but much would happen in the meantime to make his assistance necessary – starting with the creation of Bitcoin.

Chapter 2 – A Matter of Time

Lynn Wright says that Craig started showing an interest in digital currencies in the mid-2000s, as she revealed in a deposition for the *Kleiman v Wright* case:

> ...around 2004/2005, he said to me one day, he said, 'You know that the way of the future is digital currency?' and I said, 'Well, what do you mean, 'digital currency?' and he kind of explained it, 'You know, just money sort of over the like in – on computers, type thing, rather than cash in hand...'

In a June 2019 deposition for the same case, Craig claimed that Lynn knew all about his new project:

> COUNSEL: Did Lynn know about your creation of Bitcoin?
>
> WRIGHT: Yes. But she never really cared about it, and she just thought I was wasting too much time and working on things she didn't understand.
>
> [cut]
>
> COUNSEL: But how did she make the specific connection to the specific moniker Satoshi Nakamoto?
>
> WRIGHT: She saw me working. She saw me studying. She saw me get up...She was my wife. She lived there with me. She knew a lot of what I was doing. She was involved with the accounts.

As we will see shortly, the time that Wright supposedly woke up to work on Bitcoin is actually a core argument against his candidacy.

If we are to believe Wright's side of the story, he was simultaneously studying for three different master's degrees in 2005, four in 2006 and the same number again in 2007, at which time he also gained computing qualifications now cancelled because they are 'considered too difficult' and four more master's degrees in 2008. He did all this while holding down a full-time job for an international auditing firm, conducting postgraduate research, writing a hard drive wiping whitepaper with Dave Kleiman and Shyaam Sundhar of the tech company Symantec, running Ridges Estate, defending himself in a lawsuit, and, supposedly, inventing Bitcoin. He was also writing a 1,000-plus page manual on IT standards called *The IT Regulatory and Standards Compliance Handbook: How to Survive Information Systems Audit and Assessments*, which he published as an e-book on Amazon on 25 July 2008.

Wright commented on his workload at this time during the *COPA v Wright* trial, where it was put to him that it was too demanding to be feasible:

Between 2020 and 2022, I was enrolled in 23 degrees full-time simultaneously while working, and in that time, I wrote 600 papers that led to quite a number of patents. I would call that *demanding. At this time, it was fairly easy.*

Taking all this into consideration, it might, therefore, not be a stretch to assume that Craig Wright would have been living and working very odd hours at the time, something we need to compare to Satoshi Nakamoto's activity patterns. Analysis of Satoshi Nakamoto's activity is by no means an exact science, but we do have a plethora of data on his online movements that we can use to at least have a stab at his likely timezone. The moniker Satoshi Nakamoto was active online between August 2008 and December 2010, but the problem for Satoshi hunters is that we have no idea what else he might have been up to during that time; he could have been a teacher, an office worker, a shift worker, or even unemployed, so we have nothing with which to compare in the real world. The problem for Craig Wright is that we know exactly what he was doing between mid-2008 and early 2010 because he has made it public at various junctures, typically with variations in the story inserted along the way. Thankfully, Satoshi's online activities are timestamped and are not reliant on hearsay.

Analysis of over a thousand of Satoshi's forum posts, emails and other online acts suggests that he was typically inactive between 7 a.m. and 12 p.m. UTC. Given that this pattern persisted on weekends, we can assume that he was either a shift worker who worked the same shift every single day of the week and never took a day off, even on days of celebration, or this was when he slept. Assuming that Satoshi kept regular sleeping hours rather than a more anti-social schedule (which, of course, we can't), this best fits a time zone in the Americas. A New York-based Satoshi would have had sleeping hours of approximately 3 a.m.-8 a.m. local time and was most productive between 1 p.m. and 7 p.m. Similarly, a Satoshi based in San Francisco would have had sleeping hours of 12 a.m.-5 a.m. and was most productive between 10 a.m. and 4 p.m. Both of these are clearly feasible schedules, although Satoshi did post and email during his 'sleep' hours, just far less frequently. Taking these factors and others, which we shall soon discuss, into consideration, we will proceed on the assumption that Satoshi was based on the West Coast of the US.

Analysis of 118 of Craig Wright's blog posts between 2008 and 2010 shows us a very different schedule from a Satoshi based in the US. Wright's regular downtime was some six hours ahead of Satoshi's sleeping pattern, but it gets worse for Wright when we dig into the practicalities of how his Sydney timezone compares to Satoshi's known working hours, as we can see from this graphic used in the *COPA v Wright* trial:

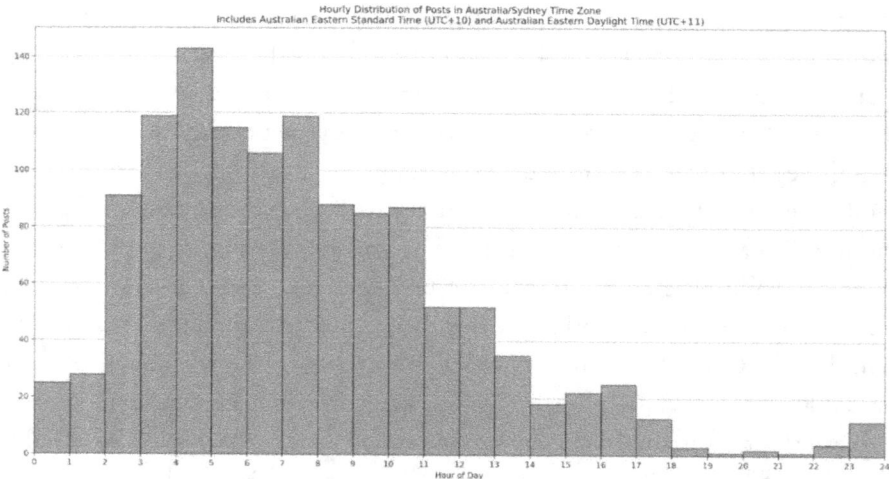

If Wright expects us to believe that he created Bitcoin, then this is how his daily schedule would have looked. Wright would have gone to bed at around 5 p.m. and slept for some six hours to wake again at 11 p.m., where he worked heavily on Bitcoin matters through the night without a break. At 3 a.m., he had a seven-hour burst of activity to take him through to 10 a.m., where he would tail off a little until stopping around 2 p.m., presumably exhausted. He would nevertheless continue to post sporadically about Bitcoin until his 5 p.m. bedtime, when the cycle would repeat. This pattern was adopted, by and large, every day of the year, Monday-Sunday, for over two years, including when Wright was working for BDO as an auditor. Amazingly, it didn't change after Wright's departure from the firm in December 2008, either, when there was seemingly no need to maintain it. The idea that Craig Wright was perpetually pulling these all-nighters and then going to work, only to continue posting about Bitcoin throughout the day until leaving the office for his 5 p.m. bedtime, is simply laughable. Unfortunately for Wright, his few comments on his timekeeping during this period don't help his argument, with one example coming in a 2019 blog post:

> I would spend mornings on Bitcoin. I got up at ridiculous times, and started by coding and checking my material before having breakfast. I am doing two doctorates simultaneously right now, but I am not doing a fraction of the study hours I was doing then. I was living on four hours' sleep for two years. I was used to being up at 3 AM or 4 AM seven days a week.

As we know, Satoshi didn't get up at 'ridiculous times'; he woke around 5 a.m. and went to bed about midnight. If Wright was trying to construct a schedule based on Satoshi's known active and less active hours, he failed miserably. Lynn Wright also confirmed Craig's typical schedule in her *Kleiman v Wright* deposition:

> COUNSEL: Did Craig typically stay up very, very late at night?
>
> LYNN: Yes, yes...I think at the time, he probably slept about four hours at the most every night. He'd...wake up in the middle of the night with an idea...

Of course, Craig Wright's 'middle of the night' was Satoshi's morning the day before, a perfectly reasonable time to wake up with an idea.

These testimonies only corroborate what the data reveals: Wright's online activity dropped off significantly between the hours of 11 p.m. and 4 a.m. Australian time, when he was almost certainly asleep. This, of course, is a not infeasible sleep pattern, but the problem for Wright is that he was going to bed right when the real Satoshi was just waking up. In order to fit in with Satoshi's suspected sleep/wake patterns, Wright would have had to have lived a vampiric existence, had a very obliging employer and possessed the work ethic of an Egyptian slave in order to create Bitcoin around such an imbalance. It is telling, therefore, that none of Wright's former employers or colleagues have ever mentioned anything odd about the hours he kept, and Lynn Wright, the person who would have been impacted the most by this impossible routine, has only corroborated Wright's erroneous schedule.

The only way it is possible for Wright to have followed this sleep pattern and still created Bitcoin is if he managed to make it appear that he was working and sleeping in a more suitable timezone, for example, by changing the clock on his computer, running through a sophisticated VPN or some other such method. However, this wouldn't account for all the forum, email and blog servers that recorded the vastly different times of his and Satoshi's interactions. To overcome the inevitable sleep deprivation and maintain this façade religiously for years without slipping up once is incredibly difficult, especially while holding down a job and studying for all those degrees. This isn't to say that Wright isn't above such antics: forensic examination of his evidence in court cases has revealed more than one instance of computer clock manipulation.

The timezone evidence, therefore, points to a Satoshi living in the Americas, which we can supplement with another clue. In 2016, an IP address for Satoshi Nakamoto was unearthed, dating back to 10 January 2009, when he was conversing with Hal Finney over issues with Bitcoin's core client. This IP address was handed out by the U.S. internet provider MegaPath, with the closest host to the user on Satoshi's side of the conversation located in Van Nuys, California (Finney was located in Lompoc, California, a two-and-a-half-hour drive away). This isn't proof that Satoshi lived in Van Nuys permanently, but the fact that the IP address was not a TOR exit node and was not related to a VPN strongly implies that Satoshi was genuinely there, at least for that day. Interestingly, Van Nuys was something of a hotbed for the cypherpunk movement, hosting Libertarian Party events as far back as 1994. Wright, conversely, has gone on record to say that he was in Australia during the week that Satoshi was in Van Nuys, which precludes him from visiting California on the 10th. Again, this isn't conclusive evidence, but, at the very least, it doesn't help Wright's claim.

The idea of a California-based Satoshi is also backed up by a statement made on 29 April 2019 by Rana Saoud, then Assistant Special Agent in Charge in the Homeland Security Investigations office of the Department of Homeland Security (DHS). During a presentation at the OffshoreAlert Conference North America, Special Agent Saoud claimed that DHS agents once met with Satoshi Nakamoto and three other members of Team Satoshi in California to discuss Bitcoin. Nothing more was said about this connection, but given the source, it has to be taken seriously.

All this leaves us with two theories:

Craig Wright worked on Bitcoin every day from 11 p.m. right through the night and all through the following day, even when holding down a job as an auditor and completing multiple master's degrees. He almost always went to bed at 5 p.m., something that his wife and former colleagues have never commented on, and kept to the same pattern when employed and, later, self-employed. He also lied about his working hours in blog posts and in courtroom testimony and convinced his ex-wife to lie under oath on the subject, as well as managing to trick a multitude of email, blog and code-hosting servers into using the wrong time zone when logging his data.

Or...

Satoshi Nakamoto was based on the West Coast of the United States, where he woke up at around 5 a.m., worked on Bitcoin and attended to other commitments during the day before going to bed around midnight.

Wright was briefly challenged over his incompatible working hours during the *COPA v Wright* trial, where he claimed that the online activity reflected the time when he was replying to emails and messages and that he did his actual work during other 'offline' hours. This is, of course, a thoroughly insubstantial response that fails to tackle the key arguments against the timezone complications. Theoretically, Wright could have reused a 2022 excuse that he had not managed his blog since 1996 to claim that someone in a U.S. timezone was posting and sending emails as Satoshi, but he has neglected to do this.

There is a third theory that Craig Wright was a member of a group calling itself Satoshi Nakamoto and that he was the brains and someone else, based in the US, was the fingers on the keyboard. The prime candidate for this role among Wrightofiles is Dave Kleiman, but Wright rubbished this notion during testimony for the *Kleiman v Wright* trial:

In all the key areas where Satoshi was speaking, Dave was hospitalized and did not have a computer and at parts not even a phone....So, being that Dave was in hospital without access to the Internet in some of these things, and being that Dave was literally under the knife during of some of it, it is not possible that Dave spoke as Satoshi, as much as some people want that.

Wright also added during the same testimony that Kleiman 'had access to his own e-mail accounts, not to the Satoshi Nakamoto e-mail accounts', although this is somewhat undermined by Wright's claim in a February 2014 email to Dave Kleiman's adopted brother, Ira, that Dave 'had the vistomail account, I had the gmx one'. Ira Kleiman asked Wright about this again three years later, whereupon Wright denied that the email exchange had ever taken place. When presented with the email in question during the *Kleiman v Wright* case, Wright responded, 'I see a document that has been created, likely by Ira.'

Wright's stance over Dave Kleiman having nothing to do with Satoshi's writings is at odds with his propensity to blame ghostwriters when work attributed to him clashes with ideas espoused by Satoshi, probably because his claim to be the sole creator of Bitcoin trumps any potential benefits to be derived from blaming others. This means that when Wright is pulled up for holding an opinion that clashes with Satoshi's writings (perhaps because Wright has forgotten about a particular Satoshi forum post or email), he is forced to contextualise Satoshi's words so that they fit with his erroneous opinion, an opinion that is never repeated once exposed.

Wright's insistence that he was the sole creator of Bitcoin, working away alone under the now infamous pseudonym, has not always been as steadfast. There have been at least three occasions when he has claimed that he was part of a group of developers working on Bitcoin, mentioning different contributors each time. However, these claims ceased when Ira Kleiman sued him in 2018 for half of Wright and Dave Kleiman's alleged Bitcoin empire, which Ira's team valued at US$600 billion. Wright's defence relied on him being Bitcoin's sole creator, so it is unsurprising that his claims of a Satoshi group ended abruptly at that point.

There are other aspects of Satoshi Nakamoto's life and work to which we can turn in order to discern the likelihood or otherwise of Wright being behind the pseudonym. In addition to differences in their daily routines, lots of inferences have been drawn (or have attempted to be drawn) between the writing styles of

Satoshi Nakamoto and the prime candidates for his mantle. Of course, the results of such analysis can never be considered definitive, but Satoshi's plentiful writings remain the best primary source we have available for an insight into his true identity. In 2016, the *International Business Times* hired Juola & Associates, a firm that uses stylometry to identify the authors of anonymous texts, to compare the writings of Satoshi Nakamoto and Craig Wright. Juola used a text analysis tool called Envelope, which, in the words of the company's Chief Scientist John Noecker, condenses 'millions of different linguistic features' collected over forty years of research to see if they could match Wright's writing style to that of Satoshi. Juola had pedigree, too: in 2013, they were hired by the UK's *Sunday Times* newspaper to help identify the person behind the then pseudonymous author Robert Galbraith, having received a tip that it could be Harry Potter author J.K. Rowling. Juola used Envelope to analyse Rowling and Galbraith's writing styles and decided that, in their opinion, Galbraith was Rowling. The *Sunday Times* broke the story, leading to Rowling admitting that she was, indeed, behind the pseudonym.

Juola's research on Wright was published in the *Journal of Digital Forensics, Security and Law* in 2016, where it analysed some of Wright's missives and compared them to work by Satoshi Nakamoto. Juola's conclusion was brief and to the point:

> *Based on linguistic evidence, we do not believe that Craig Wright authored the Bitcoin paper.*

Juola added that its investigation further revealed multiple contributors to Satoshi's writings, contradicting Wright's claim that he alone was Satoshi. The analysis concluded that no single person authored all the pieces it examined and found the writing style most closely matched that of Hal Finney, one of Bitcoin's earliest developers and a widely suspected candidate for Satoshi Nakamoto (and, lest we forget, a California resident). Wright's response to this, which he gave to *The Economist* in 2016, was unconvincing:

> *...Mr Wright says that, although he was the principal author of the white paper, he had extensive help from his friend Dave Kleiman, an American computer-forensics expert who died in 2013. Mr Wright also says that he has many different writing styles, depending on the subject matter.*

Of course, Wright would change his story over Dave Kleiman's involvement two years after this interview, but this claim to be a kind of linguistic chameleon is one of Wright's classic catch-all excuses that offers him a plausible 'out', but which is impossible to verify. Juola's research is one of a number of comparisons of Satoshi's writing style made over the years, but its study remains the only credible investigation into the linguistic differences between Wright and Satoshi carried out to date.

Wright tackled this language discrepancy in court for the first time during the *Granath v Wright* trial in 2022, where he was questioned over the fact that his writing style was different in many ways from that of Satoshi Nakamoto. Wright's response was extraordinary:

Text analysis is statistically an invalid methodology that has been basically banned in American courts now.

This startling claim is in no way accurate; text analysis, or forensic linguistics as it is referred to in the criminal sphere, was famously used to catch the 'Unabomber' Ted Kaczynski in 1996 and remains part of the FBI's investigative toolkit in cases where written content plays a part.

Even the most unqualified of armchair analysts can't fail to notice just how different Wright's and Satoshi's language styles are. Whereas Satoshi was polite and respectful, even when being challenged or sometimes insulted, Wright is frequently brash and egotistical and typically fights his way out of a corner with belligerence, foul language and aggression. He puts this down to being an Australian, but it doesn't disguise the fact that his and Satoshi's styles of communication are worlds apart. This became even more evident after Wright failed to convince the world of his Satoshi candidacy in 2016 when his writings devolved into expletive-ridden rants and self-aggrandisement of the sort that Satoshi Nakamoto never engaged in across the hundreds of emails and blog posts that have been released. Of course, it is never possible to know the person behind the keyboard, but Satoshi maintained a notable level of decorum and respect for contrasting opinions even when disagreeing with people. This is in stark contrast to Wright, who has styled himself on Genghis Khan, calling himself 'the punishment of God in cryptocurrency' and promising to 'bleed' those who opposed his views on Bitcoin in late 2018. Around the time of a 2021 lawsuit against a collection of Bitcoin developers, Wright boasted about the harm he wanted to inflict on them, which did not escape the notice of the judge in the case:

> I refer to Dr Wright's explicit threats published on social media to bankrupt developers, destroy their families, imprison them and even defenestrate one individual (the latter threat made even more graphic by the accompanying photograph of a man who appears to have just been defenestrated from a high building).

We will not print some of Wright's more vicious or disgusting diatribes, but the slide into anger and vitriol, matched only by boasts about his success, wealth, intelligence and status, are totally at odds with the shy and retiring Satoshi, the man who disappeared in 2011 and hasn't emerged even to touch his fortune, today valued in the tens of billions of dollars. One can only imagine what Juola would discern from a contemporary Wright-Satoshi comparison.

We also have anecdotal challenges to Wright's self-professed Satoshiness. One person who claimed to have been 'around Craig at Sydney pubs in the 2010s' described him as being 'Arrogant and obnoxious and overly confident without having any reason to be' and alleged that he 'Lied constantly just for the fun of it, thought it was funny, and [was] very proud when he could trick someone'. This person also said that Wright was 'Constantly asking people to borrow money or invest in his shit & scammy ideas'. Another such example comes from Australian information security consultant Nik Cubrilovic who, after Wright's disastrous 2016 reveal attempt, tracked down people who worked with Wright in the years when he was supposedly designing Bitcoin, where he came across some equally damning reports:

> ...I have come to hear – either directly or second-hand – from a number of other people who either worked for or knew Wright. The conclusion is near-unanimous: Wright is not Satoshi Nakamoto, and is not capable of being Satoshi Nakamoto. One friend described how Wright is so convincing that even tho[ugh] he knew he wasn't capable of creating Bitcoin, he would at times even doubt himself. Another said that Wright has everybody convinced for at least a short period – but then it begins to unravel as his actions do not match his word. He came away from his experience convinced that Wright is a fraud. Yet another person who worked for

Wright characterized him (via a third-party) as 'the best conman I've ever met'.

In February 2010, Wright was criticised by someone within the information security sector who disliked the 'overwhelming egoism and self-substantiating claims of your contributions to the industry' that they found present within Wright's old blog, 'Cracked, InSecure and Generally Broken' (in 2015 *Gizmodo* referred to this blog as 'an obelisk built to Craig Wright' that chronicled, among other things, 'the grandeur of his own ego'). The security critic slammed Wright's calculation methodology, asking, 'More importantly, where is the calculation for self-absorbed snake-oil selling academics with no real experience using their calculator to come up with magic numbers that represent the risk of a nuclear power plant being hacked?' They ended their piece prophetically, saying, 'People like you are dangerous and need to be exposed before someone in a position of power actually believes that you know what you are talking about.' This would prove to be far from the last time that Craig Wright was called out by genuine experts over a subject in which he professed his expertise.

In the interests of balance, it should also be noted that many people who know Craig Wright swear that he is Satoshi Nakamoto. However, once we remove family members and those who have a vested interest in Wright holding this accolade, the list is short and unimpressive. Wright can, of course, call on a collection of keyboard warriors who hang on his every word to back up his claim online, but of those who have actually taken their opinions into the witness box, none of them has testified to having seen Wright do anything Bitcoin-related at the time of its creation. Some have claimed to have received drafts of the Bitcoin whitepaper or precursor works under different names, but none of them has been able to produce these drafts or any evidence of their receipt, while others have been found to have actively lied on the stand over the matter. Those witnesses who haven't made such claims have offered nothing but vague and unproven stories that Wright was doing work related to blockchain technology at the time they knew him or, in the most valueless of instances, that he had the ability to have created Bitcoin. As we will soon see, Wright claims to have informed hundreds of people that he wrote the Bitcoin whitepaper in 2008, and yet we can count on one hand the number of people who have ever backed up this story in court. Wright claimed during the *Granath v Wright* trial in September 2022 that he had seventy witnesses lined up for the *COPA v Wright* trial, which was set to take place around a year later at that point, and was hoping to get to a hundred. However, there is no evidence that Wright's lawyers talked to more than twenty witnesses, only a handful of which actually ended up taking the stand. Wright blamed threats made by his critics as to why the others did not appear, allegations made by him alone and without any evidence.

It's also worth noting that there were millions of people across the world in 2008 who were probably capable of creating Bitcoin, including the likes of Hal Finney, Nick Szabo, Adam Back and Shinichi Mochizuki, all of whom have been named as possible Satoshi candidates, but who Wright's witnesses never encountered. Had they done so, or been presented with their work in related fields, there is every likelihood that they would have agreed that these candidates, too, had the capacity to create Bitcoin. Lynn Wright echoed Craig Wright's claim that she knew he was Satoshi in a 2024 book entitled *Hero/Villain: Satoshi: The Man Who Built Bitcoin*, telling author Mark Eglinton, 'I was not surprised that he was Satoshi, it was now public what I had thought for a long time.' This, however, differs from statements Lynn has made elsewhere; in 2016, she told *The Australian* that Craig's Satoshi claim was 'rubbish' and added that she personally did not know 'anything about Bitcoin'. She further distanced herself from Wright's story in 2020 under oath for the *Kleiman v Wright* case:

COUNSEL: When was the first time you heard the term 'Satoshi Nakamoto'?

LYNN: Probably around 2012.

COUNSEL: How did you hear about that term?

LYNN: In an article that my sister-in-law sent me.

COUNSEL: Okay. Did Craig ever mention the term 'Satoshi Nakamoto' to you?

LYNN: No.

As we will see later in this book, Lynn's comments to Eglinton may have been made against her will, meaning this deposition reflects the truth, as it should.

It is not only witnesses who have failed to corroborate Wright's Satoshi claim; Wright has done a great deal of damage himself, with instances abounding of him getting technical information on Bitcoin entirely wrong. One of the most vocal critics in this area is software engineer Jameson Lopp, who got into Bitcoin in 2012. The pair's rounds of abuse tennis stayed within the court of social media until 2022, when they escaped into the physical world during the *Granath v Wright* trial. Wright was challenged over Lopp's April 2019 claim that Wright had 'made a multitude of technical errors in his writings that call his understanding of Bitcoin and Internet technology into question'. Wright responded to this accusation by saying that in all the examples Lopp gave, he, Wright, was talking about a different Bitcoin:

> COUNSEL: Is this really technical errors, or do you have strong disagreements on the position of Lopp as regards issues on Bitcoin?
>
> WRIGHT: It's to do with the original version of Bitcoin that I issued versus the changes they made.

Here, we have another example of Wright using a sweeping claim to absolve himself of a whole host of criticisms, one that is both very helpful for his argument and impossible to prove or disprove.

Lopp is just one of a number of critics who claim that Wright doesn't know Bitcoin as well as he thinks he does, something that Justice Mellor picked up on during the *COPA v Wright* case. Having listened to Wright pontificate on Bitcoin first-hand for over a week, Justice Mellor was 'struck by the fact that all of [Wright's] knowledge and supposed insights could well have been obtained by careful study of the publicly available materials relating to the early years of Bitcoin', adding that in 'none of his evidence did he reveal any insight or knowledge unique to Satoshi'. This opinion tallies with Wright's frequent boasts of being able to absorb huge amounts of information in a short space of time on any subject, although Justice Mellor found a flaw in his strategy:

> *Furthermore, in his evidence, Dr Wright made significant errors which Satoshi would never have made, even after this length of time. Some of these relate to Satoshi's interactions with individuals not previously made public. Others relate to technical matters which Dr Wright simply got wrong but which Satoshi would not have got wrong.*

Whichever way you slice it, the evidence across all these facets of Satoshi's life and work strongly points away from Craig Wright being the man who developed

Bitcoin, and anyone who disbelieves this has to account for the glaring discrepancies we have outlined, from the timezone complications to the technical errors. To believe that Wright is the man behind Satoshi's emails, code commits and forum posts requires suspending disbelief to the most extraordinary degree imaginable and discounting clear contradictory evidence. For this reason, it is no surprise that the majority of Wright's few remaining advocates publicly support debunked conspiracy theories on a grander scale, such as phone masts spreading infectious diseases and the existence of a secret world government, quite aside from the conspiracy theories over who is running Bitcoin today. Many are also supporters of the sovereign citizen movement, whose adherents believe they are not subject to government laws, taxes or regulations and that they can opt out of these legal standards, often basing these beliefs on misinterpretations of the law that have never been supported in any legal setting. In March 2025, one of these individuals publicly aired a theory that the spread of the COVID-19 pandemic was a thousand-year-old plan concocted by shadowy elites to protect the global banking industry; initially planned for 2025, it was supposedly brought forward to 2020 due to their fear of Craig Wright and his BSV technology. Maintaining these beliefs requires the rejection of facts and rational argument for a desire to believe a specific narrative, so it is no surprise that they are attracted to Wright's Satoshi story. This belief will seem even more incredulous when we look at Wright's ever-changing story about how Bitcoin came into being.

Chapter 3 – Genesis

Craig Wright offers the following narrative for when he began working on Bitcoin:

Craig Wright R&D and the other entities as businesses representing the trusts have been registered since 29 February 2000. It was reformed under the trust business name for myself, remembering that a business called Craig Wright is not Craig Wright the person, on 10 February 2007. This is when I started creating bitcoin. At that point I changed from DeMorgan to using myself as the trustee name.

If this sounds somewhat confusing, it's just a sliver of what's to come. Thankfully, a slightly more down-to-earth version came in his deposition for the *Granath v Wright* trial in 2022:

The idea of making an Internet-based payment system and token system started right back in 1998. I'd had talks early on with people involved in the industry, including Tim May, but a lot of it came down to my work with the Australian Stock Exchange and other organizations including Lasseters and some of the banks [when] I was trying to find a more efficient global payment system.

These grand claims have never been backed up with evidence compelling enough to satisfy anyone in a position to decide on their merits, but this hasn't been for want of trying: Wright has produced thousands of documents and dozens of witnesses across his various court cases, all of which, he says, validate his claims that he was devising concepts around blockchain and alternative payment systems as far back as the 1990s. These will be explored in more detail when we cover the trials in question, but as we have already noted, Wright's witnesses have either been unconvincing in their recollections or have been found to have outright lied.

Wright credits Tim May with thinking up the concept that many see as the foundation of Bitcoin, a 1997 paper entitled 'Untraceable Digital Cash, Information Markets, and BlackNet'. Wright told Andrew O'Hagan that he had read this after its release and wanted to take BlackNet 'further', leading to his own project under the same name. Wright publicly referred to BlackNet for the first time during a 2017 iGaming Super Show presentation, but it wasn't until February 2019, just two months after May died, that Wright revealed more details on Twitter:

> *My stupidest mistake was going to the Australian government in 2001 and filing this shit.*

This tweet included several pages from an alleged 2001 funding application for Project Blacknet, whose cover page featured an abstract identical to that of the Bitcoin whitepaper. This implied that Wright had been dreaming up Bitcoin more than seven years before its launch, but this was quickly shot down when it was noted that the abstract contained changes Satoshi made to the whitepaper after August 2008, despite it supposedly being written by Wright in 2001. As Arthur pointed out in his January 2022 piece, 'Craig Wright And The BlackNet Lie', the snippets attached to the tweet were unsigned and undated, making it impossible to know whether they were from a contemporary filing or a later one. In addition, the variety of fonts on display in the 'official' form made it look like a work experience trainee using Microsoft Word for the first time. More notably, the Project BlackNet paper featured the names of two other people who had allegedly helped Craig Wright prepare it: Lynn Wright and Dave Dornbrack. Lynn was asked about her work on the BlackNet paper during her deposition for the *Kleiman v Wright* case in 2020, but her response was far from helpful for her ex-husband:

> COUNSEL: *What was Blacknet, if you recall?*
>
> LYNN: *I have no recollection of that at all. I – it's – I don't know. I – I could assume things, but that's – that's just silly.*

Craig Wright was challenged over this during the *COPA v Wright* trial, where he claimed that Lynn's testimony wasn't to be trusted because she was 'heavily sedated' and 'on opioids' at the time following treatment for breast cancer, adding that she had effectively been forced to testify by her deposing counsel. COPA's barrister, Jonathan Hough KC, pointed out that Lynn had affirmed at the start of her testimony that she was suffering from no medical conditions that could have affected her ability to provide truthful and accurate testimony, but Wright simply reiterated that she didn't know what she was saying. In February 2019, a Reddit user claimed that they had spoken to Dave Dornbrack about the idea that Wright was Satoshi Nakamoto and that Dornbrack had dismissed the notion:

> When I brought up CSW claim to being satoshi, his exact words were "bullshit" followed by a scathing character assasination.

Given the lack of an empirical source, we have to take this with a pinch of salt, but it seems that if there was an association between Wright and Dornbrack, it ended acrimoniously: in 2019, Wright referred to Dornbrack as a 'thief who lied in court' without going into detail.

During his examination of Wright, Jonathan Hough suggested that BlackNet was merely an IT security project that had nothing to do with Bitcoin, an assertion that Wright rejected:

> If you read the concept of what BlackNet is, it is an end-to-end encrypted network system that has economic security through what Tim May called 'crypto-credits'.

This links back to a March 2021 blog post where Wright mentioned such a connection for the first time, claiming that it was influential in the creation of Bitcoin:

> It is finally time to start explaining why I created Bitcoin. Why I spent nearly 25 years of my life, so far, on a project. To explain what 'BlackNet' was originally designed to be and what I transformed it into. Bitcoin represents 'CryptoCredits'.

However, the real Satoshi Nakamoto never mentioned crypto credits or its creator, Tim May, as an influence in his work, with Wright's efforts representing one of many attempts he has made, both in public and in the witness box, to link his prior work in the IT sector to what Bitcoin would eventually become. During the same examination, Wright was forced to admit that the Twitter screenshot showing the BlackNet filing was indeed from a BlackNet funding application made post-2010, two years after the Bitcoin whitepaper had been published, and that he never claimed that it had been contemporaneous in the tweet.

Wright claims that he created plenty of precursor versions of Bitcoin alongside the thoroughly discredited Project BlackNet. These include Timechain, Spyder and Tripwire, with Wright homing in on one particular entity in 2019:

In the initial stages of its development, Bitcoin was referred to as Timecoin, a term that I adopted until I transitioned to the now well-known moniker, Bitcoin, in mid-2008. Although, for some time after that, I used both terms (and a few other names) interchangeably.

Wright claimed during the *COPA v Wright* trial that 'Timecoin went on to become the commercial implementation of Bitcoin that I ran in places like Qudos bank', a claim that was put to David Bridges, Qudos' Chief Information Officer at the time, during his spell in the witness box. Bridges, however, said that while Wright pitched the bank a system aimed at speeding up their inter-bank transactions using a tamper-proof ledger, they didn't implement it. He also noted that the only thing Wright's proposal had in common with blockchain technology (the former of which was not documented in any form) was the secure nature of the system, something that would hardly have been unique to Wright's design. Wright submitted a Timecoin whitepaper dated May 2008 into evidence for the *COPA v Wright* trial, but forensic examination found that 'Rather than being a precursor document to the Bitcoin White Paper as it purports to be, this document has been created from the Bitcoin White Paper subsequently and edited in such a way that it appears as if it was precursor work.' Justice Mellor took this into account when he ruled that none of Wright's precursor work had anything to do with Bitcoin, with the reality being that 'these were simply IT security projects over a few years in the IT security sector, and nothing to do with the creation of a revolutionary cryptocurrency.'

When it comes to his other alleged influences, Wright often credits his studies at Northumbria and Newcastle universities in the mid-late 2000s as being key. There, he says, he wrote various papers featuring ideas that would all go into the mixing pot for Bitcoin, including the extraordinary claim that he submitted the first half of the Bitcoin whitepaper as part of his proposal for his Northumbria

LLM dissertation. Wright says that various people 'thoroughly reviewed' the document, including David Bridges, Lynn Wright and his Seychelles-based lawyer, Denis Mayaka. During the *COPA v Wright* trial, Wright said that his LLM centred on 'internet payment intermediaries' and that it 'provided a comprehensive analysis of the roles and responsibilities of trusted third parties within online transactions.' These, of course, ally strongly with key values within Bitcoin, and Wright posted both his proposal and his full dissertation online at the Social Science Research Network (SSRN) in 2019 as evidence of his coming up with the core concepts behind Bitcoin between 2005 and 2007. However, COPA's forensic analyst, Patrick Madden, found that the proposal submitted as evidence was in Lynn Wright's name and had been backdated to 2007, with the version on SSRN having been created on 18 August 2019, two days before it was uploaded. When questioned about this in court, Wright tried to claim that a hard copy of the proposal had been forensically dated to no earlier than 2014, evidence that had not been put before the court. This was dismissed, with Justice Mellor ruling that the proposal was 'forged by [Wright] to include references to concepts taken by him from the Bitcoin White Paper.'

There were issues with Wright's LLM thesis, too, chiefly the fact that none of the references to his ideas for an innovative new monetary system, which had been so liberally scattered in the proposal, made it into the final piece. Wright tried to explain this away in a *COPA v Wright* witness statement:

> *The feedback I received from Northumbria primarily revolved around referencing, formatting, and my use of computer science terminology. As a result, I eliminated some of the computer science jargon and ensured that I used legal terminology consistently.*

Wright maintained during the trial that 'the whole paper...is on the topic of intermediaries', referring to the nodes that help secure the Bitcoin network. However, given that all references to nodes were removed from the final thesis, readers would have needed to use a great deal of imagination to make such a leap, and Justice Mellor agreed that it 'had nothing to do with the genesis of Bitcoin.' These weren't the only issues with the thesis. Three years after Wright had published it on SSRN, a Medium article by the pseudonymous Paintedfrog (whom Wright later claimed to be one of his avowed enemies, Greg Maxwell) alleged that the work, 'The Impact of Internet Intermediary Liability', was 'heavily plagiarized' from another work, 'Liability of Internet Service Providers', a 1996 paper by Hilary E. Pearson. Paintedfrog alleged that much of the text was taken 'both in paraphrase and verbatim form— from other works with no credit given', with the opening paragraph copied word for word and Wright appropriating 'the majority of the text in Pearson's 14 pages'. Paintedfrog calculated that Wright had copied twenty-five paragraphs in full and another twenty in large part, meaning his forty-five-page thesis was as original as a Temu Barbie doll. Wright was also playing the same game with the footnotes, copying entire multi-paragraph footnotes from other works on the same matter, again without citation, only changing content when it had the potential to link to compromising works. Under questioning during the *COPA v Wright* trial, Wright claimed that the original version of the thesis had included citations to Pearson's work, but his editing software removed the citations for the later version, which was then uploaded to SSRN. Wright added that of the 200-odd references he included, the one which happened to make up almost all of the text in his thesis was the one missed. Of course, it's fairly clear what a university professor would have made of Wright submitting work that was in large part written by other people, even if he had cited it.

Wright also tried to augment his claim that his studies at Newcastle University were instrumental in helping him design Bitcoin when he submitted a paper, 'BitCoin: SEIR-C Propagation Models of Block and Transaction Dissemination', as evidence in the same trial. Wright claimed that this paper hailed from 2008, but COPA's forensic analyst Patrick Madden found that Wright had uploaded another copy of this document to SSRN and immediately smelt a rat:

> *The document contains significant portions of hidden text referring to matters which post-date the purported last modified date of [the copy entered into evidence] by several years, including 2013-2014 news articles and a US government publication which could not have been known about in 2008.*

Wright's instantly memorable explanation for the insertion of multiple contemporaneous Bitcoin references into the 2008 version and the absence of the troublesome post-2008 references was that his Citrix environment had merged two totally different documents together, resulting in the anomalies which just so happened to create a coherent, if factually incorrect, document. This was instantly jumped on by Citrix users, with one alleging that Wright was talking 'literal nonsense'. Wright also blamed his company's Citrix policies for 2019 metadata timestamps ending up in his much earlier LLM proposal, adding that metadata inconsistencies were caused by the software updating over time. Justice Mellor addressed these claims in a tongue-in-cheek manner:

> *Dr Wright provided no evidence that the ordinary use of a Citrix environment causes documents to be affected in these ways, and indeed one would expect the many blue-chip companies which use Citrix to be horrified if it did.*

Wright also credits his university studies in 2005 for the creation of the pseudonym Satoshi Nakamoto, giving a reason why he used a pseudonym rather than his own name in 2019:

> *I chose to develop Bitcoin under a pseudonym primarily due to the potential legal and regulatory ramifications associated with digital money systems. I was particularly wary of the U.S. government, which had previously posed challenges for clients like Lasseters.*

Wright had already offered a slightly more detailed explanation on this theme in a blog post a few weeks earlier, claiming that he used a pseudonym in order to protect his identity following conversations with Professors Graham Wrightson and Andreas Furche at Newcastle University, who were heavily invested in the concept of electronic money:

> *Prof Wrightson, when I talked to him, told me all about DigiCash. He is the reason that I took up a pseudonym. The Monetary Systems Engineering Research Group had a lot of resources. I read their patents and papers on transfer instruments, but more than anything else, I took away the problems that had occurred with DigiCash. I saw what had happened with ecash. I saw what had happened with e-gold.*

However, in their witness statements for the *COPA v Wright* case, professors Wrightson and Furche both denied having ever met Wright, with Professor Wrightson stating that he left the University in 2000, five years before Wright enrolled and supposedly had these discussions with him. When faced with this anomaly, Wright said that these conversations took place during his prior enrolment at the university in the mid-1990s and that 'when it comes to time and people and dates...I don't recall very well.'

Something else that Wright doesn't seem to recall very well is his motives for using a pseudonym, having claimed on Twitter a year before the *COPA v Wright* trial that he wanted the idea of Bitcoin to 'stand or fall on its own merit':

> *If I'd released bitcoin as Craig Wright, bitcoin would not have taken off. There were people in 2008 who simply argued anything I said because of who I am...The pseudonym was purely so that the people who saw my name on a paper and rejected it in this industry wouldn't have a reason to reject my ideas out of hand.*

Wright also claimed during the *COPA v Wright* trial that he wasn't trying to keep his Satoshi identity a secret, just private, adding that he 'first shared my identity with a small circle of people including my mother, my uncle Don Lynam, some close friends such as David Bridges, and my then wife, Lynn.' Bridges was called as a witness for both the *Granath v Wright* and *COPA v Wright* trials, and in neither session did he say anything about Wright coming out to him as Satoshi. Lynn Wright, as we know, only found out about the name Satoshi Nakamoto in 2012 when she read it in an article. Don Lyman claimed that he knew Wright was Satoshi Nakamoto, but we will tackle his evidence later.

Plenty of theories have been put forward over the years regarding the origin of the pseudonym Satoshi Nakamoto, with amateur sleuths suggesting everything from anagrams to coded messages. In his attempts to back up his version of history, Wright has only muddied the waters: while he has stuck to the idea that an 18th-century Japanese philosopher was behind the 'Nakamoto' name, he seems unsettled on the first name, citing over the years Tomasu, Tomagata, Tominaga and once – oddly – Tomodacta. Equally as inconsistent is Wright's narrative over the meaning behind the name 'Satoshi'. In 2019, Wright claimed that the creation of the name was 'me being Australian and taking the piss out of things', adding that it was based on the Pokémon character, Ash, whose name translates to 'Satoshi' in Japanese. Wright has also referenced the 'ashes' of the traditional financial system from which Bitcoin would hopefully rise following the financial crash in 2008 as another link to Ash, but this account is different from the one he put forward on Twitter in 2016, which he later blamed on a third party controlling his account:

> *The name Satoshi comes from Satoshi David character from the [book] House of Morgan – Casino Age.*

The fact that Wright cannot even keep the origin of the Satoshi Nakamoto name straight, let alone anything more intricate, is a damning indictment of his claim.

In a 2019 YouTube interview, Wright tried to offer proof that he was going by the name Satoshi Nakamoto prior to Bitcoin's creation by displaying a document that he said showed the roots of the name itself. The document, a piece written by Tominaga Nakamoto and taken from a 1967 edition of the Japanese journal *Monumenta Nipponica*, featured handwritten notes from Wright on the front:

> *Nakamoto is the Japanese Adam Smith. Honest ledger & micro cash. Satoshi is intelligent history. Not too hard.*

Here, we have a very handy and succinct summary of Wright's Satoshi Nakamoto origin story, albeit one that fails to mention his other influences such as the House of Morgan book, Pokemon or the ashes of the financial system. The document sported an 'accessed' date of 5 January 2008, purportedly backing up Wright's timeline, but eagle-eyed viewers noticed at once that the printout featured some oddities: the last two digits on the accessed date looked different than the two preceding it, leading many to believe that Wright had amended them to make it look like a 2008 document, either pre or post-print. This was confirmed three years later by forensic experts from KPMG as part of the *Granath v Wright* case, who opined that the accessed date originally said 5 January 2015. They also found that the IP address in the footer of the document, which had been changed to reflect an IP address used by Wright in 2008, wasn't handed out by the internet provider at that time. In March 2023, Wright doubled down on the authenticity of the document and claimed that the representative from the KPMG forensic team was 'the worst and least professional individual that I've had the displeasure of working with.' Unfortunately for Wright, the same findings were made by Patrick Madden the following year in the *COPA v Wright* case, where Wright had again used it as evidence. This time, however, Wright had his excuses ready: the erroneous figures were down to a 'cheap printer' misaligning the text, and, following his downloading of the document in 2008, his numerous enemies had manipulated and replaced the document in the online repository some time afterwards in the belief that Wright would one day use it as evidence of his Satoshi claim. The less said about this excuse, the better.

Interestingly, while he was supposedly dreaming up Bitcoin and the pseudonym Satoshi Nakamoto, Wright also wrote on a post for the Security Basics mailing list that 'Anonymity is the shield of cowards, it is the cover used to defend their lies.' Wright added, 'My life is open and I have little care for my privacy – so in my case this is an easy charge to defend.' Wright was asked about this apparent discrepancy in court in 2022, where he lectured the questioner on the difference between anonymity and pseudonymity, making it very clear that Bitcoin, and by extension Satoshi Nakamoto, were *pseud*onymous, not *an*onymous. Three years earlier, however, he seems to have been somewhat confused on the subject:

> *Do you want to know why Satoshi had to be anonymous? Think about it. My past working as a prosecution forensic expert and in other roles with the government would never lead to a system that I could have publicly stood behind.*

Interestingly, the reason for Wright's outburst about anonymity was because an anonymous user of the site had cast doubts on his qualifications, showing that such doubts go back very far indeed. As we will see, these doubts have strengthened over time to an almost suffocating degree.

Chapter 4 – Building Bitcoin

In a 2023 interview, Craig Wright made a startling claim: there had been 300 attempts at 'proof-of-work distributed cryptocurrencies' prior to Bitcoin and a staggering 30,000 different attempts at cryptocurrencies since the 1980s. Given that most people agree that there were only a handful of such attempts during this period, Wright was asked to back up his extraordinary numbers, but he couldn't. Regardless of the actual number attempted, the only successful implementation of a decentralised currency to date has been Bitcoin, which Wright says he created in reverse order, coding up the software before writing the whitepaper. This was, indeed, how Satoshi Nakamoto designed Bitcoin, but this rare collision of fact with Wright's narrative is proof of nothing but the fact that he can read, as we can judge from this November 2008 email from Satoshi to Hal Finney:

> *I actually did this kind of backwards. I had to write all the code before I could convince myself that I could solve every problem, then I wrote the paper.*

We can glean from his writings that Satoshi's overarching desire was to create a decentralised and trustless system; the Bitcoin whitepaper describes it as 'a system for electronic transactions without relying on trust'. Many of Satoshi's other writings focus on these elements, too, from which all else, such as a potential financial revolution, would spring. Wright has tended to follow this principle, but true to form, his supposed original vision for Bitcoin has shifted over time, often mirroring his legal entanglements. Wright credits Isaac Asimov's *Foundation* series with being behind the inspiration for the concept of a blockchain, while his multifaceted reasons for creating Bitcoin on top of it include:

- 'the fact that the traditional internet payment mechanisms using credit cards didn't work for small-value transactions'
- 'a sound system of money that acts to allow exchange privately but with an immutable evidence trail'
- 'a distributed timestamp and quorum system to form consensus in distributed overlay databases'

Wright also credits a desire to bring down other kinds of illegal activity as a reason for creating Bitcoin, as a 2019 blog post shows:

One thing bitcoin was created for is to end the manipulation of financial systems. This was never what we see in the west but rather criminal manipulation. It was designed to ensure that Web Money, Liberty Reserve and a group of criminals associated with things such as the Russian Business Network (RBN) were the real target.

This, however, doesn't tally with Satoshi Nakamoto's view of Liberty Reserve, which he espoused in March 2010:

[Liberty Reserve] and Pecunix have many established exchanges to paper currencies by various payment methods, and a number of vendors accept them as payment, so an exchange link between Bitcoin and LR/Pecunix would give us 2nd-hop access to all that. The possibility to cash out through them would help support the value of bitcoins.

Clearly, Satoshi had no inherent problem with Liberty Reserve and its ilk, which is just as well for Wright, who claims to have used both Liberty Reserve and WebMoney in the past, as well as an online Russian money exchanger called WebMoney IRK (WMIRK).

Wright says he began coding the Bitcoin client in early 2007, using 'some of the code from earlier with Lasseters', with the whole thing based, supposedly, on his BlackNet creation. Conversely, Satoshi Nakamoto never mentioned a date earlier than 2007 for designing Bitcoin and certainly never mentioned any gambling roots for the code. Wright said in a witness statement for the *COPA v Wright* case that he had a preliminary version of the code ready by early 2008, supplying two printouts of this early code with 'handwritten annotations' as evidence. When the veracity of this evidence was called into question, however, Wright backpedalled and said that it was never intended to be evidence of code from 2008, despite his solicitors defining it as such in their submission to the court. Wright revised his story, stating that the earliest date he could confidently assign to the code was mid-2011, claiming it was based on work from 2008 that had been updated over time.

There exist grave doubts that Wright had the ability to code the Bitcoin client at all. In 2008, he failed three elements of his Master of Information Systems Security certification at Charles Sturt University: IT Management Issues, Principles of Database Level and, most damningly of all, Theory of Computation. In August 2021, programmer Joseph Gardling pointed to an August 2011 post from Wright's now-deleted blog, which stated that it was continuing from a prior blog post on 'securing code'. Wright added as an introduction to this second post that he was 'following up with…more tips of coding that seem to be neglected by the text books', and it was immediately clear to Gardling why textbooks neglected it. Gardling noted that 'Practically everything is wrong' with what Wright had to say and added that it bore all the hallmarks of a 'non-programmer', noting that one of the many errors made by Wright was one that Satoshi had tackled correctly in 2009, two years before Wright got it wrong.

Gardling continued his analysis by looking at a follow-up piece on the same subject by Wright, noting that the new attempt was 'almost entirely shamelessly plagiarized' from a third party, including the comments, which he tried to change 'just enough to avoid being detected' (this is not the last time Wright will be accused of such an action), adding that Wright made just one original contribution to the script which he 'completely screwed up in the most amateur way possible'. Gardling's analysis showed that by 2011, two years after Bitcoin had been coded up and released, Craig Wright still couldn't write error-free code, continually making mistakes where Satoshi previously hadn't. It seems, then, that Wright took a shortcut to adulation by plagiarising the work of other, more proficient coders and passing it off as his own.

A further insult came in 2018 when Wright joined a Twitter conversation over the subject of his alleged inability to code, posting a screenshot of what he claimed was his version of some elementary 'Hello World' computer code. However, a respondent quickly noted that Wright had simply copied and pasted the code from an existing website that showed users how to do it, which led to another castigation:

> *I'm pretty sure 'hello world' is one of the first things any of us learned about coding, if you have to plagiarise hello world code then you definitely know fuck all.*

Wright tried to defend this to his followers in November 2019 when he claimed, 'ALL devs copy and paste code' and that he 'added Easter eggs to my extra long hello world'. Nobody has ever claimed to have found such Easter eggs, and Wright has never revealed them. Interestingly, the reason why the Twitter debate sprang up in the first place was down to Calvin Ayre, Wright's cheerleader-in-chief and part of the group that rescued him from financial ruin in 2015. Ayre claimed that Wright 'invented the internet' due to the number of degrees Wright said he held at the time, but the 'hello world' debacle put paid to this extraordinary claim.

Wright discussed his coding skills at a 2019 Bitcoin conference in Amsterdam, where he said that they were 'shit', claiming that 'like every other academic coder out there, I have no idea about real-world coding.' He clarified this in 2022 by saying that his skills were only inferior to those who code every day, but this, and all his other coding claims, were brutally exposed two years later during the *COPA v Wright* trial. On what was supposed to be the last day of his testimony, Wright was asked to define an unsigned integer, which is essentially used to determine whether a string of data will have a plus or minus prefix and is something that is considered foundation-level knowledge in C++ coding. Wright aborted several attempted answers before seemingly giving up and slumping forward in his chair, admitting that he was 'not sure' how to define it. His interlocutor, Alexander Gunning KC, allowed the agonising silence that followed to go on for almost ten seconds before helping Wright out by defining the term through his use of a very prescient book, *C++ for Dummies*, written by its creator, Bjarne Stroustrup, who was giving evidence against Wright at the trial. The revelation that Wright could not define this fairly basic coding concept stunned even those who already doubted his coding abilities, with crypto advocate and BitcoinersWithoutBorders co-founder Michael Parenti pointing out on Twitter that the unsigned integer function featured in the original Bitcoin source code on over 300 occasions, and so Craig Wright really should have had at least a basic handle on what function it performed seeing as he had supposedly coded it in so many times.

Wright discussed the Bitcoin code during a fireside chat following a 2019 conference, saying 'most of it came from me' but that some cryptographic code came from B-money creator Wei Dai and others. During the *Kleiman v Wright* trial, Wright claimed that he had exchanged both code and viewpoints over Bitcoin with Dai:

> *[Dai] was more interested in how the code would work. Wei pointed me to a project he had been running called B-money. Wei discussed how B-money was very similar to what I was talking about, but he thought that my project wouldn't scale. So he thought it would fail.*

This is false on a number of levels, as anyone who has read the three interactions between Satoshi Nakamoto and Dai, all of which have been publicly available online for many years, can testify: Satoshi asked if he could cite B-money in the Bitcoin whitepaper, Dai replied to say that he could and recommended some other papers, and Satoshi emailed again months later with a draft of the Bitcoin whitepaper. There was no discussion over the potential or otherwise of Bitcoin and certainly no exchange of 'a block of code' as Wright testified during the *Kleiman v Wright* trial. Dai also featured in one of the pieces of manipulated evidence used during the *COPA v Wright* trial when Wright submitted an alleged precursor draft of the Bitcoin whitepaper as evidence, which he said was dated to May 2008. However, this version cited B-money in the footnotes despite Satoshi not finding out about it until August 2008, three months after the date on the draft.

Wright has also offered a different version of history regarding Satoshi's interactions with computer scientist Adam Back, whose creation, Hashcash, is also cited in the Bitcoin whitepaper. In a July 2020 interview, Wright retold his version of Back's introduction to Bitcoin:

> *Adam came into this in 2013, and basically, the whole thing was, 'I got mentioned in the whitepaper, aren't I wonderful?' And that's all he's ever done.*

Wright's animosity towards Back was apparent during the *COPA v Wright* trial when Wright claimed that it was Dai who had pointed him towards his own B-money paper, whereas the Dai-Satoshi emails clearly show Satoshi crediting Back with this. Wright could produce no evidence to support his version of events, consigning this story to the same fate that befell another claim he put forward during the same trial:

> [Back] showed little interest in Bitcoin. His attitude was quite dismissive; he stated that digital cash had been attempted before and was bound to fail. At the time, I did not understand he was pointing at issues associated with creating a cryptocurrency and not digital cash.

Wright had previously voiced this claim during a 2023 interview where he said that Adam Back would never release all the emails between himself and Satoshi because he had 'zero faith in Bitcoin'. Unfortunately for Wright, Back did just that for the *COPA v Wright* case, and nowhere was there any hint of him denigrating Satoshi's ideas or claiming they wouldn't work. When faced with this on the stand, Wright argued that there were other communications from social media platforms and forums that Back hadn't released, a claim Back denied under oath and which Wright did not back up with any evidence. It is not hard to fathom why Wright might seek to downplay Back's influence in the creation of Bitcoin: he has been waging an ideological war against the Englishman for many years due to Back's role in creating Blockstream in 2013, a company Wright claims is intentionally crippling Bitcoin for profit. This is something we will discuss in more detail in later books, but it explains why Wright has tried to airbrush Adam Back from Bitcoin's history. In a deeply ironic twist, Wright accused Back in September 2024 of allowing the world to believe that he, Back, was Satoshi Nakamoto, equating such a notion to a 'fraud' calculated to 'gain credibility and attract investment' to Blockstream. Within minutes, however, a respondent highlighted multiple occasions where Back had said on social media that he unequivocally was not Satoshi Nakamoto; when challenged on these discoveries, Wright failed to respond. Back continues to this day to deny suggestions that he is Satoshi Nakamoto, frequently offering his opinion that the matter should be left alone.

Wright also chose the *COPA v Wright* trial to throw another individual into the mix over his Bitcoin creation claims:

> In early 2008, I discussed the Bitcoin code with Mark Turner, a friend and fellow developer. I communicated with Mark using my real identity, as he was someone I knew personally and trusted. Mark provided candid feedback on the user interface, expressing his honest opinion that he found

it 'ugly' in its current state. As a result of Mark's input and other similar discussions, I tried to improve the front-end software, considering his expertise in user interface design.

This slice of history was erased in a subsequent witness statement and never made a return, suggesting that Turner might have had a change of heart over putting his neck on the line for Wright. Having seen how Justice Mellor felt about the testimony and behaviour of Wright's other witnesses during the *COPA v Wright* trial, Turner's credibility is undoubtedly better for it.

Wright says he finished the code for his Bitcoin minimum viable product in March or April 2007. When he was happy with how this prototype worked, he allegedly began drafting the whitepaper, producing the first-ever example of a handwritten draft for the *Granath v Wright* trial in September 2022. This document, which clocked in at a hefty seventy-six pages, was notable due to the fact that it contained, as one observer noted, 'Very few scratches out/edited sentences, no grammar/spelling corrections, all written in one go, in perfect order, 'neatly' organized.' This is particularly noteworthy as Wright claimed during the same trial to have made almost thirty drafts of the Bitcoin whitepaper, including working on multiple versions at the same time:

> Now, when you use Word, it has one version, and it keeps updating. Back then, I used to work on multiple copies and save multiple copies and cut and paste between them.

To add to this complicated process, Wright said during the *COPA v Wright* trial that he also made changes to documents, producing new ones in the process, before abandoning the changes and going back to the original. This approach makes the already questionable seventy-six-page handwritten version with barely any corrections all the more unlikely. Another clue as to its lack of authenticity is that Bitcoin was referred to by name around the midpoint of the document, despite the fact that Satoshi didn't settle on that name until at least a year after Wright's purported timeframe. Even more damning for Wright was the fact that, on a list of candidate names he had written on the document's inside cover, 'Bitcoin' was not present. Wright also produced dozens of other earlier drafts, written and typed, in 2023 for the *COPA v Wright* case, all of which were flagged by forensics experts on both sides as having multiple issues and inconsistencies. These will be discussed when that trial is examined in a later book, as will

Wright's claims, introduced for the first time in 2023, to have written the whitepaper using software called LaTeX.

The bumper handwritten version of the whitepaper was pointedly hand-dated 'August 2007', written and boxed off at the top of the front page, a date which just so happened to tie in with a story Wright had been telling for some years: in that very month he had a meeting with Alan Granger, the IT manager of BDO, the company the pair were working for at the time, who Wright hoped would allow him to develop Bitcoin in-house for the company's use. Wright said in 2022 that he had written 'maybe 10-12 pages' of the whitepaper by the time this meeting took place, producing evidence for the *Granath v Wright* case in the form of a copy of minutes on a company meeting notepad. This note, which Wright had supposedly kept since 2007, stated that he and Granger had discussed and then delegated such items as a 'p2p ecash as paper' and the completion and testing of related but unspecified code. The document carried such details as the time of the meeting, the venue and a detailed agenda but neglected to state the actual date on which it took place, with 'Aug 07' haphazardly stated in its stead. When commenting on this during the *COPA v Wright* trial, Wright was less than convincing over this omission:

> *I know I had the meeting. I don't remember the exact day of the meeting. I should have actually put it down, but I didn't.*

Like Wright's attempt to claim that he dreamed up elements of the Bitcoin whitepaper at Northumbria University, the truth about this meeting was also revealed during the *COPA v Wright* case. COPA's lawyers tracked down the Chinese manufacturer of the notepad, Quill, whose representatives informed them that the pad featuring that particular design wasn't created until 2009, two years after the meeting between Wright and Granger supposedly took place. In addition, it wasn't released to the market until 2012, suggesting that Wright had gotten hold of one of these more recent versions and manually dated it to 2007. Wright's response to this discovery was astonishing: under questioning, he claimed that he knew more about the manufacturer of the notepad than Quill, having had dealings with the company since the 1990s while working for Staples, blaming a merger for their mistake with the production dates. Justice Mellor ruled that Wright's story, which did not come with any evidence, should be 'rejected as dishonest'.

Wright also says that he sent Alan Granger the final draft of the whitepaper in mid-2008 under the title 'Timechain', which is another name for Timecoin. This claim makes it all the more odd that, when questioned by the *Herald Sun* newspaper on the day Wright was 'unmasked' by *WIRED* and *Gizmodo* in December 2015, Granger, who was by then working for Wright's company DeMorgan, said that he had 'no idea' whether Wright invented Bitcoin or not, adding that he was still 'coming up to speed' on how the cryptocurrency worked. This was despite apparently discussing the concept behind it with Wright during this meeting in 2007 and then, a year later, reading all about it in the whitepaper. This absence of recollection from Granger, plus the fact that the only evidence for his exposure to Bitcoin is a meeting which never took place, suggests that Granger legitimately knew nothing of Bitcoin or Wright's supposed role in it until he joined DeMorgan years later, when he was informed of the notion. This is hardly surprising, however; as we know, COPA's forensic analyst Patrick Madden found that the Timecoin whitepaper was nothing but a revised and backdated copy of the Bitcoin whitepaper.

Wright says that Granger rejected his request for funding for Timechain but passed the idea on to others in the company for their consideration, with Wright naming several such individuals during the *COPA v Wright* trial. When asked why none of these individuals had come forward to testify, Wright claimed that they had all been 'trolled extensively', although he didn't say by whom, while Granger had allegedly received death threats from 'a multitude of people' and had been scared away. One of those who apparently felt safe enough to go into bat for Wright during the *Granath v Wright* and *COPA v Wright* trials was Neville Sinclair, although his testimony during the former trial was hardly clear-cut:

> *I remember a meeting I had with Craig Wright...he came to see me in my office and mentioned that he...talked to Alan [Granger] about possible support for systems that he was in the process of developing...gave me a brief outline and thought whether or not any of our clients might be interested in supporting him in that regard.*

Sinclair went on to give a slightly more detailed description of this technology, saying that what Wright had described to him was 'somewhat similar to what we currently look at in terms of the description of blockchain, but it wasn't referred to in that context.' This is hardly the smoking gun that Wright has proclaimed it to be, with this assertion rendered even more moot by the fact that Sinclair also testified that neither the names Bitcoin nor Satoshi Nakamoto were referenced during either of these meetings. Sinclair also says that Wright only mentioned the name 'Bitcoin' to him for the first time in 2011, a feature that runs through Wright's story like a motif through a stick of Blackpool rock. Unlike the Granger meeting, the Sinclair meeting doesn't seem to have been minuted, which might be to Wright's advantage.

Wright claims to have written about this rejection on another notepad, this one made by DataStation, which was entered into evidence for the *COPA v Wright* case:

> *I cannot get BDO in on this. Alan is OK but other than Neville, no partner wants to listen.*

Unfortunately for Wright, this notepad fared as well as the Quill exhibit; COPA contacted DataStation director Ben Ford, who, through his own dogged investigation, found that the notepad in question was produced no earlier than 22 May 2012. Faced with this, Wright changed his story to claim that the notes related to an ATO tribunal, which just so happened to take place in 2012, rather than relating to anything pre-Bitcoin. This was even more doubtful given that the notes also referred to a forthcoming meeting with Microsoft, something Wright first discussed in January 2021 and which he said took place in mid-2008, where he tried to pitch Bitcoin to the company. Wright said that he had been discussing the prospect of helping Microsoft introduce a Bitcoin-based system as a competitor to their extant ad-based model, a point he expanded on during the *COPA v Wright* trial when he said that Microsoft was interested in 'developing a commercialised internet platform, with integrated micropayments' and that he 'envisioned Microsoft operating Bitcoin at scale, pushing it into the mainstream'. This was borne out on the DataStation notepad:

> *Visiting Microsoft in a few weeks. Need to get the Bing team to understand the option of a micropayment token over an ad-based model.*

COPA, however, had seen the 2008 emails between Wright and Microsoft and found that at no point was there any discussion of Bitcoin, tokens or anything related to them in the lead-up to the interview. Wright claimed that the crucial emails were on a Ridges Estate email account to which he had lost access and added that the mention of Microsoft on the notepad was because they came back to him in 2012 over the potential of micropayments. Ruling on this matter, Justice Mellor found that 'The emails that we do have appear to present a reasonably full picture of a set of communications about a regular job interview process and nothing more than that.'

Another factor in the argument against the claim that Wright was happy to let Microsoft develop Bitcoin stems from his hatred for Silicon Valley, an example of which we find in a 2018 blog post:

> This is the entire purpose of Bitcoin. To make money that is stable, and yet this is the one thing everyone tries to alter, that is to make Bitcoin a typical Silicon Valley 'screw with it and hope that it works' experiment. That's the thing, Bitcoin will never work in this manner.

Wright was even more effusive during the *Granath v Wright* trial:

> I hate Silicon Valley! I can't stand them! I think they're the whole problem of the world right now.

Reading this, we have to ask why Wright claimed to have been in discussions to sell the idea of Bitcoin to a Silicon Valley giant if he despised them so much. Wright revealed his Microsoft claim in early 2021, right at the start of his entanglement with COPA, a collective he described the following year as 'a bunch of Silicon Valley a-holes' who hated him because he '[didn't] want to proverbially rape everyone out because of their data and information.' Wright added that he believed his blockchain platform BSV to be a threat to the business models of the likes of Meta, a COPA member at the time, something he trumpeted ad nauseam in the lead-up to the trial in February 2024.

Wright says that he typed up his handwritten Bitcoin whitepaper in early 2008 and sent the resultant forty-page document to Donald Lynam, Max Lynam (son of Donald) and Zoren Illievich, who Wright described in court in 2021 as 'a person who does a lot of government contract work in Canberra, Australia.' However, a Google search for Zoren Illievich brings up no results at all other than Wright's testimony, although it's possible that Wright was referring to Canberra-based forensic scientist Zoran Iliev, who does indeed have an extensive history working for the Australian government. Wright says he then cut the whitepaper down from forty to twenty pages, sending the resultant copy to Gareth Williams, the MI6 spy who died of suffocation inside a holdall in 2010, who also allegedly helped Wright with 'analyzing graph theory associated with the creation of Bitcoin and some of the mining algorithms that I was planning to implement.' This is as strange as it sounds, but it is not the strangest (or most improbable) involvement of Gareth Williams in Craig Wright's story, as we will see later. If a March 2008 email is to be believed, Wright also sent a copy to Dave Kleiman:

> *I need your help editing a paper I am going to release later this year. I have been working on a new form of electronic money. Bit cash, Bitcoin ...*
>
> *You are always there for me Dave. I want you to be a part of it all.*
>
> *I cannot release it as me. GMX, vistomail and Tor. I need your help and I need a version of me to make this work that is better than me.*
>
> *Craig*

However, this email was proved to be a forgery during the *Kleiman v Wright* case, whereupon Wright alleged that it was not a true version of the real email and blamed Dave's brother, Ira, for introducing a 'slightly modified version' of the email into evidence in order to 'build the case around his brother.' The problem for Wright was that in July 2015, he sent this 'modified' version to his associate Stefan Matthews as proof of his Satoshi claim, which was brought up during the *COPA v Wright* case. Once again, Wright dismissed all knowledge of the message, claiming that his emails had been compromised by a 'wolf in the hen house' inside one of the companies and that he hadn't been the sender. When it was pointed out that in an earlier witness statement, he had confirmed, 'This is an email to Stefan Matthews dated 9 July 2015 at (08.46), in which I forward an email from me to David Kleiman,' Wright tried to claim that the inclusion of the comma in the sentence changed its nature and that his defence that he didn't send it was valid.

Max Lynam confirmed in a roundabout way during testimony for the *Granath v Wright* trial in 2022 that he received 'iteration after iteration' of a document containing elements he would later recognise as being part of the Bitcoin whitepaper, adding that he ran a 'validation script' on a laptop in 2008 as a favour for Wright, with no mention that it was anything to do with Bitcoin. Wright allegedly told the Lynams over dinner in 2013 that what they had actually been doing was mining bitcoins, but claimed during the *COPA v Wright* trial that he didn't feel any need to tell them at the time:

COUNSEL: *You never told them, did you, that they were gaining block rewards, which might have any value?*

WRIGHT: *Oh, it was never about value back then.*

COUNSEL: *You didn't tell them that they were getting block rewards that might have value, did you?*

WRIGHT: *That was never the point. The point was to create a timestamp server. At the time, block rewards weren't valuable.*

Lynam told Wright during their 2013 dinner that the laptop in question had been trashed when the family left their property in 2011, at which point Wright claimed that it had been mining bitcoins the whole time and that there would have been around 6,500 on there. However, this revelation occurred at a time when Wright was getting into extremely hot water with the ATO over his Bitcoin claims, so this may simply have been Wright looking to plant another Bitcoin-related seed that might bear fruit later. In February 2023, Wright was pressed on why he didn't tell the Lynams that they were running the Bitcoin software, to which they could have testified in court. His response was hardly convincing:

Why does that matter? It didn't have a marketing name. I'm not a good marketing person.

Lynam twice testified that he had been mining bitcoins for Wright, but in neither case was he able to say that Wright used the name 'Bitcoin', and there is no evidence other than Wright's word that the laptop had been doing anything of the sort. During the *Granath v Wright* trial, Lynam said that Wright had told him at that 2013 dinner that the coins on the laptop's drive would only have been worth a few hundred dollars at the time it had been dumped, adding that it 'definitely wasn't worth going and trying to find a computer that was put into landfill a couple of years ago.' This is far from accurate: the coins on the laptop could theoretically have been worth as much as US$125,000 by late 2011 and US$6.5 million by the time of the dinner in late 2013, so it's no surprise that

Wright tried to throw the Lynams off the scent, given that he couldn't risk them finding the bitcoin-less laptop.

In May 2008, Satoshi Nakamoto sent Adam Back and Wei Dai a draft of the Bitcoin whitepaper, but this represents a problem for Wright, who claims the pair were both dismissive of the very concept of Bitcoin in their earlier exchanges. As we have seen and as we will continue to see, when someone crosses Craig Wright, they can typically expect negative repercussions, and so it is extremely out of character to believe that Wright seemingly tried to get them back on board again. Equally as unlikely is the suggestion that Wright would neglect to mention any prior disagreements between himself and the pair in the follow-up emails, and yet there is none.

Satoshi sent the drafts via a link to file-sharing site upload.ae, which Wright claimed during the *COPA v Wright* case to have owned:

> *I also operated a secondary server in Melbourne, known as upload.ae, to mirror some of the directories. Upload.ae was linked to my Bigpond company account. I established a mirroring process between the Malaysian and Melbourne servers to ensure data consistency and availability.*

However, when COPA's counsel Jonathan Hough pointed out that upload.ae was operated by one Faisal Al Khaja, a citizen of the UAE, Wright claimed that Al Khaja ran the service and he, Wright, 'had a subdomain on it', something he had never mentioned in his earlier witness statements and had no evidence of. Wright added that he sent the same whitepaper draft to Gareth Williams, Zoren Illievich and Donald Lynam, of which there is also no evidence. This all points to a simple narrative: Satoshi used upload.ae to host the whitepaper draft, which he sent to Wei Dai and Adam Back for their thoughts following their earlier help.

Wright claimed during the *Kleiman v Wright* trial that Donald Lynam had a much bigger role in Bitcoin's creation than that of mere whitepaper recipient, alleging that he helped Wright to 'set everything up'. Uncle Don didn't remember it this way, however:

> COUNSEL: *If someone said that you edited that paper, that would be incorrect?*
>
> LYNAM: *That would be incorrect.*

> COUNSEL: *If someone said that you helped set up Bitcoin, that would also be incorrect?*
>
> LYNAM: *Yes.*

Lynam added that he received a 'highly technical' copy of the Bitcoin whitepaper from Craig Wright in mid-2008, which he decided not to attempt to edit because of its complexity, although he added that there were 'no doubts in my mind whatsoever that [Wright] was the sole creative author' of the Bitcoin whitepaper. He also added that Wright informed him of his plan to publish under a pseudonym 'when it came to the point he said he was planning actually to [launch Bitcoin]' and confirmed Max's story that the family had mined bitcoins between 2009 and 2011. However, having reviewed Lynam's testimony as part of the *COPA v Wright* trial, Justice Mellor rejected it:

> *I have little doubt that Mr Don Lynam wanted to believe the best of his nephew but also that he had been carefully prepared for his evidence in his Kleiman deposition. In all the circumstances, I conclude that his account was made up. Accordingly, the extracts from his Kleiman deposition carry no weight at all.*

There are some as yet unmentioned alleged recipients of the Bitcoin whitepaper from Wright's various accounts that are worth discussing. The first is 'some people at the university I was with in Newcastle, Australia', who, Wright says, received both the first and second typed drafts. This is problematic because, as we know, Wright was supposedly trying to keep a low profile at the university and remain 'just another postgraduate researcher and student' rather than opening up as Bitcoin's creator. If this was his goal, it seems counterproductive to send staff a copy of the Bitcoin whitepaper. Wright could argue that the document was labelled Timechain/Timecoin rather than Bitcoin or that he sent it under his Satoshi Nakamoto pseudonym, but this presents another problem: we are asked to believe that this collection of individuals, who must have been incredibly surprised to see a whitepaper for a cryptographic digital currency land in their inboxes from a random Japanese man, never thought to mention it to Craig Wright, even in passing. He was also relying on them not to put two and two together and conclude that it might be he who had sent it in the first place. Wright has never stated to whom he sent these versions of the whitepaper at Newcastle University, so this claim is impossible to verify.

Wright summarised the level to which he allowed his Satoshi mask to slip in a witness statement for the *COPA v Wright* case, where he listed twenty-one people to whom he sent the whitepaper in his own name and fourteen who received it from him as Satoshi Nakamoto. This included sending drafts to representatives from the Australian Stock Exchange, RailCorp, News Ltd, Hoyts, Sporting Bet and Qudos Bank. He also apparently discussed the concepts behind Bitcoin with teaching staff from Charles Sturt, Newcastle and Northumbria universities and members of the SANS Institute, but has no idea who. This, then, firmly puts paid to his claim, made in a deposition for the *Kleiman v Wright* trial and repeated many times since, that 'I did not reveal myself to anyone.' During the *COPA v Wright* trial, Wright was questioned as to how many of the twenty-one alleged recipients had confirmed their receipt publicly, which COPA alleged numbered two. Wright tried to argue, again, that his project morphed along the way, saying, 'You're mixing up my larger Timecoin implementation and Bitcoin' to excuse COPA's calculation.

Another person to whom Wright says he gave the whitepaper at this early stage was Stefan Matthews, who was working as Chief Information Officer at Sydney-based online sports betting operator Centrebet at the time. In 2005, Centrebet's owners brought in BDO to perform audits, and among the four-person team sent out to work on it was Wright. Being locally based, Wright was the individual in touch with Matthews and the Centrebet team on a regular basis, and Matthews claimed in a 2021 interview that Wright started pitching him various ideas to do with electronic cash during their time together:

> *[Wright] was constantly trying to get me involved in concepts around electronic cash, e-cash, digital gold, gold-backed electronic cash, all sorts of things during a six or seven-month period from early 2008 to... third quarter of 2008.*

This is problematic because, as we know, Satoshi Nakamoto began working on Bitcoin in 2007 and published the whitepaper in October 2008, so it doesn't make sense that Wright was pitching Matthews all these alternatives while at the same time ramping up to launch Bitcoin. Matthews changed his story for the *Granath v Wright* trial a year later, presumably following a quick but important word from Wright, where he got back on script, saying that it was indeed 2007 in which Wright began pitching him these ideas, not 2008.

Matthews's story of how he received the whitepaper is also riddled with inconsistencies. In 2016 he told Andrew O'Hagan that Wright gave him 'a document written by someone called Satoshi Nakamoto'; in a June 2021 interview, he said 'hand on heart' that the paper did not have the name Satoshi Nakamoto on it; a year later, *CoinGeek* reported that Matthews 'can't recall if the document was credited to Satoshi Nakamoto'; and two months later at the *Granath v Wright* trial, Matthews went back to his 2021 story that the paper had no name on it whatsoever. Matthews stuck to this story for the *COPA v Wright* trial in 2024 when he said 'with certainty' that it had no name on it, at the same time disowning his 2016 explanation, claiming that he 'never told Andrew O'Hagan that it had the name Satoshi Nakamoto on it'. Matthews also claimed in a 2021 interview to have seen versions of the whitepaper with Wright's name on it after August 2008, but unless Wright was studiously dating his versions (which, as we have seen, is not his strong point), Matthews would have had no way of knowing whether they were later or earlier versions, particularly given the thirty versions Wright was supposedly working on simultaneously.

It isn't just the paper's author that represents a problem for Matthews; the format is also an issue. Matthews claims that Wright handed him a USB stick in August 2008, from which he printed the paper, the same month that Satoshi Nakamoto uploaded the draft copy for Dai and Back. Unfortunately for Matthews, Wright's story is different; Wright has said that he handed Matthews a hard copy, claiming that he gave his then-client the 'second to last iteration'. Wright attempted to smooth out the cracks in this story during the *COPA v Wright* trial when he said that he gave Matthews multiple copies of the paper under different names at different times and in different formats, but this only led him to dig himself another hole: when asked why he only mentioned one such occasion in his witness statement instead of listing all of them, Wright responded, 'I didn't think I had to' (Matthews has only ever said that he saw one copy of the whitepaper). Justice Mellor ruled on his interpretation of the Wright-Matthews story following the *COPA v Wright* trial, noting that he was 'satisfied that Mr Matthews did not receive a copy of the Bitcoin White Paper in 2008 and his evidence about receiving a copy of it before it was made public was made up.'

When it comes to the contents of the whitepaper he never received, Matthews's story is that he wasn't surprised by what he read, given that it represented a combination of the ideas Wright had been pushing on him since 2007 (or 2008). He claims that he told Wright he wasn't interested in the concept of Bitcoin, completing a hatrick of alleged rejections for Wright, but Wright went ahead anyway. A few months after this, Wright supposedly asked Matthews if he could borrow a sum of money, offering Matthews 50,000 bitcoins as collateral. Matthews, however, didn't want 'this Bitcoin stuff' and refused. This highly insubstantial anecdote has even been used in court as an example of Wright's access to bitcoins at this time, and yet it comes with its own problems: according to *CoinGeek* and Matthews's testimony for the *COPA v Wright* case, the sum of money in question was $500, but according to Wright it was $100. Unsurprisingly, Wright and Matthews cannot back up this story with any evidence, and Justice Mellor ruled that it was one of a number of fabrications the pair had come up with to bolster Wright's fictional Satoshi claim. As we will see, Matthews became heavily invested in the success of Wright's projects in 2015, adding to the lack of impartiality when it comes to his evidence over such matters. Indeed, Andrew O'Hagan noted in 'The Satoshi Affair' that Matthews spent more time 'selling the idea of Wright as Satoshi rather than investigating it', which, in hindsight, is a very telling observation.

Another controversial recipient of the August 2008 draft copy of the Bitcoin whitepaper was, according to Wright, Dave Kleiman. Wright first referenced Kleiman's supposed involvement as a Satoshi contributor in February 2014, claiming that the Floridian assisted in both the design of Bitcoin and its early mining. However, this changed in February 2018 when the *Kleiman v Wright* lawsuit was filed, which was based on Wright and Kleiman's supposed work on Bitcoin. In order to win this case, Wright and his team had to maintain that Wright created Bitcoin alone, which was problematic because Wright had spent four years telling various individuals, including the Kleiman family, that he and Dave had developed it as a partnership. This will be explored more in Volume II, but the filing of this lawsuit represents the moment when Wright began to airbrush Dave Kleiman from Bitcoin's history and paint himself as the sole creator.

It's worth stopping here to examine a key claim of Craig Wright's that falls down the moment we look at the evidence offered to support it. Ever since he first addressed the 2015 *WIRED* and *Gizmodo* 'doxxings', Wright has vehemently stated that he never wanted to be identified as Bitcoin's creator.

However, this argument looks as hollow as a cheap Easter egg when matched with Wright's own version of history, as outlined here (some of the claims below will be addressed later in the book):

- Wright says he provided early copies of the Bitcoin whitepaper to family members, clients of his employer, friends, associates, and forgotten members of academic institutions. These were allegedly sent under Satoshi Nakamoto's name and under his own name.
- Wright claims to have shown a draft of the Bitcoin whitepaper to a group of students as part of an exercise on how to amend metadata within a document.
- Wright's public blog contained references to Bitcoin before it was launched (these were subsequently found to have been backdated).
- Wright believed that up to four hundred people within the ATO knew he was Satoshi Nakamoto following his 2009/10 tax return and subsequent battle.
- Wright emailed multiple people in 2014 to tell them that he, Dave Kleiman and others created Bitcoin.
- Wright claimed in 2024 that 'most of the people working at my firms knew who I was'.

These are just some of the more egregious ways in which Wright has undermined his claim that he wanted to keep his alleged Bitcoin creation quiet over the years, even maintaining during the *COPA v Wright* trial that this still amounted to a 'small circle of people'. It is interesting to note that not one of these individuals came out in support of Wright in the wake of the December 2015 *WIRED* and *Gizmodo* pieces or the year after when he faced ridicule over a failed proof event. In fact, it took until the *Kleiman v Wright* trial in 2021 for a handful to back Wright's Satoshi claim on the stand, with the most supportive testimony being that Wright *could* have created Bitcoin. Since then, Wright has typically relied on the same select band of individuals whose testimony has only ever had a neutral or negative impact on his defence; across the three trials in which Wright has used witnesses, their testimonies have been found to be either inconsequential or fictional. When the *WIRED* and *Gizmodo* 'doxxings' broke in December 2015, Wright's long-term project manager Alan Pedersen told Andrew O'Hagan that he believed Wright wanted to be recognised as Satoshi, saying it was 'in his personality' and that he was 'pushing for [the December 2015 exposé] to happen'. He also added that it had only taken two weeks of working with Wright to come to the conclusion that Wright wanted public recognition for the creation of Bitcoin. This goes against Wright's claim that he was determined to remain private.

Put simply, even if we are to believe that Wright wrote and distributed this plethora of Bitcoin whitepaper drafts between 2007 and 2008, this doesn't stack up with his later claims to have wanted to stay in the shadows. The paucity of evidence backing up his version of history from this period, plus the unconvincing and sometimes fraudulent witness testimony in support of it, is telling. In stark contrast, the real Satoshi Nakamoto was so successful in ensuring his anonymity that no one has even gotten close to knowing any personal information about him apart from the fact that he was in Van Nuys for one day in 2009.

The question of whether or not Wright wrote the Bitcoin whitepaper was a central tenet of the *COPA v Wright* case, and Wright's assertions looked to have been obliterated when Patrick Madden used forensic analysis to destroy the authenticity of all Wright's whitepaper drafts and precursor works. Just days after Madden's report dropped in September 2023, Wright supposedly found a whole host of earlier drafts on storage devices in a drawer, managing to get the trial delayed so that they could be entered into evidence. However, these new files were found to have been forgeries created in the weeks leading up to their 'discovery', with the court shown an animation of Wright effectively reverse engineering the whitepaper into the LaTeX source files he claimed to have just found. In his ruling, Justice Mellor was unequivocal about Wright's LaTeX claims:

> *It is likely that the first time that the content of the Bitcoin White Paper encountered LaTeX was in September 2023 when Dr Wright set about trying to create a forgery or forgeries which he thought (mistakenly) would not suffer from having metadata which would reveal it or them to be forged.*

The creation of the LaTeX files was the latest in a long line of whitepaper forgeries by Wright, adding yet more hours to the hundreds he had already dedicated to perpetuating his myth. Throughout the three trials that featured discussions over Wright's Satoshi claim, which took place between 2021 and 2024, Wright was found to have carefully edited and backdated professional papers to include references to Bitcoin or blockchain technology as well as combing through his academic papers to find passages that might, however tangentially, connect to its concepts. He was found to have coached witnesses to imbue conversations from decades ago with similar levels of retrospective importance, applying the same principle to documents which were also unconnected to Bitcoin or blockchain. He even went to such extremes as creating that seventy-six-page version of an early whitepaper draft, attempting to complete the mirage with artificially rusted staples and coffee marks like a child's tea-stained treasure map. These examples highlight the lengths Wright was forced to go to as the walls closed steadily in, seemingly unaware that each new forgery saw him sinking further into a quicksand from which he would never emerge.

Wright conjured up many forgeries for the ATO between 2013 and 2015, a feat he repeated four years later when he kicked off his libel lawsuit frenzy, but it was the *COPA v Wright* case that really pushed his activities in this arena into overdrive. His perpetual forgeries were debunked almost as quickly as he could make them, leaving him facing a race against time to come up with the perfect, incontestable forgery. Unfortunately for him, his sloppiness was matched only by his hubris and the underestimation of his opposition, leading to Justice Mellor ending Wright's campaign once and for all with one simple sentence:

> *...the suggestion that Dr Wright drafted the Bitcoin White Paper or anything like it is pure fabrication. The account he gave in his witness statement(s)...was pure fantasy.*

Wright's claim to have written the Bitcoin whitepaper, born in early 2014 and castrated in May 2024, was backed by nothing but a cavalcade of confabulation and messy forgeries, leaving none but his most blindly loyal supporters distinctly unimpressed by his efforts. If Craig Wright's Bitcoin whitepaper evidence was unconvincing, however, then his claims over its launch were simply extraordinary.

Chapter 5 – Life on the Mining Farm

On 22 August 2008, Satoshi Nakamoto again uploaded a draft of the Bitcoin whitepaper to upload.ae, but more importantly, he also bought the domain Bitcoin.org through the Anonymous Speech service. At least, we assume this was Satoshi, given that Anonymous Speech hid the buyer's identity. Craig Wright asserted in a 2019 blog post that he paid Anonymous Speech for the domain with a credit card, claiming that he had bank records showing the purchase, a claim he pushed on more than one occasion over the following months without offering up the records themselves. He promised the same later that year in an unpublished interview with *The Financial Times*, where he agreed that the records were his 'big bit of evidence' and claimed that he hadn't released them before then because he 'didn't want to'.

The perpetually promised records finally came to light in 2022 as part of the haul collected from Wright's systems for the *COPA v Wright* case, where a 10 June 2019 email from Wright to his 'litigation liaison' at the time, Jimmy Nguyen (pronounced Nu-win), was presented:

> *Anonymous Speech is vistomail. 4557-0256-7578-1583 is my old credit card. All the credit card shows is 'AnonymousSpeech'. You need to have the Vistomail document as well.*

The email was accompanied by screenshots from a National Australia Bank (NAB) credit card statement showing an expenditure of $687.12 on 30 August 2008 and an associated international payment fee, supposedly representing Wright's purchase of the domain and Satoshi's Vistomail email account. COPA was immediately sceptical over the legitimacy of the screenshots and had them analysed by Patrick Madden, who found that timestamps dated them no earlier than June 2019, the month Wright sent the email to Nguyen. This was important because of another discovery: in 2019, it wasn't possible for an NAB customer to access records as far back as 2008 on the bank's online portal; a request to the bank was necessary for such information. This, Madden concluded, meant that 'content of the webpage cannot be relied upon.' Anonymous Speech closed its virtual doors in 2021, signing off by thanking its users and issuing a final, appropriately misspelt notice:

> *and lastly Craig Steve Wrigh[t] is not Satoshi! He is just a lone[l]y person looking for real friends.*

Following Patrick Madden's analysis, Wright changed his story, admitting that the records *were* fake but claiming that he had known this all along:

> *The two screenshots of the National Australia Bank ('NAB') credit card statements...were sent to me by Rivero Mestre, a law firm in the US. I recollect that Amanda McGovern sent these screenshots to me using WhatsApp, on the 9th or 10th of June 2019 for the purpose of discussion related to the US Kleiman case. The images had been sent to her using a direct message from a pseudonymous Reddit user, whose identity remains undisclosed.*

Wright added that the purpose of the email to Jimmy Nguyen wasn't to prove he had bought Bitcoin.org but was instead reflective of him asking the lawyer for help in confirming they were fake, which he said was obvious to anyone not reading the email without preconceived notions. In the box, Wright was asked if he believed the person who had made the fakes was out to help him or harm him:

> *I don't know. I have a lot of people who think they are helping me but actually harm me. They think that they're helping when they do things, but they're not.*

This statement raises the suggestion that someone within Wright's orbit faked the screenshots and sent them to his U.S. law firm in order to bolster his case without informing him of what they were doing, a scenario as unlikely as the alternative: that one of Wright's enemies faked a credit card statement that they knew would turn out to be exposed as a forgery in order to discredit him and seeded it through Reddit and his gullible lawyer.

One of the more glaring issues with Wright's story is that at no point did he tell COPA that he considered the screenshots to be fakes, instead allowing them to proceed under the assumption that they should be considered genuine right up until they were exposed as forgeries. Wright explained this away by suggesting that many documents had come from laptops belonging to former employees of the companies he ran between 2011 and 2014, whom he believed were out to sabotage his businesses. As such, he said, all documents entered into evidence from these devices should have been considered tainted. When asked why he hadn't made more of an effort to flag the documents he considered fake, Wright stated that it should have been obvious in transcripts from prior lawsuits, primarily the *Kleiman v Wright* case, that all documents originating from ex-staff laptops should have been considered suspect. However, COPA discovered that there was no record of any such disclosures in the Kleiman files, which left Wright scrambling for an excuse. In desperation, he invented a lawyer in whom he had supposedly confided, hiding behind legal privilege to avoid naming them. Justice Mellor, however, was having none of it:

> J MELLOR: *If they told you not to reveal something, you should identify them.*
>
> WRIGHT: *Um... er... Johnny... um... I can't remember Johnny's last name; I haven't dealt with him in a while. He's a Sikh.*
>
> J MELLOR: *Which firm was he from?*
>
> WRIGHT: *An American firm that was basically dealing with one of the American entity companies. He's a corporate lawyer.*

Wright promised to find Johnny the Sikh's last name, but never did. Worse was to come for Wright when his genuine credit card records from the period were presented in court and showed no purchases relating to Bitcoin.org or Anonymous Speech. This genuine credit card number matched the 'fake' number in the 2019 email to Jimmy Nguyen, leaving Wright unable to explain how the Redditor who supplied the records to his lawyer, Amanda McGovern, had managed to get hold of his credit card details.

Wright also chose this debunking as the moment to change his story about how he paid for Bitcoin.org and the Vistomail account. Having said for four years that he had used his credit card, in October 2023, Wright pivoted, stating that he 'never claimed that the Bitcoin domain was purchased using my NAB credit card' and added that, now, he couldn't actually remember how he paid for it. When pressed on this matter during the *COPA v Wright* trial, Wright embarked on a never-before-told explanation, claiming that he had used the New Zealand branch of online payment provider WebMoney to make the purchase. Wright said that although he remembered using WebMoney, he wasn't sure which credit or debit card was actually used within the WebMoney wallet, which explained his prior lapse of memory with regard to the payment method. This story, of course, is totally at odds with his prior claim that he possessed bank records that could back up his purchase of Bitcoin.org, leading to the following assumption by COPA:

> *It was an obvious fiction made up on the spot, Dr Wright having forgotten what he had said in a previous statement.*

Wright's final effort to prove access to the Vistomail account came through four separate videos he submitted as evidence for the *COPA v Wright* case, which he claimed were taken in 2019 and purported to show him having access to Satoshi Nakamoto's Vistomail account, including proof of his purchase of Bitcoin.org. Wright's supporters, of course, took these videos as a slam dunk, but Patrick Madden wasn't so sure: he found that the footer in Wright's videos did not match the footer actually present on Vistomail in 2019, with Wright arguing that the site showed a different footer when logged in, something he couldn't prove as the site had since shut down. Wright was not shown logging into the site, and rather than taking one video of himself navigating it, he took four videos of him scrolling through individual pages, having already supposedly navigated there before pressing record. His rationale for doing this, as he explained to Jonathan Hough, was unconvincing:

HOUGH:	*Why record a separate video for each page, though? Why not navigate between them on the video?*
WRIGHT:	*Because then you have to put down your phone and move round.*
HOUGH:	*You can't operate a mouse and a phone at the same time? Is that your evidence?*
WRIGHT:	*And hold the thing still? No.*

This is quite the admission from the man who claimed in May 2025, 'I climb vertical cliffs for fun—because walking on flat ground with the herd is too dull for someone who prefers gravity as an adversary.' To further undermine the evidentiary value of the videos, COPA noted that the address bar had been carefully cropped out of the video, meaning it was impossible to know which website Wright was actually on. There was also a problem with the date the videos were supposedly taken. Wright had claimed during a March 2020 deposition for the *Kleiman v Wright* case that he had no way of accessing the Vistomail site, and yet here were four videos of him doing just that a few months earlier. Had he forgotten about them? When this was put to him by Jonathan Hough, Wright blamed confusion over sub-accounts and had an interesting explanation as to why he hadn't mentioned such a distinction in 2020:

> *I was very hostile. I was very upset. I felt betrayed by Ira Kleiman, and I reacted badly in the court. So I admit that.*

This doesn't tally with the transcript of this part of his deposition, however, where we see Wright at his calmest, giving lengthy and composed explanations of various matters, with no signs of him being upset or hostile whatsoever. Discussion of this matter led to Wright making a stunning admission to Hough:

WRIGHT: I was being particularly difficult...I did get really annoyed with that case and...I didn't lie, but I didn't give information about the site. So you're correct.

HOUGH: So you may have told the truth and nothing but the truth...but not the whole truth?

WRIGHT: I wasn't asked the rest of the question and I'm doing beyond what I need to now. I should have actually said how it worked; I didn't.

Wright also claimed during the *COPA v Wright* case that Simon Cohen, a partner at this former law firm Ontier, had accessed the Vistomail site in 2019 before Wright lost access, but Wright could not provide any evidence of this, and Cohen never confirmed getting such access.

Wright's actions regarding this single piece of evidence are symptomatic of his modus operandi across many aspects of his legal affairs: if a previously authenticated document is proven to be a forgery, he will dismiss it and blame someone else for contaminating it or secretly slipping it into his files. This specific example of the Bitcoin.org purchase serves a double purpose regarding Wright's methods in that he will also often blame other people who, for various reasons, are unable to counter his allegations. In this instance, Wright's story of Amanda McGovern and the mysterious Redditor only appeared after McGovern had passed away, making it impossible to question her about the incident. As we will see, Wright also has a nasty habit of using such devices to throw out wild accusations in the witness box, knowing that his targets often cannot respond in kind.

On 31 October 2008, the Bitcoin whitepaper was uploaded to Bitcoin.org. Satoshi Nakamoto posted about it in the Cypherpunk Mailing List, opening with the summary, 'I've been working on a new electronic cash system that's fully peer-to-peer, with no trusted third party.' He linked to the paper before replicating the process on another cryptography mailing list, Metzdowd.com. Wright, however, disputes this version of events:

> *Bitcoin was never, never released on a Cypherpunk mailing list. Anyone who ever tells you that is either stupid or lying.*

Wright's theory on this matter dates back to 2019, having failed to mention it to any noticeable degree in the three and a half years since he was first connected with its creation through the *WIRED* and *Gizmodo* pieces. That year, however, he became publicly vehement that Bitcoin had nothing to do with the cypherpunk movement, claiming that the cypherpunks embraced the ideals of WikiLeaks and its founder, Julian Assange, with whom Wright had quarrelled in the mid-1990s. This vehemence only grew in the years that followed and is neatly summed up in a February 2022 message to his followers:

> *If you bullshit, [and] you are fucking brain dead stupid and a total cunt and dumb as a dead slug, then you may think bitcoin had ANY connection to the cypherpunk movement in its development. It didn't.*

In December 2022, Wright publicly offered 50 bitcoins from the first block on the Bitcoin blockchain to anyone who could show him where 'Satoshi (me) posted bitcoin on the cypherpunk mailing list', adding, 'The cryptography mailing list has no links, and nothing to do with the cypherpunk list.' No one took Wright up on the offer, which may have had something to do with the fact that Wright had already blocked all dissenters, leaving a collection of sycophants as his only followers. This is a favoured tactic of Wright and his backers, a strategy that has allowed Wright to exist in an echo chamber where he only ever receives praise for his comments and ideas and avoids difficult questions. Despite claiming that the Bitcoin whitepaper 'provably wasn't' posted to the Cypherpunk Mailing List, Wright has never offered public proof of an alternative passage the whitepaper took to publication. As we have mentioned, there is a good reason why Wright wants to disassociate Bitcoin from the cypherpunk movement: he was never accepted into the cypherpunk clique, and given that he supposedly created Bitcoin, he cannot allow it to stem from the cypherpunk ideology, seeing as it didn't match his personal outlook. This misdirection was neatly summarised in an October 2022 post on the BSV website:

> *The propagation of the idea that [the Bitcoin whitepaper] was released on the cypherpunks mailing list creates a loaded premise that Satoshi Nakamoto was in alignment with the ideological underpinnings of that mailing list, rather than a serious professional who wanted to keep abreast of the latest developments in the field of cryptography.*

And who could this 'serious professional' be? No prizes for guessing.

In mid-December 2008, just three weeks before Bitcoin's launch, Wright headed to India to present his data-wiping paper with Dave Kleiman and Shyaam Sundhar. This is notable for two reasons. First, it would have been at a crucial time in Bitcoin's development, and so it would have been a particularly awkward moment for Wright to have to focus on something else. Second, Satoshi's online activity around this time didn't change, suggesting that Wright persevered with his 5 p.m. bedtime, which would have been around midday in India. Sundhar told *Gizmodo* in 2015 that neither Wright nor Kleiman ever mentioned anything related to Bitcoin or digital currencies during the time they spent together, which is odd considering that at that point in time, according to Wright's pre-2018 statements, Kleiman was heavily involved in Bitcoin. Sundhar also didn't notice Wright nipping off with his laptop at all hours to work on something else or sleeping the afternoons away.

Wright's lead solicitor in the *Kleiman v Wright* case, Andrés Rivero, referenced this period in a 2023 interview, where, while discussing months' worth of emails between Wright and Kleiman, he inadvertently undermined Wright's pre-lawsuit claims that the pair were working on Bitcoin at this time:

> *You'll notice that something they haven't mentioned is the word 'Bitcoin' because in these emails between these two men at the critical time period, the word 'Bitcoin' never appears [and] the word 'blockchain' never appears.*

If the pair had designed Bitcoin together, it is clearly inconceivable that they would not have been discussing it in any context just weeks before its launch. It is also similarly implausible that, had he designed it on his own, Wright wouldn't have mentioned his creation to his best friend at this crucial point.

The 2008 financial crisis forced BDO to cut staff and offer redundancy packages, with Wright using this as an opportunity to work on something new, as he claimed in an email to Dave Kleiman on 27 December:

> *Dave. My wife will not be happy, but I am not going back to work. I need time to get my idea going. Alan told me they are trying to make people redundant and I will walk into it and use the funds to keep me going...I need your help. You edited my paper and now I need to have you aid me build this idea.*

This email, which elsewhere references the implementation of multiple racks of servers for the unnamed project, may well be genuine as it discusses merely 'my idea' rather than Bitcoin, which could reference any of the various projects Wright would start in his post-BDO years, all of which required servers. Wright described this moment again during testimony for the *Granath v Wright* trial in 2022, saying that it was the catalyst for the breakdown of his marriage:

> *I came home one day and I told my wife, 'I've taken a redundancy, and I'm not getting another job. I've got this project I'm doing.' And...she wasn't terribly happy.*

This is hardly surprising, although as we will learn, it was, in fact, a relationship with another woman that ultimately cost Wright his marriage. Wright also claims that around this time a Professor Dawn Song convinced him to leave BDO, telling his followers in April 2018 that Professor Song 'was the first person to listen to me as me and not think bitcoin a joke.' This conversation allegedly took place during the lunch break at an unnamed conference, with

Professor Song helping Wright to 'decide to accept a redundancy from BDO' and advising him to 'trust in my passion and dreams'. Wright has, however, never called on Professor Song to testify to this in court, and Professor Song has never publicly referenced Craig Wright, Satoshi Nakamoto or Bitcoin.

The truth about Wright's situation at this time is, perhaps unsurprisingly, markedly different from what he has publicly claimed. Wright established Information Defense Pty Ltd (Information Defense) on 29 January 2008, weeks after he left BDO, which purported to be in the business of securing and maintaining code for various online casinos and sports betting operations. Wright set about creating a network of computers to serve his clients, some at his home in Lisarow, a town positioned between Sydney and Newcastle on Australia's east coast, and some at a farm he owned in Port Macquarie near Bagnoo, a small agricultural region some 250 miles north-east of Sydney. This seemed to keep Wright busy, as Lynn recalled in her testimony for the *Kleiman v Wright* case in 2020:

> COUNSEL: *Speaking of computers, did Craig have a lot of computers?*
>
> LYNN: *Yes, he did. Well, we had to have servers in here and at the farm that we had, because of the 24/7 monitoring of our clients. He had to be available, if something happened with one of the clients, that he could do remote work from.*

Wright indeed spent time on the road nipping up to the farm to ensure that the servers were still ticking over and his clients supported, building up enough of a base to branch out with another company, Integyrs Pty Ltd (Integyrs), which he founded two months later. This, he said on his LinkedIn profile, was a risk modelling company involved in 'Algorithmic and secure software design and code analysis' and which had a deal with 'a major multinational gaming company'. Wright argued in a 2021 blog post that the two companies were successful enough to have staff:

> *Few people seem to understand that Information Defense and Integyrs each had staff. Contrary to the popular opinion that seems to be floating around, I was not acting alone in 2009. I had people working for me.*

This 'popular opinion' was not just shared by any old Tom, Dick and Harry; it was shared by the only person who was there at the time – Lynn Wright:

> COUNSEL: Do you know if anyone else worked at Integyrs besides Craig?
>
> LYNN: No, I – I think it was just him.

The evidence of this period makes it clear that, far from creating Bitcoin following his departure from BDO, Wright used his golden handshake to launch several companies connected to the IT security sector, which was, after all, his forte.

Satoshi Nakamoto launched Bitcoin on Saturday, 3 January 2009, with the first block (called the Genesis block) created that day and the next block, block 1, coming along six days later. Why the delay? In April 2019, Wright explained that the fault lay with Microsoft's patching program:

> *I had configured all of the machines with the same time zones, even those in different countries. They all shut down to patch at the same time. The entire Bitcoin network stopped following the genesis block, and needed to be started again.*

Wright's story, in case you hadn't guessed by now, is that his Bagnoo server farm wasn't created to support the clients of his new businesses; it was, instead, where Bitcoin was born. Wright claims that he painstakingly built a network of mining machines ('69 computers plus other equipment') at a cost of some $600,000 and had a high-speed cable internet service installed in the region, with everything up and running until Microsoft scuppered his plans with the rollout of its monthly 'Patch Tuesday'. Wright stated in June 2019 that the impact was severe:

> *Literally on that Tuesday night, everything updated, turned off and restarted.*

This is a nice little story, but it doesn't survive scrutiny. First, Lynn testified that Wright only had 'about four or five' computers at the farm, which is damning in itself, but it's also important to note that this particular Patch Tuesday took place on Tuesday, 13 January 2009, rather than ten days prior, as Wright claimed, which, as we know, was a Saturday. This was put to Wright during the *COPA v Wright* trial, where he offered a multitude of reasons why he was correct, including the fact that Patch Tuesday was a generic term for updates and didn't always happen on a Tuesday. This is true in that there have been a handful of occasions over the years when the rollout has been delayed, but this was not the case on 13 January. Wright then claimed in the witness box that he was part of the Microsoft Developer Network (MSDN), something he had never mentioned before in any court case, CV, email, blog post or forum comment, and for which he provided no evidence. Wright claimed that his MSDN membership allowed him to receive patches early and that it was the early application of these patches that caused the computers to crash on the 3rd. Of course, someone who has achieved the level of MSDN member should have been aware of the dangers posed by a Microsoft patch to their system in the first place and mitigated against it. The real reason for the six-day gap between the Genesis Block and Block 1 is straightforward: Satoshi was still preparing the downloadable Bitcoin client. This software package was released on 8 January 2009, during which time Satoshi deliberately refrained from mining, with his own mining activity beginning only after other users, like those mentioned, had started. Satoshi also noted no outages of the Bitcoin system on 13 January, certainly none that forced the entire system offline for days on end.

Wright maintains that he spent the week Bitcoin was offline driving back and forth between his home and the farm, trying to bring it back up. This was a seven-hour round trip, with Wright claiming his mileage as a business expense, something he says was a source of contention with the ATO when it came to his tax affairs. As we will see, however, this is a red herring that Wright is keen to bring out and wave in front of naysayers on the rare occasion he allows himself an encounter with them. The frequency of his trips was such that Wright claimed to have had computers and even a satellite system installed in his car to assist him, although he has never expanded on the purpose and efficacy of such a setup.

Following the six-day gap in Bitcoin's blockchain, Wright says he managed to get the system up and running again, resulting in the first two users of the Bitcoin Core client joining the network: Hal Finney and security research scientist turned entrepreneur and venture capitalist Dustin Trammell, who may have actually beaten Finney to the punch. Wright said during the *Granath v Wright* trial that he shared early versions of the Bitcoin code with Trammell prior to its release, but Trammell refuted these claims shortly afterwards in an interview:

I was involved with Bitcoin from the very beginning, but I didn't actually have any contact with the real Satoshi for a few days after the first public release of the code. Satoshi at no time ever sent me any early copies of anything. I found out about Bitcoin as the rest of the world did when the whitepaper was published, and then the first copy of the code...I downloaded myself after it was publicly released. So to hear that claim come from Craig on the stand under oath was quite surprising to me.

When this was repeated to Wright during the *COPA v Wright* trial, Wright had an answer ready: Trammell was being 'disingenuous' because Wright had sent him a link to the code rather than the code itself, hence why Trammell was able to say, truthfully, that he had never been sent any code by Satoshi.

On 12 January 2009, shortly after Finney joined the network, Satoshi sent him ten bitcoins in the first-ever Bitcoin transaction. Wright told Andrew O'Hagan that this was, in fact, just one of four he made that day, with the other three going to 'Dave [Kleiman], myself [and] another I cannot name as I have no right to do so.' We can infer that Wright means Gareth Williams and is claiming some official secrets nonsense here, as he has done in court cases since. Under questioning for the *Kleiman v Wright* trial, Wright called this recollection a 'half truth' and said that he, in fact, couldn't remember to whom he sent the coins. He also told O'Hagan that he was emailing Wei Dai and two future Bitcoin developers, Gavin Andresen and Mike Hearn, at this time, but when asked for proof, Wright claimed that all the emails had been wiped following his departure from Australia to the UK in 2015 (as we know, no such further communications with Dai ever took place). As O'Hagan noted, 'It seemed odd, and still does, that some emails were lost while others were not.'

Satoshi, Finney and Trammell used low-powered PCs and laptops to mine their bitcoins, which was all that was needed at the time. Wright, however, was allegedly operating at a much larger scale:

Around 10 machines, maybe 12, mined Bitcoin between 2009 and 2011. They included churches and charitable organisations that I did work for freely. Any Bitcoin they had remained with them, and if they have them, they have them, and if not, it's lost until someone later in history recovers them when the keys become exploitable. I had between 60 and 100 machines running at the time, of which an average of 55 or 56 would be mine personally. In the beginning, 75 were mine personally.

Wright said he generated a pile of 'between 80,000 and 100,000 bitcoin' through mining at these churches, none of which he seems to have left with them as payment for stealing their electricity, saying in an unpublished interview with *The Financial Times*, 'I donated the machines, so the fact that I also used them to mine Bitcoin, well, you can't complain too much.' There is likely as much truth in these stories as there is in Wright's claim that he operated machines in Malaysia and Tokyo; such proclamations sound worldly and impressive but are never backed up by any evidence. In a 2018 interview, Wright claimed that 'my son was mining in 2010', but this can't be true because Wright didn't have a son with Lynn and couldn't have been said to have had any custody over his future wife's children until mid-2011 at the earliest.

There are also issues with the amount of power Wright would have been throwing at the nascent network, given that his ultra-powerful setup would have sent Bitcoin's mining difficulty through the roof immediately, entirely centralising the mining pool and making it impossible for others to join in. When this theory was put to Wright during the *COPA v Wright* trial, Wright claimed that critics were 'misrepresenting Bitcoin mining and nodes', arguing that because he was running 'the majority of the network' at the time, there were more demands on his system. However, at this time, barely any transactions were being conducted on the network, rendering the need for such computational power moot. These criticisms were taken on board by Justice Mellor, who labelled Wright's claim about launching the Bitcoin system 'pure fantasy' and said that his story over the operation of his beefed-up mining farm in Bagnoo 'does not ring true'.

While Wright's Bitcoin birthing tales have been swallowed unquestioningly by his followers, other individuals have proved more sceptical. One such individual was a Twitter user with the handle DebunkingFaketoshi, known otherwise as Jim. Jim smelt a rat when reading Wright's version of history, particularly when Wright said that he 'had the whole road ripped up' and paid for fibre internet not just for himself but for 'maybe 50,000 people' in the region. As someone who knew New South Wales well, Jim felt he was uniquely placed to investigate Wright's claims over the farm, and so he did, finding them to be impractical, implausible and, ultimately, non-existent. Jim found that the fibre internet run would have had to have been 3.75 miles in length and that none of Wright's neighbours knew anything about it. When Wright was informed of this, he told his followers that the fibre hadn't been laid in Bagnoo at all but had instead been installed in his house in Gordon, calling Jim a 'Szabo Core wanker' and threatening 'We will sue him in time.' By this point, however, Wright had already rowed back on his claims in typical style, denying in an interview that he had a full-fibre connection and saying instead that he had 'fibre to the exchange and copper to the home'.

As if it needed any more confirmation, in 2021, a Wright supporter went on a kind of sad pilgrimage to the alleged cradle of Bitcoin and immediately debunked the story for himself. The pilgrim, Mark Heron, revealed that 'the 2 local farmers I spoke to were clueless as to their famous former resident', but worse was to come when the conversation turned to Wright's supposed gift of high-speed internet: they noted that there was still no fibre in the region, adding that the exchange was 'a good 5km by road' from the farm, tallying with Jim's calculations. Other individuals have since tried to confirm Wright's claims, but all have been rebuffed, the latest attempt being in March 2022, when it was found that there was 'still no fibre on the premises', getting on for thirteen years after Wright said it had been installed.

When it comes to where the bitcoins Wright supposedly mined ended up, it will come as no surprise to hear that he has made contradictory claims on this topic over the years. In a 2019 declaration for the *Kleiman v Wright* case, Wright stated that he 'mined Bitcoin during the years 2009 and 2010', which went 'directly into a trust...located in Panama'. Five years earlier, he had told the ATO that details of the Panama trust were 'all on Dave's hard drive', adding that the trust was set up by Kleiman and 'a few people I know of in Panama and Costa Rica.' In 2020, while being deposed for the *Kleiman v Wright* case, the mining story changed:

> COUNSEL: *Did you ever mine Bitcoin into a Panama trust?*
>
> WRIGHT: *No, I did not mine Bitcoin into a Panama trust.*

So, if not Panama, then where? The Seychelles, as it turned out, to which Wright had pivoted in between these depositions, explaining that he had mined on behalf of one of his companies, Wright International Investments (WII):

> *I was the person employed by Wright International. I, for Wright International, acted as the IT person for my company and ran the computers that created the ledger; and thus, straight into the company that was owned by the trust, created Bitcoin... The trust controlled the company, and the company had ownership of the coin.*

Wright clarified matters during the *COPA v Wright* trial when asked about his companies' involvement in mining:

> *It's only in the very first week that anything was mined by me. All the mining was done by Information Defense and transfers from Information Defense were made to the other company. The Australian company Information Defense was the entity right from January doing mining.*

Given that Information Defense was only registered on 29 January, it would have been hard pushed to do much mining that month and, as we will see, there is no evidence other than forged documents to back up Wright's claim that any mining was done anywhere. Doubts over the purported creation date of WII – 4 August 2009 – had always plagued the company since Wright first aired his story, and Patrick Madden confirmed these when he found a 17 October 2014 invoice from offshore company specialists Abacus, which purported to be for ongoing services for WII. However, it was, in fact, a manipulated copy of the sale invoice for WII made to look like it was for ongoing services. COPA found an Abacus advert from the time of Wright's purchase promoting its 'vintage' shelf companies for sale, but it seems that their companies weren't vintage enough for Wright's needs.

All this was to come, however; in 2009, Craig Wright was on the cusp of his first entanglement with what would turn out to be an arch-nemesis, a battle that would last for more than a decade and whose ramifications were solely behind the birth of his Satoshi cosplay.

Chapter 6 – A Taxing Situation

Wright's long-running battle with the ATO first came to light when the agency took part in a raid on his property on 9 December 2015, the same day as the *WIRED* and *Gizmodo* 'doxxings' were published. Little more was known about Wright's tax affairs until the *Kleiman v Wright* case was filed in 2018, where the full scale of his entanglements with the agency was laid bare. Until that point, Wright had claimed that the issues had been over his early Bitcoin mining, suggesting that the ATO had a vendetta against him, a story still peddled by his backers years later, as Stefan Matthews noted in a 2021 interview:

> ...there were factions within the Australian Tax Office that were victimising Craig. I think their decisions and their actions were highly personally motivated to destroy anything Craig was associated with.

This, as we shall see, is pure conjecture and another of the conspiracy theories woven by Wright and echoed by his supporters to explain away troubling behaviour. All the evidence we have seen suggests that the ATO had the facts on their side when investigating Wright and his activities, with Wright's allegations seeming to stem from one or two isolated incidents, which will be discussed.

Wright's troubles with the ATO began in 2009 when he submitted his personal tax return for the 2008/09 tax year, wherein he claimed to have sold intellectual property (IP) to Information Defense and Integyrs for $1.35 million and $896,000, respectively. When offset against a number of claimed deductions for that tax year, Wright's net capital gain was just $34,713 despite these huge sales. In a July 2021 blog post, written due to the upcoming inclusion of his tax affairs in the *Kleiman v Wright* trial (which Wright fought to prevent), Wright naturally tried to link the IP back to his work on Bitcoin:

I claimed the transfer of intellectual property, which included rights to the database and other aspects of Bitcoin, from an overseas company and associated trust to the Australian company. I paid the GST [Goods and Services Tax] on both sides of the transactions. I valued the intellectual property and database at around US$1.3 million. The amount was transferred to two companies [Information Defense and Integyrs]. My accountant applied the required GST amount, with Information Defense having a balanced amount with the registered trust entity.

In the post, Wright fleshed out Information Defense's alleged purpose:

The company I set up in January 2009 called Information Defense aided in managing the Bitcoin network by running nodes. The company ran computers in several locations, which acted as the initial Bitcoin nodes from 2009 and until 2010.

The ATO rejected Wright's tax return, with Wright later claiming that his Bitcoin operations had been classed as a hobby and not related to his businesses, hence the ATO's refusal to deduct associated costs. The agency imposed administrative penalties on Wright for recklessness in completing his tax return and for making false and misleading statements, but Wright appealed, taking his case to the Administrative Appeal Tribunal. In January 2013, Wright won this appeal, resulting in the ATO lifting the administrative penalty and allowing various expense deductions. The costly battle put the fire in Wright's belly over the ATO:

The dirty tactics that the damn government in Australia did was to try and close my company -- stop my court case before I won it. The way they wanted to stop my court case was basically to screw me over by bankrupting me, which they didn't get to do. I won.

During its investigation, the ATO asked Wright to explain how he came to the valuation of his IP, with Wright responding that it was the result of almost twenty years of personal study and research, including professional training and university degrees. Wright even claimed back interest on loans provided by Lynn, the capital of which, by 2009, had exceeded a staggering $815,000, double the average Australian house price at the time. Wright, however, insists that all the money he spent was his and even had the gall to complain in 2021 about how little Lynn contributed:

> *Wives have this habit of not appreciating when the husband goes off on a boondoggle project that they fail and waste all of your savings with a 1 in a million chance of success on a digital cash system... When I spent over $1 million of my money gaining the knowledge and education to create the system, think about how little you gave me.*

Lynn, it seems, gave everything, ending up bankrupt after their 2011 divorce, with evidence emerging in August 2023 that Wright's backers used her parlous financial situation, exacerbated by having to pay for cancer treatment, to file a lawsuit supportive to his cause.

On the surface, then, it seems that Craig Wright was in a pitched battle with the ATO about the merits of the Bitcoin mining he was doing through Information Defense and possibly Integyrs, having used his education up to that point to design Bitcoin in the first place. This couldn't be further from the truth, however; the ATO's issue with Wright was solely in relation to his IT companies. As well as contesting some of his expenses, the agency also argued that deals Wright had conducted between his companies carried no actual liability and were merely attempts at wash transactions. Once Wright's Satoshi story became public, he began to use his ATO filings to push this new narrative, as this 2016 report from the agency into the activities of Integyrz Pty Ltd (a separate company from Integyrs) shows:

> *We dispute Dr Wright's contention that the ATO audited and disallowed deductions related to Bitcoin mining on the basis that Bitcoin mining was a hobby and that he tried to transfer equitable interest in Bitcoin to related companies. The audit report contains no references to Bitcoin.*

Unless the ATO was lying, therefore, none of Wright's tax dealings in 2008/2009 ever mentioned Bitcoin, and Wright has never presented evidence to the contrary.

Regardless of this fact, Wright persisted with this version of events during the *Kleiman v Wright* trial, claiming under oath that the simple act of registering Information Defense in the first place had eviscerated his shield of anonymity:

I filed in June 30, 2009 a number of tax returns. I filed a March return. And I was in a court process between '11 and '13 with the tax office. So the people in the court, the judges, it was a private -- it wasn't public. It wasn't published. But each of those people knew [he was filing Bitcoin-related returns]. My lawyers knew. My accountants knew. The tax office knew...if I filed for Bitcoin in 2009, saying that I'm selling the IP into my company, then the tax office knows.

Wright added that the ATO therefore 'knew exactly who I was' in early 2009, which is true only in the sense that its officers knew he was Craig Wright. More evidence against Wright's argument comes from his own accountant, John Chesher, who noted in a meeting with the ATO in February 2014 that the disagreement was 'in relation to transactions that occurred relating to Intellectual Property', transactions that were wholly unrelated to Bitcoin. An important question to ask here is: why couldn't Wright present his own copies of the tax filings or any correspondence from the three-and-a-half-year legal battle with the ATO? Alas, as Wright had revealed in a July 2021 blog post, he had thrown it all away:

In total, we had to put together around 11,000 pages of documents. There were electronic copies and paper copies, although I don't have any of them now. In hindsight, I should have kept them, but the reality is that after years of dealing with lawyers and accountants and the tribunal in court, I wanted nothing to do with any of it.

However, one of Wright's lawyers miraculously found this stash of files on her first trip to his house, which he decided to utilise:

...I shall be setting up a project to put the full story out without any redaction / I will start with the 2008 to 2013 tax filings and battle. In 2011, the ATO accused me of all sorts of things because of Bitcoin. / there are hundreds of binders / hundreds of thousands of pages / all of the things that the ATO said in court / all of the things that were implied / all of the layers that they tried to make up / and, from that links to the apologies that they had to make to me

These files can't have been too convincing, however: at the time of writing, not one document from the haul has seen the light of day.

Wright clearly placed great importance on this initial battle with the ATO, inadvisably carrying the supposed Bitcoin connection into the *COPA v Wright* trial in 2024, where it met a predictable fate: Justice Mellor dismissed his account as a 'total fabrication'. Wright addressed this period in a 2021 blog post where he merely said, 'The resulting argument was based on rather obscure laws, concerning transfers between hobbies or organisations that are not designed for profit and ones that are profit-making and hence have to pay GST.' Seeing as Wright has not followed through with his promise to provide evidence of this battle, we will never know if this is true or not, but one thing we do know is that the clash certainly wasn't over Bitcoin.

Wright's claim that the ATO dismissed Bitcoin as a hobby rather than a business was, he says, rooted in another criterion: they didn't think the enterprise would generate any income. As we know, however, Wright was of a similar mindset, which was why he never told Max and Donald Lynam that they were mining bitcoins, so he can have no complaints on that score. Similarly, Stefan Matthews said in an interview in 2021 that at the time Wright supposedly launched Bitcoin in 2009, he, Wright, had 'no idea whether it would be successful or not.' This proves that, even if Wright's imaginary conversation with the ATO over Bitcoin's potential had taken place, they were both apparently on the same page over its potential profitability.

Wright's battle with the ATO cost him Information Defense and Integyrs, both of which went into liquidation prior to his victory, something that he acknowledged in a March 2011 blog post:

> *Integyrs Pty Ltd was a company I started. It is now going into receivership. Why? As small minded people from the Australian Tax office see that it has no value. The IP is to do with Risk, algorithmic analysis, crypto and more. I helped design the world's first on-line casino and more, but hey, they fail to understand. So, as the IP is worth nothing, I will give them nothing. Dave K and a few people I know from Playboy Gaming are setting up a trust. We move this overseas and we will make it work. Bitcoin has value. It is not a hobby. It sells for $5,000 now. Let us see just how much they cry when it is valued in 2020.*

The reason for the $5,000 reference is rooted in Wright's alleged attempt to sell around a million mined bitcoins, as well as the aforementioned Bitcoin-related IP, to Information Defense and Integyrs, which would be offset against his tax. This, of course, the ATO rejected, and Wright's claim in the blog post was that, in some sort of fit of vengeance, he had instead sold it all to Dave Kleiman for $5,000, something that will become important later on when we discuss the Tulip Trust. In its audit report on Integyrz that March, the ATO dryly noted that, rather than supplying a record of this sale, such as a blockchain transaction, Wright instead merely provided 'a blog post as evidence of this intention', noting that 'ATO forensics advises it is possible to backdate blog posts.' The blog post is typical of Craig Wright's efforts from this era, many of which were found following his 'outing' in December 2015 to have been retrospectively edited to include crucial information which aided his connection to Satoshi Nakamoto. Indeed, the post in question also drops in several mentions of crypto, Bitcoin and trusts, and yet the Internet Archive has no record of this blog post appearing at all in 2011 when it was supposedly published; its presence wouldn't be felt until 25 March 2015. The ATO clearly wanted Wright to know that it believed he had seeded this information well after the fact to augment his argument.

With regard to the bankruptcy of Information Defense and Integyrs, it's worth exploring why Wright didn't sell some of his mined bitcoins to keep the companies afloat or at least pay the legal bills to fight the ATO. Wright addressed this in a 2021 blog post:

> *I mentioned that I personally could not allocate any of the bitcoin that I had issued. My inability to allocate bitcoin stems not from technical issues, as some people try to claim. It is a legal issue, under the unilateral contract defined through the rules. If I reallocate the amount of bitcoin, or if I change how my system works, then there is the issue of my being liable, and even if I was pseudonymous, which I wasn't as much as people believed, I could be sued.*

There is, of course, a more straightforward theory: he never had any bitcoins in the first place. Wright added in the blog post that, had the ATO gotten its way, ownership of the Bitcoin protocol and its twenty-one million coins would have gone to the Australian government, but, luckily for the world, 'the plan by the ATO failed dismally'. Here, Wright paints himself as not just the creator but also the saviour of Bitcoin, as he would do again in 2018.

The last word on Wright's first battle with the ATO and the companies at its heart comes from Lynn Wright, who was asked during her deposition for the *Kleiman v Wright* case about what business Integyrs was actually conducting. Lynn replied that she didn't have 'a great deal of knowledge' about what Integyrs had done, but she was pretty sure why it folded, and it wasn't to do with the ATO investigation:

> COUNSEL: *Why was Integyrs in liquidation?*
>
> LYNN: *...my first response would be a bit flip, so I'm not going to respond to that, because I don't really know.*
>
> COUNSEL: *And what was your first response?*
>
> LYNN: *Probably because it wasn't making any money.*

Craig Wright's attempt to blame the ATO for the collapse of Integyrs and Information Defense, therefore, might be a little wide of the mark.

Wright has hung this first entanglement with the ATO up as proof that it had a vendetta against him; a rationale he has used to explain the actions it took against him in later years. He still claims to this day that his three-year legal fight was about the ATO's treatment of his Bitcoin enterprise, despite all the evidence to the contrary, and his complete inability to produce any documentation to support his story hasn't swayed his core of supporters, who explain away the ATO's findings that Wright never mentioned Bitcoin to them before 2013 as an institutional coverup.

This initial tangle with the ATO was a drop in the Tasmanian Sea compared to what was to come down the pipeline in the years ahead for Wright, but in the midst of this battle came a significant event that would shape the Bitcoin world – and Wright's future – for more than a decade.

Chapter 7 – Satoshi Bows Out

2010 saw Bitcoin's popularity increase, including witnessing the first purchase using the cryptocurrency, while more people experimented with mining the coins. Soon, miners began using computers with graphics cards due to their higher dedicated power, leading to 3.39 million bitcoins being mined in Bitcoin's first full year. Bitcoin experienced its first, and to date only, compromise on 15 August 2010 when someone was able to temporarily create 184 billion bitcoins out of thin air. Wright commented on this incident in a filing for the *Tulip Trading Ltd v Bitcoin Association for BSV & Ors* case in 2021, where he claimed that 'as a core developer of Bitcoin at the time', he, as Satoshi Nakamoto, resolved the issue by essentially re-running all of the legitimate transactions that had taken place and removing the illegitimate ones. An in-depth report on Satoshi Nakamoto's history and legacy by *Bitcoin Magazine* in April 2021 found that this exploit led to deeper discussions over Bitcoin's design and purpose, issues that it seems Satoshi didn't want to engage with:

> On these questions, Satoshi was less collaborative, less clear about what his choices implied. Complicating matters is that he appears to have been open, at least tacitly, to repositioning the software's selling points in the name of adoption.

This, the report said, resulted in 'a questioning of Satoshi's authority, a bristling at the boundaries between his directions and what developers and users might decide.' This divide grew throughout the second half of 2010, with Satoshi criticised as a Godfather figure at the head of the Bitcoin table, dictating its direction and its methods of getting there. As a result of this criticism, he withdrew, interacting less frequently in open forums.

On 4 December 2010, payment processing giant PayPal closed the account of the website WikiLeaks after it published around 250,000 confidential cables sent by U.S. diplomats, an episode that had global political ramifications. Following this action, members of BitcoinTalk, then the preeminent Bitcoin forum, urged WikiLeaks to accept Bitcoin donations, but Satoshi warned against this:

> *No, don't 'bring it on'. The project needs to grow gradually so the software can be strengthened along the way. I make this appeal to WikiLeaks not to try to use Bitcoin. Bitcoin is a small beta community in its infancy. You would not stand to get more than pocket change, and the heat you would bring would likely destroy us at this stage.*

This led to more criticism of Satoshi's attitude, with one poster arguing that 'satoshi basically needs to be removed from leadership.' In the immediate aftermath of the WikiLeaks episode, Satoshi began removing his name from Bitcoin-related statements and posts, seemingly preparing his exit. A week later, Gavin Andresen stated that he had received Satoshi's blessing to start 'more active project management', suggesting that Satoshi was finally stepping down. When discussing this exit in a May 2019 interview, Craig Wright claimed that he, as Satoshi, made a request of Andresen during their conversations at this time:

> *One of the things I said to Gavin at the end was, 'Stop trying to make me into this shadowy figure', which is what everyone kept doing.*

Andresen has never attested that Satoshi asked him this, however, and Wright's claim is rather problematic given that Satoshi chose to work through a pseudonym and never intentionally revealed anything about himself, which is the very definition of living in the shadows.

Satoshi's last message on BitcoinTalk came on 12 December 2010, where he discussed some technical points about the protocol, giving no hints that he was just hours away from resigning from the project. This he did, however, changing the copyright in Bitcoin's Massachusetts Institute of Technology (MIT) license from 'Copyright (c) 2009-2010 Satoshi Nakamoto' to 'Copyright (c) 2009-2010 Bitcoin Developers', signalling a signing over of the rights to the developers which allowed them to use, copy, modify, merge, publish, distribute, sublicense and sell copies of the software. Soon after, he handed Gavin Andresen the Bitcoin 'alert key', in many ways the Bitcoin killswitch, signalling his formal resignation.

Around this period, discussions were also taking place regarding a potential move of the coding repository from Sourceforge to GitHub. Most developers were supportive of the move, given GitHub's more impressive toolset and its ability to handle bigger and more sprawling projects, and there was an informal agreement in the community that this would take place. Having taken control of Bitcoin, Andresen accelerated the migration to GitHub, publishing his first post there on 19 December 2010. Satoshi Nakamoto was never heard from publicly again, with emails to select developers being his only communications until he sent his last communique in April 2011.

This is the widely accepted version of Satoshi's exit and Bitcoin's transfer of power, but, unsurprisingly, it's not the story Craig Wright tells. Equally as unsurprising is the fact that Wright's story has changed with the wind since he first discussed it in 2016. Wright addressed the WikiLeaks-Bitcoin argument during a public interview on stage following a conference in 2019 where he was asked why, as Satoshi Nakamoto, he didn't want Bitcoin to be used by WikiLeaks. Wright's response had nothing to do with the argument put forward by Satoshi on BitcoinTalk, however, instead blaming Julian Assange for inciting war in exchange for popularity:

> *Risking soldiers' lives so that you can be famous is fucking evil. There's no other way to put it. It's fucking evil.*

Wright's interviewer, Jimmy Nguyen, tried to steer Wright back towards the actual reason Satoshi gave for not wanting to hook up with WikiLeaks, which, in case Wright had forgotten what he had supposedly written nine years ago, was represented on a giant screen behind them. Wright, however, wasn't playing ball:

> *I didn't want Bitcoin to be the back door to helping Mr Assange avoid the US government.*

Nguyen eventually cajoled Wright back to the discussion over the scaling of the Bitcoin blockchain, which was the whole point of the tortured exercise, but the fact that Wright's antagonism towards Assange trumped what Nguyen had thought was going to be a simple revisiting of history makes for painful viewing. Wright's criticism of Julian Assange here is nothing compared to how he spoke about his fellow Australian six months previously in an unpublished interview with *The Financial Times*:

The guy is the biggest piece of scum, and I hope they fucking hang him. I don't even say that about child molesters. The guy killed more people than anyone I fucking know personally and I don't know personally because he freaking has leaked operational data. The guy is scum. He basically works for the Russians; he takes fucking money. He's like that other scumbag from the NSA who fucking was a treasonous piece of scum, and that's my opinion of him.

This latter reference is to Edward Snowden, who, coincidentally (or not), has publicly criticised Wright's Satoshi claim, joking in October 2022 that Wright 'can't even commit fraud properly' following his defeat in the *Granath v Wright* trial. In response, Wright described Snowden as 'an angry little turd' who committed treason in a fit of vengeance, having failed to earn a promotion within the National Security Agency.

Wright also has issues with the way Bitcoin was licensed. Satoshi Nakamoto released the Bitcoin code under an MIT license, making it open source and free for anyone to use and adapt, which was key to the principles of a non-closed system. Wright, however, claims that this wasn't the case, and in 2021, he started legal battles to assert his viewpoint:

...it is important to note that Bitcoin was not released under a GNU General Public License. The MIT License is incredibly patent-friendly, and it doesn't cover any of the associated files such as images or white papers. To cover such files, it would be necessary to use the Creative Commons license in association with the MIT License, which was never done with Bitcoin.

In a blog post the same year, Wright also added:

...the database rights under copyright and the associated IP rights are all maintained by the owner, unless otherwise assigned. The rights to the IP of Bitcoin have never been assigned outside my control.

Wright has faced fierce criticism over this claim, not least from the lead counsel for the Creative Commons, one of the biggest open-source license issuers in the world, and arguments on this matter have come down to such fine details as which files were included in which folders in the initial upload. Wright took a collection of Bitcoin companies and developers to court in 2022 over the

Bitcoin IP issue, the details of which will be covered in Volume III, but he summarised his position during the *Kleiman v Wright* trial:

> *By saying Bitcoin is set in stone, as the issuer, creator and developer of the system, I have said 'you cannot change my protocol'. Not 'it's a community project'. I have never once said it's a community project. I said 'This is available to everyone to use.' Not to change. Going out there and changing my protocol and misrepresenting fraudulently what it is...leaves [perpetrators] open to lawsuits.*

Wright claimed during the *COPA v Wright* case to have sent Gavin Andresen a file containing a copy of the alert key as far back as October 2010, with Wright keeping a copy himself, adding that he had granted Andresen access to the Bitcoin code on SourceForge on a lower-level administrator basis. However, Wright produced no evidence to support this, and Andresen has never supported this version of events.

Wright gave us the first insight into his supposed departure as Satoshi during a fractious encounter with *GQ* magazine in April 2016, telling reporter Stuart McGurk that the reason he quit Bitcoin was due to a 'friend's death' and because 'The burden of being Satoshi...became too great.' Which friend Wright referred to was not discussed, and conversely, in the same round of interviews, *The Economist* revealed that Wright had told them that he had left Bitcoin because 'there was a media storm at the time and he wanted to remove himself from it.' This, however, is simply not true; there was no media storm over Bitcoin during late 2010 and early 2011, with the Bitcoin element of the WikiLeaks incident never making it any further than the BitcoinTalk forum.

Wright didn't discuss his reasons for leaving Bitcoin again until the *Kleiman v Wright* case really kicked into gear in 2019, and even then, the reason for his departure wasn't widely discussed. In a February 2019 blog post, Wright opened up on his rationale, giving a reason which won't surprise anybody:

> *I didn't run away from Bitcoin, but I needed to know more about the system I created. Most critically, I needed to know that it could work at scale as I had planned. Towards the end of 2010, WikiLeaks had started promoting Bitcoin as an end to their woes. WikiLeaks and I have not had a good relationship. I needed to go away, and I needed to prove to myself*

that the system I had created worked the way I'd intended. It does, and it always did.

Wright expanded on this four months later in another blog post:

I left Bitcoin as a project so that I would not be the benevolent dictator. I left to be an absentee dictator. One who set rules in stone. I explained it well, I would have thought, but obviously it went over everyone's head.

The following month saw a different take from Wright on why he quit, as he explained to his counsel during a deposition for the *Kleiman v Wright* case:

I left Bitcoin, or started leaving, in August 2010. I did not want to be associated with the public name Satoshi at all after that point. The problem occurred because in June 2010 people...who had been working on Bitcoin, decided, when I was pushing for a commercial application, to make the first commercial application as a heroin market.

Wright added during this deposition that 'Between August and December of 2010, I pleaded, I said [a drugs market] was a bad idea with Martti [Malmi] and with Michael [Marquardt]'. However, no record of these conversations has ever emerged, and while there were indeed discussions on BitcoinTalk about users setting up a heroin market in June 2010, Satoshi didn't comment on any of them. Indeed, there is no public indication either way that Satoshi encouraged or discouraged the use of bitcoins to buy drugs, or anything else for that matter, meaning there is no evidence to back up Wright's assertions.

Wright also claims that Malmi and Marquard 'locked me out of the domain and took it over', adding in the same deposition that he 'finally left publicly as Satoshi in 2010 because they launched Silk Road.' Silk Road, founded by Ross Ulbricht, didn't actually launch until February 2011, but in 2019, Wright alleged that the idea was born inside the forum:

It was [Michael Marquardt] and Martti who moved the idea to hard drugs...and sold Ross...on it.

Wright claimed during the *COPA v Wright* case that Ulbrich discussed his ideas for a heroin market on BitcoinTalk under a pseudonym, by which time he had already been selling his wares through Silk Road for six months, alleging that Malmi's emails, which Malmi released for the *COPA v Wright* case, discussed an exchange that would be the Silk Road backend. Other than Wright's interpretations of Malmi's emails, there is no evidence this ever happened, and author Nick Bilton's authoritative work on Ulbricht and Silk Road, *American Kingpin*, completely disputes Wright's account. In his witness statement for the *COPA v Wright* case, Malmi called the allegations that he was behind Silk Road 'ridiculous and false', and Wright's counsel did not put these allegations to the Finn under cross-examination; Justice Mellor agreed that such accusations were baseless. Wright claimed in 2019 to have archived copies of the Silk Road site that promoted the use of Bitcoin for child pornography, but these have never seen the light of day.

This apparent takeover of Bitcoin by heroin peddlers also didn't make it into 'The Satoshi Affair'; during the seven months Wright and Andrew O'Hagan spent together, Wright apparently showed no animosity towards those who allegedly turfed him out of Bitcoin. Instead, Wright simply sent the author a collection of forged emails that showed Wright supposedly leaving Bitcoin due to a kind of existential crisis over the pressure of being its figurehead. Something else that didn't make it into O'Hagan's piece was any mention of Julian Assange or WikiLeaks from Wright, suggesting that, as late as 2016, Wright had no intention of including them in his Bitcoin exit narrative. Another indication of this is the fact that the last person O'Hagan had shadowed in a similar fashion was none other than Assange himself, publishing his unauthorised biography in 2011, a job which, incidentally, helped O'Hagan land the Wright gig. Wright would almost certainly have had something to say about O'Hagan's potential involvement at the time had it mattered.

In March 2019, Wright gave his followers yet another insight into his reasons for leaving:

> *I was at the end [of] my rope in 2010 / Hal and others telling me how it will not scale. / So, I left and needed to find a way to make it scale. It turned out, the way I planned worked. The issue was Hal and others never wanted it as Bitcoin, they wanted socialist coin.*

Wright gave another, and this time less coherent, reason why he left Bitcoin during a conference talk two weeks later:

> *Part of why I fucking disappeared was to have things not controlled, and I have to come back to control things to get it fucking not controlled; that's the freaking irony of this shit!*

Shortly after this, Wright flipped back to the heroin angle, telling his followers that when Bitcoin Talk users began discussing 'drug sales and other dark websites', he feared for the future of his project. He combined these two elements almost a year later when he told them that he had retreated into the shadows because he 'needed to work on making the controls needed to stop' the rogue heroin-loving developers.

In three years, then, Wright's reasons for leaving Bitcoin shifted and morphed between the death of a friend, the burden of being Satoshi Nakamoto, a non-existent media storm around Bitcoin, a need to prove Bitcoin worked, the desire to not be a benevolent dictator, developers' plans for heroin markets, Hal Finney telling him it wouldn't scale and to not have things controlled. Of course, there may be more than one reason why Satoshi might have left Bitcoin, but the fact that Wright has hardly, if ever, mentioned more than one of the above explanations at any one time in interviews or in blog posts through the years is telling. It is also telling that there is no evidence to prove that these were Satoshi's thoughts at the time, and there is plenty of evidence to back up the prevailing theory that Satoshi had simply had enough by late 2010.

In 2020, Wright began to settle on one story: he was forced out of Bitcoin by the heroin-loving cabal of developers. In a blog post of February that year, Wright said that he stopped mining Bitcoin in August 2010 after he 'started to lose faith in my own project', adding that things began 'falling apart' for him at that point as he was 'losing control' of Bitcoin and was 'being pushed out'. Of course, it appears that Satoshi himself also felt pushed out, but the difference in Wright's claim, which he cemented in 2022, is key:

> *I did not agree to move the servers as people dud in 2011 as I DID NOT GIVE THEM ACCESS. Technically it was a crime.*

In the space of one forum post, Wright had advanced the actions of the cabal from mere ideological foes to the perpetrators of a coup d'etat. This coup, Wright explained, was essential so that Bitcoin's new overlords could fulfil their ambition to create the ultimate libertarian underworld currency:

> *I did not think that three months after I left everything would be moved on to GitHub or that those associated with dark websites and other nefarious activities would take over.*

Wright further claimed that the motivation behind the move from Sourceforge to GitHub wasn't borne out of practicality but was instead to allow the developers to circumvent the administrator controls he had used to manage the old codebase. This allowed them to use their new privileges to make all the dastardly changes they wanted, as he explained on Twitter in March 2023:

> *...all of my accounts were removed by Peter Woolley [Wuille] and he set up access and migrated away from SourceForge into GitHub removing all access. So, this goes back a long way but unfortunately I wasn't paying attention because, well divorce.*

Wright doubled down on this theory in a July 2020 interview:

> *When I left everything...the way it was, I thought I could work in the background and fix things without being involved. But I abdicated not...delegated. There's a big difference.*

Wright expanded on this in his first witness statement for the *COPA v Wright* case in July 2023, where he claimed that he had always intended to 'maintain ultimate control and oversight of the development process' of Bitcoin but that developer Wladimir van der Laan pushed the GitHub move through, severing Wright's ties with the codebase. This, Wright said, was aided by Gavin Andresen following Wright's handing over of the alert key, with the whole thing done, Wright said, to wrestle power away from him, a claim he repeated in a *Forbes* piece the same month where he said the developers 'set up completely new sites, and moved me out.' Again, Wright implicated van der Laan, who denied the claim in a statement to *Forbes*, pointing out that the GitHub repository was established before he began working on Bitcoin. Wright denied this during the *COPA v Wright* trial, maintaining that van der Laan was responsible for setting it up and he 'convinced Gavin to move to it', despite Andresen being the one who first mentioned GitHub to Satoshi in July 2010. This action, incidentally, 'bore significant implications for the governance and trajectory of the project' according to Wright, wreaking changes that led the developers to 'effectively assume control of the project.' This, Wright said, led to developers stepping into leadership roles and 'steering the system's future development and protocol amendments'.

Wright's claim of being forced out was further cemented in 2022 thanks to a letter sent to multiple Bitcoin developers by Ontier on behalf of Wright's company, Wright International Investments UK Ltd:

> *WIIUKL asserts that the Bitcoin protocol and database were copied by you and/or the other developers of the BTC network to create that new network and that the protocol and database used on that network is owned by WIIUKL.*

One of the recipients of this letter was another of Craig Wright's long-term nemeses, then Bitcoin developer and Blockstream co-founder Greg Maxwell, who told us that the idea that van der Laan, or any of the developers, hatched a plot to oust Satoshi Nakamoto was 'just nonsense'. Maxwell also denied the suggestion that Satoshi's Sourceforge access was revoked during the move:

> *Satoshi's access wasn't removed from Sourceforge at all, leading to an incident years later when his account was hacked. Even after that, there were passwords to the databases on Sourceforge that were set by Satoshi and never changed.*

This is backed up by a September 2014 email from Gavin Andresen to the Bitcoin Foundation press team:

> *Satoshi has no special powers, so Bitcoin users don't have to worry about his old email address getting compromised. In hindsight, I should have removed Satoshi as an administrator or deleted the old Sourceforge project. I didn't because I wanted to avoid drama (I'm sure some people would see that as some kind of "shun Satoshi and grab power" move).*

Andresen was to be proved right, although from a rather unexpected source.

Maxwell, Wuille and van der Laan were among the dozen-plus developers targeted in multiple lawsuits Wright initiated between 2021 and 2022, but conspicuous by his absence on the defendants' list was Gavin Andresen, despite his apparent position of supreme power in the alleged coup. Indeed, when Wright was asked his opinion of Andresen in a July 2022 interview, Wright said that Andresen was '[A] very interesting guy who got too much shit'. Wright's hatred for Maxwell, which is rooted in their differing views on Bitcoin and

Maxwell being a chief critic following Wright's 'outing' in 2015, is well documented, as Wright noted in August 2022:

> *I don't want to see Mr Maxwell charged with mere civil charges. I want to see him imprisoned, and when I'm done with him, he will be.*

Wright's antipathy towards Maxwell has occasionally strayed into the unorthodox. In March 2022, Maxwell, a keen astronomy photographer, published a photograph of a 'relativistic jet believed to be ejected from a supermassive black hole'. Just a week later, with no prompting, Wright promised, of all things, a new scientific theory debunking Einstein's theory on black holes, first espoused in his 1915 general theory of relativity. Wright argued that black holes didn't exist in the way Einstein had suggested and implied that Maxwell, therefore, couldn't have seen what he saw:

> *I propose to demonstrate that time is not necessarily infinitely divisible; rather, it must occur in finite slices while simultaneously acting as a medium to update information throughout the universe.*

Wright released his new theory to the world in September 2022 under the title 'The Philosophy of Time'. The paper has never been peer-reviewed, the reason for which might be explained in comments made on the paper by a published philosopher attached to an academic institution:

> *This paper resembles the random emails I get from people claiming to have disproved relativistic physics more than it does a plausible masters thesis. / This would fail as an undergraduate thesis at my institution.*

Running the paper through OpenAI's ChatGPT 4.5 model yields further criticisms, most notably oversimplification, a misunderstanding of established relativistic physics, lack of evidence and a reliance on 'speculative analogies and intuitive reasoning, neglecting deeper philosophical counterarguments and rigorous scientific validation.' For those already aware of Craig Wright's modus operandi, this will hardly come as a surprise.

Having seemingly settled on a story over why he left Bitcoin, Wright stirred the pot again for the *COPA v Wright* case:

> *Around April 2011, I began to phase out my communications under the pseudonym Satoshi Nakamoto. By this time, the Bitcoin system had been*

successfully established and was functioning autonomously. With the framework in place, I felt it was time to divert my attention to other pursuits.

Here, rather than Wright saying that Bitcoin had been derailed by heroin markets, WikiLeaks or the coup that stripped him of access, he was now suggesting that everything had, in fact, been working as planned, and he voluntarily stepped away to focus on other things. Wright added that 'Other personal reasons influenced my decision to withdraw as Satoshi Nakamoto, chief among them being an ongoing investigation by the Australian Tax Office', marking the first time that Wright referenced his ATO investigation as having anything to do with him leaving Bitcoin. Wright's most recent comment on why he quit Bitcoin came in *Hero/Villain*:

> *'People fail to understand that I stepped away from direct involvement with communicating about Bitcoin as Satoshi because I had other things happening in my life that needed my attention more,' Wright says. 'Bitcoin was out, it was working and users were coming around to the idea. But it didn't need Satoshi and my other business interests needed me. Also, people forget that I was going through a stressful divorce. As much as Satoshi was a myth, I was also a person.'*

Again, there was no mention of Julian Assange, drug markets or coups, with Wright suggesting that Bitcoin was running like a charm when he stepped away. As anyone with even a passing interest in criminal matters knows, when a defendant perpetually changes their story, it usually only means one thing.

As we have established, Wright has never presented any evidence to back up his claims of a forced ejection from Bitcoin, and there is plenty of evidence from Satoshi's writings to show that the decision was his alone. Satoshi was also seemingly happy with the few arrangements the transfer necessitated and had no intention of remaining in the background as the kind of shadow dictator Wright supposedly envisioned. Satoshi told Bitcoin developer Mike Hearn over email in March 2011 that he was 'happy to answer any questions' about Bitcoin even after he had left, a promise he kept for another month, and there is no sense from any of these later communications that Satoshi felt ousted in any way or was concerned about his dwindling level of control. A great example of this is his last email exchange with Hearn in April 2011, where the pair discussed various technical aspects of Bitcoin, among other things, before Hearn asked if Satoshi would consider coming back. Satoshi, however, rejected the notion:

> *I've moved on to other things. It's in good hands with Gavin and everyone.*

It goes without saying that if Satoshi had felt that Gavin Andresen had been part of the cabal to oust him, he would not have praised the Australian's capabilities when it came to looking after his creation. Wright was asked about this message during the *COPA v Wright* trial, with Wright saying that he never wanted to leave Bitcoin development and the 'other things' were other areas of Bitcoin he had planned to work on. Mike Hearn testified during the same trial that had Satoshi asked for his access back, it would have been granted without question, while Greg Maxwell told us that Satoshi's departure actually caused problems:

> *[Satoshi] was not forced out and I'm confident that *everyone* at the time would have been delighted if he continued. The loss of his participation no doubt resulted in delays in moving the project forward since it took some time for other people to understand the software comprehensively to the point where they could make more complex changes.*

Satoshi's final email to Martti Malmi was described by Nathanial Popper in his book *Digital Gold: Bitcoin and the Inside Story of the Misfits and Millionaires Trying to Reinvent Money*:

> *Satoshi's final e-mails went to Martti, whom Satoshi asked to take full ownership of the Bitcoin.org website. "I've moved on to other things and probably won't be around in the future," Satoshi wrote to Martti, in early May, before transferring the site to Martti and disappearing into the ether.*

Here, again, Craig Wright's version of events leaves us with more questions than answers. Why was he still liaising in a friendly manner with individuals he considered traitors? If he was so concerned that Bitcoin was going to be used for criminal means against his wishes, why was he still offering technical advice to those doing the deed? Would Satoshi Nakamoto really have kept his growing displeasure over Bitcoin's potential use to himself, only to file multiple lawsuits about it a decade later? And why would those eventual lawsuits exclude Gavin Andresen, whom Wright names as someone directly involved in the coup? As we will find out in the second book in this series, Wright and Andresen have a history that extends beyond their supposed interactions in 2011, which may account for Wright's decision to preclude him from his legal activities.

Setting all these questions aside, an overarching one that we will instead turn to is: why did Craig Wright change his story? As we have already alluded to, the change in narrative in 2022 took place right before he sued a collection of Bitcoin developers, claiming that they were infringing his copyright over the Bitcoin whitepaper, database and file format. For this, Wright needed to make it clear that he didn't willingly hand over his creation to the developers and quietly exit stage left; rather, he was the genius inventor pulled kicking and screaming from his laboratory by evildoers wanting to steal his creation for their own nefarious desires. This narrative also played nicely into the image that *CoinGeek* writers had been portraying of Ira Kleiman following his decision to file a lawsuit against Wright in February 2018: Kleiman was a greedy chancer looking to take advantage of the man who gave the world Bitcoin and who was now forced to defend himself and protect his rightfully held assets. The fact that Wright never mentioned this supposed coup until some eight years after it allegedly happened, right when he needed such a story to back up not one but two court cases, is more than a little suspicious.

All the contemporaneous evidence relating to Satoshi Nakamoto's departure from Bitcoin, which consists almost exclusively of his emails and forum posts, shows a person who endured more and more criticism as 2010 progressed, leading to him withdrawing from the Bitcoin social scene towards the end of the year, seemingly having realised that the game was no longer worth the candle. It is much more likely that Satoshi, having spent some three years dedicating his life to Bitcoin, felt like he had taken it as far as he could by 2010 and no longer wanted the stress. An intensely private person, he was also likely aware that Bitcoin's growth would lead to investigations into his own life and a potential search for his identity, an assumption that would prove correct. In short, the moment was right to leave Bitcoin, and he did – just in time. It is telling that while Satoshi Nakamoto has successfully hidden his identity and remained in the shadows, Craig Wright has actively and aggressively sought the limelight.

It's worth examining another of Wright's claims about his reason for leaving Bitcoin that fails to stand up to scrutiny. In an already-referenced 2019 on-stage interview with Jimmy Nguyen, Wright said he created Bitcoin 'not thinking it was going to be a crime coin' because of the public nature of the blockchain. This, however, is dangerously short-sighted for a so-called computer security expert and worrisome for those who relied on Wright's foresight to secure their systems against wrongdoers. Wright says he was paid in Liberty Reserve dollars for much of his casino work in the early 2000s, and the fact that he couldn't see the potential similarities in use case between Bitcoin and this pseudo-currency either makes him a less than impressive security consultant or an outright liar. Wright may have hated Silk Road, but he was happy to share a payment platform with the people who sold their wares through it, highlighting the shallowness of his moral argument. Of this, Wright merely says that it was 'ironic that the only way I saw to fix the problem that I have created [Bitcoin] was to utilise something even worse [Liberty Reserve]'.

Despite supposedly moving tens of millions of dollars through Liberty Reserve, Wright was never traced by U.S. authorities when they shut it down in 2013, even though he was, so he said during a March 2020 deposition for the *Kleiman v Wright* case, the only person on the platform to have completed anti-money laundering checks. This means he was either very lucky or he never used the site at all (later in this book, we will see evidence that points firmly to the latter). Wright also claimed to Ira Kleiman that, as well as having some 300,000 bitcoins from his mining activities, Dave Kleiman owned a company in the U.S. that had significant Liberty Reserve holdings at the time of the seizure. No evidence of this has ever emerged in any legitimate correspondence involving Dave Kleiman, but Wright's current wife, Ramona Watts, was still forced to confront it in response to an email from Ira in June 2015:

One of Dave's companies had significant investments in Liberty Reserve— the US government shut that down and confiscated all his money. I do not have the full details—I only know that happened.

This story is too close to the version Wright had already spun Ira Kleiman to be coincidental, especially when it comes with no evidence, suggesting that Ramona was simply regurgitating Wright's words.

When we compare the publicly accepted version of Satoshi's exit to Craig Wright's, it is clear to anyone with an unbiased outlook that Satoshi Nakamoto was in no way forced out of Bitcoin by other developers. Even if we take out the claims and denials from the major players, the facts speak for themselves: there is not a single example of Satoshi Nakamoto complaining, either at the time or months later, that he felt excluded, a stance supported by his behaviour at the time of his exit and Craig Wright's in the years since. There is also no evidence that Satoshi planned to stay on after announcing his departure, with his desire made obvious by his words and actions. Any alternative theories have to be accompanied by convincing evidence, and all Craig Wright has ever produced to back up his version of history is an interpretation of the existing material.

Until he can produce emails or forum posts that show Satoshi being distressed about the conversations that were taking place in late 2010 or offer any unequivocal proof that Satoshi didn't want to leave Bitcoin, Wright's claims of a coup will remain floundering in the digital dust.

Chapter 8 – D.I.V.O.R.C.E

Craig Wright says he took a rather remarkable sabbatical after being kicked out of Bitcoin's development circle, spending January 2011 working for anti-human trafficking organisations in South America. During this time, Wright claims that he was in the 'jawbreaker' team, which was concerned with the prevention of such crimes, expanding on this a little in his June 2019 deposition for the *Kleiman v Wright* case:

> *I had worked for police in a combination as an expert witness in taking down peer-to-peer networks is how I understood them, and I worked on anti-child grooming and antipornography for a long time.*

Wright even claimed he was shot twice during this period, despite his job being 'accessing systems and information', and complained in a February 2019 blog post that 'evidence of it is likely to still exist on the Internet for all my efforts to have destroyed it'. Journalist Thomas Watson, who interviewed several former covert operatives for a piece on Craig Wright's inner circle in 2023, was told that there was 'zero chance' any civilian would be in the line of fire working beside a jawbreaker operation.

In the blog post outlining his crime-busting escapades, ~~James Bond~~ Wright claimed that he was 'what some people would call an 'agent of influence" and added that during his time in South America, he realised why human cruelty is allowed to be perpetuated:

> *I have witnessed children as young as 10 with AK-74s and women who have been forced to watch the death of their children knowing that other members of their family are being held and, if they try to escape, will be killed. All of it exists because of a system that allows records to be lost.*

Critics immediately jumped on Wright's claim that one of the key reasons behind the prevalence of South American guerrilla groups is inadequate record-keeping and mocked his sudden transformation from accountant into someone who 'disappeared...to heroically fight sex traffickers in Venezuela.' In Wright's favour is the fact that his blog went very quiet in late 2010 and into 2011, with no posts at all between 14 November and 16 January, picking up again in February with an average of one post per day on subjects as diverse as the minimum wage, socialism and the perils of ethanol. One such blog post covered the link between gold, the sex trade and cybercrime in Colombia and Venezuela, with Wright explaining how the process worked. There was no mention of him having first-hand knowledge or experience of these, however, and everything he mentioned was publicly available at the time. One can't help but think of the episode of *Blackadder* where the eponymous hero and his manservant, Baldrick, hide away in their home for a week while pretending to be in France rescuing the Scarlet Pimpernel, hoping to gather the plaudits when they emerge with a random Frenchman in tow.

What doesn't work in Wright's favour regarding this timeframe is a claim he made during a June 2019 deposition for the *Kleiman v Wright* case, where he said that he held a half-hour virtual meeting with Dave Kleiman and Gareth Williams while he was on his way to Venezuela. Wright said that he first met Williams at 'BlackNet conferences' and that he had trained the spy in analysing international money flows, imbuing his work with a certain gloss when he said that Williams later 'took software that I wrote and...used it to break into American servers'. There is, of course, no proof that any of this happened, which Wright put down to national security restrictions. Wright claimed he was in New York for this call 'sometime in 2011' (we assume January, going by his timeline), where he said he asked Williams and Dave Kleiman to help him erase his Satoshi history:

> *I agreed with Gareth that if Mr. Williams deleted all the records of what I was doing and helped me, that I would help him with software that was necessary for some of his investigations that were outside the scope of his normal work.*

This would have been difficult, however, because Williams had famously died padlocked inside a bag in his bathtub four months earlier. When challenged on this during the *COPA v Wright* trial, Wright said that he had made an error with the date, with the true timeframe just happening to fit perfectly with the narrative he had held until that point. The correct date, he said, had been August 2010, when he had been 'departing the [Bitcoin] scene', a claim which landed him in another bear trap:

> COUNSEL: *That's convenient, isn't it? Because, of course, Mr Williams was found dead on 23 August 2010. Did you have this video call just before he died?*
>
> WRIGHT: *No. I get dates wrong.*

The phone call would also have been a stretch for Dave Kleiman, given that he was at the start of what would end up being an 850-day spell in the West Palm Beach Veterans Affairs Medical Center due to various complications with bedsores, brittle bones and infections. Wright had stated four years earlier during his deposition for the *Kleiman v Wright* case that Kleiman's hospitalisation had precluded him from posting on BitcoinTalk under the Satoshi name, but he was apparently perfectly able to join the call, despite it necessitating 'technical solutions that aren't actually a videoconference' from his hospital bed. By the time of the deposition, where Wright first brought up the alleged phone call, however, it had been six years since either of the two other supposed participants might have been in a position to confirm or deny whether it took place.

Wright alleges that this conversation with Williams was his last communication with the spy, but there is an illuminating coda to the story. When Lynn Wright was testifying for the *Kleiman v Wright* case, she was asked if anyone had reached out to her following Dave Kleiman's death:

> ...I did get some emails...and then letters, physical snail mail, two from Dave himself, which was rather upsetting for me because he had been dead for quite a while, and another one from a Gareth – I can't remember his last name – who I later learned was also dead. So it had nothing to do with the shares but it had to do with – I don't know if it's mining of bitcoin or what, but it meant nothing to me.

The idea that Lynn Wright received emails and then written letters from two dead men, one of who had been deceased for almost three years by that point, should ring alarm bells in itself, but the suggestion that Gareth Williams may have written to Lynn Wright about Bitcoin mining is beyond ludicrous, even if it was sent when he was still alive. Upon receipt of the missives, Lynn asked Craig about Gareth Williams, who told her of his death in 2010 (something he seemingly forgot when it came to his depositions) and then advised her what to do with the communications:

> *When I received…I guess the first or second email from Dave and this Gareth fellow, I didn't know what to do with it, so I got in touch with Craig and he said to give it to his solicitors.*

It's worth remembering that Lynn and Craig had been separated for three years by the time the messages arrived, and Lynn had no idea of Craig's theoretical link to Bitcoin when they were together. It is, therefore, beyond odd that Dave Kleiman and Gareth Williams would think of contacting her about Bitcoin at all. It could be purely coincidental that the communications just so happened to bolster Wright's contemporaneous story that Williams and Kleiman had parts to play in the creation of Bitcoin, but there is an obvious alternative explanation: Craig Wright penned them himself. Seeing as the letters and emails have never seen the light of day, we must consider that whoever wrote them, they were far from convincing.

Prior to the call with the deceased Williams and the hospitalised Kleiman, Wright had been keen to divorce himself not just from Lynn but from Satoshi and his haul of bitcoins, too:

> *Back in 2011 [Satoshi's haul] was not worth a lot of money, and I thought it was a millstone that would drag my life to hell. It was already dragging other people's lives to hell. Drug markets, terrorist markets, they're not about freedom. They're not honest. Dave talked me out of destroying it utterly. If I had my way, I would have put a hammer through the hard drive that held those [private keys to the Satoshi wallets].*

These early 2019 depositions also saw Wright remember 2011 itself very differently:

> *After I left [Bitcoin], I stopped being a pastor; I stopped going to church. I couldn't face anyone I knew anymore. My first marriage fell apart. My life fell apart.*

This claim was markedly different from the tone Wright had struck in an interview just six months earlier:

I wasn't depressed. The first time I saw something fail, I was for a while, but you get over it, and you get back on your feet, and you keep going.

Here, then, we have Wright inconclusive over the issue of when, or indeed if, his life fell apart because of his exit from Bitcoin. Blockchain critic David Gerard noted in 2019 that, according to Wright's LinkedIn profile, the Australian was 'working at a string of fairly normal-sounding IT companies in Australia' rather than wallowing in self-pity, suggesting that Wright's stoic side had won out. Wright has, incidentally, disavowed his LinkedIn profile, telling *The Economist* in 2016 that his profile was a 'joke' to 'take the piss out of myself' and to stop people bothering him, which makes little to no sense whatsoever. Wright went a step further in a 2019 blog post via a familiar refrain:

I do not even manage my LinkedIn profile. To tell the truth, I haven't even looked at it.

Nevertheless, Wright's profile claims that in early 2011 he was still the director of Integyrs and Information Defense; CEO of GreyFog, a company Wright set up in 2009 which was involved in 'security software and solutions to the digital media industry'; the Vice President of Asia Pacific for the Whitehats IT security conference; mentor and 'Stay Sharp' instructor at the SANS institute; Technical Director of the Global Information Assurance Certification (GIAC); Vice President of the Forensics Services department at iVolution Security; and subject coordinator/lecturer at Charles Sturt University, to name but a few appointments. Let's not forget, too, that Satoshi Nakamoto was still discussing technical matters with Bitcoin developers in January 2011, meaning that Wright was simultaneously helping the very people who had ousted him overcome complex issues with Bitcoin, holding down roles with multiple companies and institutions and being shot by South American people traffickers. All of this was done while maintaining his peculiar work-sleep schedule, suggesting he benefited from very amenable employers indeed.

Wright was also able to enjoy the trappings of being an apparently successful CEO at this time, as this 31 January blog post extolling the virtues of flying business class shows:

I have 4 companies, 2 of which are in the stages where they are in need of constant attention and I can be there 24x7 even as I fly now. I only have the small sections for take-off and landing where I have to be internet deprived. As a work-a-holic, the ability to stay connected from 3G on the parts of my travel and manage and monitor client needs and staff is absolutely tremendous.

Wright was suggesting that his companies couldn't survive without him being offline during a four-hour flight, so how they were able to cope while he was dodging bullets and prizing AK-74s out of the arms of Venezuelan children is a mystery. This blog post also doesn't seem to reflect the actions of a man who has lost his purpose in life; instead, it shows someone making the most of the opportunities afforded him and with a firm grasp on his direction.

As if this wasn't enough for the depressed recluse to be getting on with, Wright had other irons in the fire. A particularly notable instance came on the back of a request by the Cyber Security Division of the DHS in January 2011, which sought proposals aimed at improving cyber security across federal networks and the Internet while developing new and enhanced technologies for detecting, preventing and responding to cyber attacks on the nation's critical information infrastructure. Wright and Dave Kleiman took up the challenge, and on 14 February, Kleiman formed W&K Info Defence Research LLC (W&K) in Florida, the vehicle through which the pair would submit their technological proposals. In 2019, Wright downgraded his involvement in the establishment of W&K and massively upgraded Lynn Wright's role, claiming, 'Lynn set everything up with Dave.' This would prove to be the basis of a 2020 lawsuit, but it was Craig and Dave Kleiman who dusted off some old hard disk wiping whitepapers and got to work, eventually submitting four proposals which, if all four were selected, would net them US$5.85 million in research funding. None of the proposals, it should be noted, featured Bitcoin or blockchain technology in any way, with titles such as 'Software Assurance through Economic Measures' and 'Software Derivative Markets & Information Security Risk'.

And there was more. According to his blog, Wright was also looking for others willing to help him develop 'a new revolution in payments' during this period; not Bitcoin, but instead an 'online gold trading system alone the lines of a PayPal.' This is exactly the sort of idea that Stefan Matthews claims Wright was coming up with in 2007, which begs the question of why Wright would pitch him various ideas around digital cash and gold-backed cash, create Bitcoin and then return to his 'PayPal for gold' idea three years later. Wright claimed in court in 2022 that this was because, as Satoshi, he had 'mentioned how other assets in 2010 could be embedded into Bitcoin' as a 'Bitcoin solution'.

And there was more still. Incredibly, Wright was also supposedly getting involved in the 'development of large-scale storage and data distribution' through another company he set up called Cloudcroft, a shelf company bought in Lynn Wright's name on 3 March 2011. Wright said in a 2019 blog post that Cloudcroft, despite fulfilling its brief to create and offer large-scale computing environments, didn't have many takers, leading to Lynn having to go out and get a second job to make ends meet. However, this was more likely because, as the imminent divorce agreement would state, Lynn 'in lieu of payment of wages or salary has received and accepted promises of payment from Craig to assist the survival of those businesses.' Apparently, promises don't pay the bills or repay loans.

This plethora of jobs, projects and other activities doesn't exactly paint the picture of a man reduced to human rubble by the theft of his life's crowning glory. Indeed, Wright's claim that he was booted out of Bitcoin and spent the months afterwards lost in a fug of despair couldn't be further from the truth: according to the man himself, he was involved in heading up multiple institutions, running several companies, travelling in business class around the US, teaching, working with Dave Kleiman on those DHS projects and rescuing children in South America. While we can question the feasibility of some of these escapades, Wright nevertheless had more irons in the fire than a blacksmith at this time, which is incompatible with his supposed inability to face his friends and family and the suggestion that his life was falling apart post-Bitcoin.

On 27 February 2011, Wright allegedly decided to cash out his Liberty Reserve earnings into bitcoins, using Russian money exchanger WMIRK to facilitate the deal. This was an odd move, seeing as WMIRK's business model was the on-ramping and off-ramping of WebMoney payments and had no affiliation with Bitcoin whatsoever. As late as 2013, the company was still advertising WebMoney transfers only, and yet Wright claims that in 2011, he called them up on the phone (thankfully, they spoke English) and arranged to swap his Liberty Reserve holdings for bitcoins. This story echoes another pattern that runs through Wright's tales, in that certain key interactions took place through phone calls, Skype calls, Internet Relay Chat or unspecified encrypted communications – in short, anything that doesn't leave a paper trail. This is true even for deals supposedly worth tens of millions of dollars, but the necessity for such assertions will become clear when we come to the assessment of Wright's documentary evidence over his Satoshi claims.

WMIRK was an odd choice for multiple reasons, but Wright's decision looks particularly strange given that Bitcoin exchange MtGox had a direct link to Liberty Reserve built into its backend at the time. This would have allowed Wright an instant transfer of Liberty Reserve coins into bitcoins, but instead, he chose a WebMoney company based in Siberia, which advertised less than US$100,000 in readily available liquidity and which didn't deal in bitcoins. Wright says that he was already familiar with WMIRK from his gambling days, but this story didn't come out until 2022, leading to his critics alleging that he simply alighted upon an exchange from which his adversaries would find it hard to obtain contradictory records (he only named the exchange for the first time the following year). Part of WMIRK's offering was full documentation of the on-ramp and off-ramp process, which clients used for compliance or tax purposes, whether legitimate or not, something that Wright never seems to have received, making him another exception to their practices.

WMIRK apparently told Wright that, for his holdings, he could get 80,000 bitcoins, and the resultant purchase order claimed that Wright had paid $1.68 million for the coins. Bitcoin's value on the date of the purchase order, 27 February 2011, was around $0.90 per coin, meaning that 80,000 coins should have cost him $73,000, not $1.68 million. When questioned about this for the *Tulip Trading Ltd v Bitcoin Association for BSV & Ors* case, Wright initially blamed this discrepancy on the fluctuation of the Liberty Reserve dollar, which raises the theory that the currency, which was pegged to the U.S. dollar, suddenly devalued by 95% just when Wright was making his purchase. In 2023, however, Wright changed his story:

> There was no established market for Bitcoin at that time. I made the decision to pay an inflated price…in order to generate a healthier Bitcoin market. I considered that a higher price would assist with the discussions taking place at that time between myself and the ATO.

This is, of course, utter nonsense; if the deal had ever happened, it would have been a private affair where the bitcoins would (or should) have changed hands away from the open market and would not have benefited anyone other than the seller. It seems plausible that the valuation on the purchase order is merely more Wright sloppiness; the 80,000 bitcoins would have first hit $1.68 million in value in early February 2013, suggesting that Wright merely put the wrong year on the purchase order. Nevertheless, seemingly satisfied with the shocking exchange rate he was being offered, Wright agreed to the deal on behalf of Craig Wright R&D Trust (a trust that doesn't exist anywhere other than on the purchase order created for this sole transaction), and WMIRK sourced the coins, with Wright instructing its agents to take the payment out of his Liberty Reserve account. 79,956 bitcoins were duly deposited into the Bitcoin address listed on the purchase order, an address which began '1Feex', on 1 March 2011.

In October 2013, the ATO quizzed Wright over how he came to be in possession of Bitcoin addresses containing almost 500,000 coins, including the 1Feex address, with Wright putting the acquisitions down to 'a matter of fate and other circumstances' (nowhere was there any mention of a Russian exchange). Wright was quizzed on the meaning of this odd phrase in a June 2019 deposition for the *Kleiman v Wright* case:

> *I mean exactly the meaning of the word. Fate means circumstances beyond control, so the fact that my best friend died is fate, misfortune. It would not be a random occurrence. When someone commits suicide it is still fate.*

This, obviously, referred to Dave Kleiman, but when Wright was asked the same question at the trial two years later, he seemed to suffer a memory lapse:

> COUNSEL: Dr. Wright, when you said: "These addresses are now in my control as a matter of fate and other circumstances," you meant because Dave died, did you not?
>
> WRIGHT: No, I did not.

WMIRK was first referenced by name in the aforementioned purchase order, which was submitted as evidence for the *Tulip Trading Ltd v Bitcoin Association for BSV & Ors* lawsuit in 2023. The purchase order itself was soon found to be a forgery, with Craig blaming Lynn as soon as this was revealed. In a witness statement following the debunking of the purchase order, Wright altered his account regarding the purchase of the 1Feex coins, claiming that it was a 'test transaction' as part of a previously undisclosed plan to find a way to utilise his Liberty Reserve dollars. The fact that TTL ended up paying $1.68 million for bitcoins valued at just $72,000 indicates that the test failed badly. Craig also used this new story to reverse back over Lynn:

> *TTL's position is that the Purchase Order was not authored by me but was instead created by my ex-wife, Lynn Wright, whom I had entrusted with the administration of the 1Feex transaction. It is essential to note that I believe the Purchase Order remained under Lynn Wright's control (either directly or via administrative staff) throughout our separation in December 2010, with my physical departure from our joint residence occurring in February 2011.*

Given that the deal supposedly took place in late February 2011, it's not clear how Lynn was able to get her hands on the purchase order pertaining to it three months beforehand. It didn't matter anyway, as Craig binned the document the moment it was exposed:

> *For the avoidance of doubt TTL's position is not that the Purchase Order represents contemporaneous proof of the transaction.*

Perhaps unsurprisingly, Wright's absurd story doesn't stand up to scrutiny. Had the ATO not closed its investigations into his companies in 2016, its officers might have been interested to learn that the coins in the 1Feex address had come not from WMIRK but, in fact, from MtGox. The exchange suffered a hack in late February 2011, with the hackers sending the spoils to the 1Feex address on 1 March, where they remain to this day (many believe that the hackers accidentally sent the coins to an inaccessible address). Emails, online chats and transactions on the MtGox database, produced through investigations into the exchange's collapse, proved that the coins belonged to MtGox and had nothing to do with Craig Wright or his companies. The 1Feex-MtGox connection was made public in 2016, by which time Wright had already told the ATO that his companies controlled the address, catching him in yet another lie. Worse, the year before the MtGox revelation, Wright had used the coins as collateral for a US$15 million bailout, which we will discuss in Volume II.

The 1Feex coins also played a tangential role in Craig and Lynn Wright's divorce, which Craig says was partially caused by his reaction to his ejection from

Bitcoin. However, he admitted under oath that he and Lynn had been having issues since 2009, and the pair had been heading for separation well before his alleged Bitcoin exit. During the *Kleiman v Wright* trial, Wright dated their informal separation to August 2010, with him moving out 'a few months later'. However, in her deposition for the same case, Lynn remembered things differently:

> COUNSEL: And how long did you stay married to Craig after you discovered the relationship with Ms Ramona?
>
> LYNN: I don't know. She wasn't the first one that he was mucking about with, and no doubt won't be the last, but probably I found out about her in December – or in November, and we separated then.
>
> COUNSEL: So you separated in November of 2010?
>
> LYNN: Yes.

Given this 2010 separation, the notion that Craig Wright entrusted the administration of the WMIRK purchase to Lynn rather than the woman he was leaving her for makes no sense whatsoever.

Lynn made no mention of anything happening in August 2010 in her deposition, stating only that her discovery of an affair between Craig and Ramona Watts in November 2010 was the catalyst for the separation (in a February 2019 blog post, Craig said the 'marriage ended' in October 2010). This clashes with another of Craig's claims: that he met Ramona in 2011 through charity work and that the pair started dating at 'the end of 2011.' We only have the word of each as our guide here, but Lynn's more specific recollection is given buoyancy by the inference that the events impacted her more than Craig; a jilted wife doesn't mistake the year in which she confronted her husband and his mistress over their affair. Lynn testified that this confrontation acted as the trigger for the dissolution of their marriage, which took some seven months to play out. Incidentally, evidence gathered following the *COPA v Wright* trial in 2024 showed that Craig may not have ended his adulterous ways: a Tinder Gold subscription featured among his contemporaneous credit card expenses, showing that he may not have ceased his 'mucking about'.

Among the documents Lynn submitted as part of her deposition for the *Kleiman v Wright* case was a divorce agreement dated June 2011, which carried some interesting details. Lynn was awarded all the income from Cloudcroft and use of the IP related to Greyfog, although given that she told her deposing attorney that the Greyfog device was only bought by 'a couple of clients', it's debatable whether that IP was actually worth anything. What's more notable is something noted under 'intellectual property' on the agreement on Craig Wright's side:

> *Any and ALL Bitcoin, private keys, trusts and software associated with Bitcoin.*

This document, then, should act as a smoking gun that Wright had a stash of bitcoins, private keys and IP related to Bitcoin's creation and operation in mid-2011. However, Wright rather undermined this possibility during a June 2019 deposition for the *Kleiman v Wright* case:

> COUNSEL: Did the divorce settlement deal with any Bitcoin assets?
>
> WRIGHT: Indirectly. It dealt with companies.

This claim of indirect ownership was in stark contrast to what was stated in the divorce settlement, but Wright expanded on the theme of indirect control:

> *All of the Bitcoin, IP, et cetera, that I had that was mined and created into a company I owned called Wright International Investments. Wright International Investments was set up to own everything I was creating. I attempted to move that into other Australian companies, but that fell through because of the tax office. The issue was which companies went to who, which other assets went to who. I kept Wright International Investments.*

Nowhere on the asset split breakdown is there any mention of WII, despite this supposedly being the vehicle that held all of Wright's bitcoins and IP since its establishment in 2009.

As we know, Lynn confirmed in her testimony that Craig never mentioned Bitcoin or Satoshi Nakamoto to her during their time together, which makes it all the more strange that the agreement she signed specifically mentions Bitcoin. Indeed, Lynn stated in her *Kleiman v Wright* deposition that she recognised the document in question, potentially setting her up for a charge of perjury. There is another explanation, however:

> *It was sent to me by Craig's solicitor a week or so ago...I guess I said I didn't...have a copy of it. I just had my divorce decree.*

What we have, then, is Lynn Wright relying on Craig's copy of the split agreement rather than her own, a version which just so happens to back up the story spun at the trial and runs contrary to Craig's own prior comments. It is not a stretch, therefore, to believe that Craig Wright amended the genuine document to insert the references to Bitcoin before sending it over, perhaps knowing that Lynn wouldn't read it thoroughly or dare to question it. This issue came up later in proceedings, leading to Ira Kleiman's legal team doing some digging:

> *...the document is another forgery. Plaintiffs obtained the Wrights' divorce records directly from the federal Magistrates Court in Australia, which include no such copy of the agreement...The fabrication of this document also explains why Ms. Wright testified she did not have a copy of the relevant agreement, and that the only copy she had was provided to her by Wright's counsel, a week before her deposition.*

Craig Wright's legal team had also claimed that Lynn had 'no reason to lie for Dr. Wright', but the plaintiffs argued that she, in fact, 'has a strong incentive to lie: she is financially dependent on him, lives in fear of him cutting off her support, and has lied for him in the past due to that.' This was evidenced by Lynn's explanation of why she had helped Craig out with some research in 2013, two years after their divorce:

> *... probably because Craig was supporting me and I didn't want to run the risk of him saying, "I will just stop giving you the money".*

The suggestion of cash for testimony came to light again three years later when Christen Ager-Hanssen, the former CEO of Wright's long-time employer, nChain, published an email from an unknown source to one of Wright's backers, noting that they had visited Lynn to inform her that she would receive US$30 million if 'the case goes well'. We will discuss the case in question in Volume II, but what was evident from the email was the hold that Craig Wright still had over Lynn more than a decade after their divorce:

> *I asked her about the court case she was involved in. She seemed a little uneasy when she talks about Craig. She mentioned that just thinking about him gives her stress and it is not good for her health. She said she wishes people just leave her alone.*

This email, and more that cannot be published for legal reasons, speaks of a disturbing level of control by individuals within Wright's camp for years after the divorce, but it is the way their divorce was conducted that shows how deep-rooted this control appears to have been. On the surface, the divorce seemed amicable: rather than hiring legal representation for themselves, the pair drew up a settlement and asked a solicitor, Michael Shehadie, to formalise it. This process meant that Lynn didn't have anyone going in to bat for her in the negotiations, with her *Kleiman v Wright* testimony suggesting she might have needed the help:

> LYNN: *Michael Shehadie was our solicitor from – like, we had retained him for quite a few years, and then during...our divorce, he represented...I thought he was representing me, but I – I – I don't know, to be honest.*
>
> COUNSEL: *Was he acting for both of you?*
>
> LYNN: *I thought he was acting for me, but I think that was more – see...we did the divorce ourselves. We...didn't go through a solicitor to go...through the courts for us. We put the paperwork in ourselves, and then the agreement...was developed with Michael Shehadie.*

Lynn added that she was so preoccupied with concerns over how she was going to support herself following the divorce that she 'didn't ask a lot of questions I should have' over the details, adding that it 'probably would have been better for my future' if she had. Craig Wright, however, claimed in 2019 that things were the other way around:

> COUNSEL: *Were you represented by counsel?*
>
> WRIGHT: *Lynn was represented by counsel; I wasn't.*

Wright added in his deposition that he destroyed his copy of the settlement agreement in 2014, leaving Shehadie as the only person with a copy to send to

Lynn. Given that the document Lynn received had clearly been manipulated, this means that either Wright lied about destroying it or Shehadie doctored the document on behalf of his client before sending it over. It wasn't just in the financial realm that Craig appears to have exerted control over Lynn: during her deposition, Lynn retold how Craig convinced her to 'cop the points' when he was caught speeding in a school zone due to his being one point away from a driving ban and a possible prison sentence.

Craig Wright has publicly stated that he and Lynn were flat broke at the time of the divorce, which may have been the reason why the pair avoided the court process. There may, however, have been another more sinister motive. Lynn was asked in her deposition whether Craig had ever mentioned any dealings in Costa Rica, to which she replied that he hadn't. This is important, given that Wright told the ATO that the source of funding for hundreds of thousands of bitcoins he spent on his companies was through his holdings in the Costa Rica-based Liberty Reserve. This, he told them, amounted to US$30 million at the time the divorce was being finalised in May 2011, which is particularly impressive given that he had supposedly used all his Liberty Reserve holdings on that bitcoin purchase from WMIRK just three months previously. This means that Wright either accumulated the US$30 million between February and May 2011, or he had a separate Liberty Reserve haul. Either way, Lynn clearly had no idea about any such funds, despite Craig claiming that she had written out the purchase order for the alleged WMIRK deal. This was likely Craig's way of deflecting criticism over its multiple inaccuracies, but it undermines his entire Liberty Reserve story, suggesting that Lynn knew about its existence when she told her deponent for the *Kleiman v Wright* case that she had never heard of any Costa Rica-based investments.

Craig Wright's Liberty Reserve holdings are not mentioned anywhere in the divorce settlement, and with Lynn admitting that she had very little involvement in his business activities beyond the work she was hired to do, it's clear Craig never mentioned the pot of Costa Rican gold to her. If we are to believe his claim, the decision to settle divorce matters privately allowed Craig to keep his Liberty Reserve funds out of Lynn's reach, even as she went bankrupt after the divorce. If the pair had divorced through the law courts, Craig would have had to either reveal his holdings or face huge concealment penalties if they were later uncovered. It seems, therefore, that Lynn Wright may well be, to use her own term, one of the bodies Craig Wright left by the wayside as he pursued his goals.

There is, of course, another explanation as to why Lynn Wright had never heard of any Costa Rica funds: they never existed. Such an eventuality would exonerate her from the accusation of lying under oath and would instantly erase the multitude of questions that arise if we are to believe Craig Wright's side of the story. Craig has never provided a shred of evidence to back up his Costa Rica story, and all testaments to this possibility by third parties are rooted in his word alone. The existence or otherwise of the Costa Rica funds is irrelevant to how Lynn Wright felt she was treated in the divorce, and it's impossible not to feel sympathy for the way she seems to have been thrown out of the speeding car that was Craig Wright's ambition. It must be noted, however, that Craig has not given his version of the divorce proceedings under oath, and so all such assumptions about his conduct must be viewed through this lens. However it happened, by early 2011, the Wrights were divorced, and Craig and Ramona Watts were starting a new life together, a life that would see Wright take his corporate chicanery to a whole new level.

Chapter 9 – From Panama to Panopticrypt

Despite swapping his wife for his mistress, Craig Wright says that by mid-2011, he was still drifting with 'no idea what to do'. This, as we have seen, is at a time when he had more on his plate than the greediest all-you-can-eat diner. Wright says that he sold all but 'the back 350 acres' of the farm at Bagnoo and engaged in 'isolated forensic jobs [including] work for a number of casinos and sports betting sites' to keep the pennies rolling in, but, again, this doesn't tally with the suggestion he had US$30 million sitting in Liberty Reserve. It also brings into question the wisdom of his supposed decision to spend over one and a half million dollars on $72,000 worth of bitcoins a few months earlier, although this gamble would have paid off had he actually taken it; by June 2011, their value would have increased to $2.9 million. Then there was his 'PayPal for gold' idea, which was only topped by, of all things, a Bluetooth-enabled NFC payment glove. A video from mid-2011 shows a youthful-looking Craig Wright wandering around a Woolworth's store with a friend, talking about how he is going to buy some energy drinks with his new accessory. The video has all the marks of a bout of university high jinks, and indeed, Wright is wearing a navy hoodie emblazoned with Patrick Henry University on the front, something he clearly forgot about when he posted the following in 2021:

> *So, when you hear claims that Craig Wright was ever in hoodies you will iinstaantly know that these are complete and utter lies that other people want to use to create a false story...there are no pictures of me ever wearing a hoodie...because it never happened.*

Around this time, the supposedly directionless Wright was invited to add yet another position to his bursting curriculum vitae. Wright had recently been introduced to the Global Institute for Cyber Security and Research (GICSR) by its International Executive Director, Richard Zaluski, who helped get Wright appointed as its Asia Pacific Director. Wright's now-deleted LinkedIn page states that he held this position from April 2011, but articles announcing his appointment appeared that June. Wright's responsibilities were reported to include the establishment of 'a regional 'centre of excellence' in cyber security with the region's leading research organisations and cyber security universities'; ensuring that 'government intelligence communities, intelligence services, law enforcement agencies, major universities and research and development agencies' had access to the work that GICSR was doing; and establishing relationships with 'regional intelligence agencies, governments and security vendors to those that GICSR have in place with the NSA, FBI, DHS, NASA and NIST in the USA'. This was quite a long list of responsibilities for Wright, who, in a series of interviews connected to his new role, seems to have been fully focused on his new job and showed no signs of career drift. However, the truth may have been a little different: during a December 2019 deposition for the *Kleiman v Wright* case, GICSR founder and CEO Deborah Kobza opened up about Wright's role, saying that he was, in fact, an unpaid volunteer whose role was 'trying to help bring people in' for a research project.

Wright lasted around a year in the job, but his stint may have been much shorter had a stunning revelation about his conduct come to light during his time there. During email discussions in February 2014 with Dave Kleiman's family, Wright told Ira Kleiman that his brother had 300,000 mined bitcoins split across various trusts, with Ira referencing one called the GICSR Trust in Belize. The trust was brought up during Wright's first deposition for the *Kleiman v Wright* case in 2019, where he said that Dave Kleiman's role had been merely 'putting information onto computers' and referenced no held bitcoins. Wright tried to draw on national security concerns in order to prevent further questioning over the trust, given the non-profit's work with U.S. intelligence agencies, but when Deborah Kobza was deposed seven months later for the same case, she had no such compunctions. Kobza revealed that no staff had ever set up trusts in the GICSR's name, nor were they allowed to, which made it all the more obvious that Wright's GICSR Trust had either been fraudulently created or was a complete fiction spun for Ira Kleiman. She was then informed that Wright had told the ATO that Craig Wright R&D had entered into a licensing agreement with the GICSR worth a staggering, and oddly precise, $28,181,818.18, with

Wright trying to claim back the tax levied on the deal from the ATO. Kobza's attention was then brought to the paperwork concerning the deal:

> COUNSEL: Have you ever seen this page before?
>
> KOBZA: No.
>
> COUNSEL: And can you see who is identified on the signature lines?
>
> KOBZA: Yeah, I see Craig Wright, director, and through GICSR, Deborah Kobza. I don't know if it would have executive director, NH-ISAC, there. That's a completely different organization. So I don't understand why that's there.
>
> COUNSEL: So is that your signature?
>
> KOBZA: No, it's not.
>
> COUNSEL: Does it resemble your signature?
>
> KOBZA: No, it doesn't...This definitely does not resemble my signature.

In another document related to the GICSR, Wright tried to claim a $31 million deal with the National Aeronautics and Space Administration (NASA) over peer-to-peer technology, which Kobza said was impossible as the organisation had never done any work with NASA. The revelations left Kobza close to tears in the witness box as she grasped the scale of Wright's fraud against her and the GICSR:

> *Seeing written evidence of somebody that's stolen your identity and is committing fraud and, you know, using your name and the name of the small nonprofit I had is -- is shocking and appalling. I'm very, very upset. To the point of filing my own lawsuit for fraud and identity theft. I mean, it's -- it's shocking that someone that was represented to me that worked for a university could move on to do things like this. You know, you see things about people getting impacted by crime and things like that and how they feel helpless, and that's how I feel. It's -- it makes me sick to my stomach.*

CoinGeek covered this issue in its typical pro-Wright manner, totally underplaying the seriousness of the fraud over the Belize trust:

> *The general takeaway from the Kobza deposition was that Kobza knew little to nothing about Dr. Wright and his business affairs and that Dr. Wright was not authorized to obtain that license on behalf of GICSR, or at least not authorized to do this without making the GICSR's founder aware of the transaction—which he didn't do.*

Wright also perpetrated a slightly lesser fraud on the GICSR in 2013 when he spoke at that year's Datacon conference as the outfit's Vice President for Australia, affording himself not just a return to the institute he had left more than a year prior but a retrospective promotion into the bargain.

It goes without saying that Wright's activities during this period contradict his assertion that he was languishing in a 'deep abyss of despair', a claim that would not actually come out until years afterwards when he was riding high on his Satoshi Nakamoto hobby horse. Wright paints the picture of someone experiencing a kind of existential crisis following his ejection from Bitcoin while at the same time starting up multiple new ventures, taking up exciting new job opportunities, flying business class and larking about with friends over wearable tech.

Despite his plethora of jobs and other appointments – and his supposed malaise – Wright decided that mid-2011 was the perfect time to set about 'fixing the problems that I'd created' with Bitcoin. Wright told *Forbes* in July 2023 that he divided the IP he had created for Bitcoin among four of his companies: Information Defense, which received IP related to the Bitcoin database; Integyrs, which received cryptographic research; Greyfog, which received IP related to real-world use of smart technology (today called the Internet of Things); and Strasan Pty Ltd (Strasan), which received information concerning 'sharding', the splitting up of blockchain transactions into smaller pieces to aid throughput. Wright, however, neglected to say exactly when he had done this, and there is, as we will see, nothing but a few rejected tax rebate claims to back up his tale.

Wright's Bitcoin salvation mission would come in the form of yet more companies, which he hoped would put Bitcoin back on the path he had supposedly intended for it. The first of these companies was Panopticrypt Pty Ltd (Panopticrypt), which means 'everything hidden in the open'. This would be a Bitcoin-based technology that Wright said in 2019 would help him 'prove that Bitcoin worked', a claim he undermined four years later in his first *COPA v Wright* witness statement when he said that Bitcoin was working as planned when he left. We get an idea of the level of document forgery that has dogged Craig Wright's career when we learn that the Australian Securities and Investments Commission (ASIC) registration certificate for Panopticrypt was found to be a forgery; forensic investigator Dr Matthew Edman found that the certificate, which purported to date from the time of the company's registration in June 2011, had been created on 23 October 2014 by someone in an Eastern Australia time zone using a modified copy of the ASIC registration certificate awarded to another of Wright's companies, Coin-Exch Pty Ltd (Coin-Exch), on 17 April 2013. The forgery seems pointless, seeing as Panopticrypt was registered in June 2011, but this creation date will be explained later.

Wright hoped to prove Bitcoin worked through a project run through Panopticrypt: Sukuriputo Okane (scriptable money), which 'would have allowed for tokenisation of shares, gold, digital currencies like central bank digital currency, all on top of Bitcoin.' As he would later do with Tulip and C01N, Wright also attached the name to a supercomputer he was allegedly building as a get-out clause after the ATO cornered him on certain aspects of the scriptable money project. As well as supposedly trying to prove Bitcoin's workability, Wright also 'spent millions testing alternatives' to it, right at a time when he also says the ATO's attacks on him were bleeding him dry, but we know where these millions supposedly came from:

> *I had money put aside from operations concerning casinos that I was involved with and had a large amount of money overseas, and I spent that buying other assets in Bitcoin...*

This, of course, is Wright's famous US$30 million Liberty Reserve fund, which he decided to cash out 'between May and June 2011', right after his divorce was finalised. As he had done months with his prior Liberty Reserve haul, Wright decided to transfer his money into bitcoins, again following in the footsteps of those Silk Road sellers he so loathed. Wright claimed in his August 2019 deposition for the *Kleiman v Wright* case that he wanted to buy a million bitcoins but ended up with 'somewhere between 650 and 700,000'. This would have been around 10% of all the bitcoins in existence at the time, with Wright saying in a sworn declaration for the same case that he used the Panamanian company Signia Enterprises Corp (trading as High Secured) to 'acquire Bitcoin on the market and hold it on behalf of the Tulip Trust'. Just weeks after this declaration, Wright expanded on this $30 million Bitcoin purchase:

> *The market, at the time, was very illiquid, and I didn't realize exactly how much it would impact the market. And so I caused a price spike when I bought this, a significant one. The price of Bitcoin temporarily went from cents to about $30 and then dropped back down again. And I was not able to purchase all of the Bitcoin that I had planned.*

This story doesn't check out for multiple reasons, not least because we are asked to believe that, after WMIRK helped him pay twenty-three times over the odds for his first large-scale Bitcoin purchase, Craig Wright once again entrusted his fortune to companies that had no history of dealing with it. This was also despite this haul representing his last throw of the financial dice; the capital through which he planned to resurrect Bitcoin. We are also asked to believe that whichever of the two companies that made the purchase bought $30 million worth of bitcoins on a highly illiquid market in one go rather than setting a bid and waiting for it to fill, which is the kind of error that even the tea boy at a wealth management company would know to avoid. Even after the company made this colossal error, Wright was apparently forgiving enough to allow it to custody the coins for him, even though it had just as much experience with Bitcoin storage as Bitcoin trading.

It's also worth examining Wright's claims of moving the Bitcoin price with the purchase. Historical data shows that the Bitcoin price did indeed spike to US$30 in June 2011 across all exchanges, which would appear to be the genesis of his assertion. However, Bitcoin had been on a steady rise since the turn of the year, so he was far from the catalyst for this spike, while the suggestion that his purchase sent Bitcoin to US$30 from mere cents is erroneous, given that it was already at US$3 by the start of May. It's also impossible that any exchange at this time had enough liquidity to handle 10% of all the bitcoins in the world in one go, and the only one we still have data for, MtGox, never recorded such a trade on its books. If the trade did happen, therefore, it couldn't have been on the open market, and so couldn't have impacted the price.

Wright's cavalier attitude over funds that were crucial to his future endeavours beggars belief, but there is a simple explanation for all of it: it never happened. Apart from the profusion of inconsistencies and the lack of empirical data to back up the purchases, Wright has never produced any evidence of a deal or even negotiations over a Bitcoin trade with High Secured or Signia Enterprises, with the companies themselves also failing to confirm any such deals. Wright has also failed to produce evidence to support any part of the process he followed to buy the coins, while the only proof of their receipt into his companies was found by Justice Mellor to have been 'plainly forged by Dr Wright.' It is also telling that Wright's story has, once again, changed along the way, with key elements added over time. As ever, these revisions were only ever provided to try and plug holes that were exposed in his stories and never with any proof.

As is evident, this purchase never took place, but if it had, it would have turned out to be a shocking deal: Wright bought at the very peak of the first Bitcoin bull run, and within six months, his US$30 million investment would have been worth just US$1.54 million. Setting aside the nonsensical nature of the purchase, Wright claims that High Secured custodied some 700,000 bitcoins on behalf of Craig Wright R&D, which was tasked with managing Wright's treasure trove and sending the coins out to Wright's companies on behalf of Panopticrypt. This, Wright told the ATO, was done 'so that bitcoin would not come into Australia because there were GST implications and other tax implications at the time', with Wright later saying that Bitcoin software was also sent over to keep it away from the ATO's greedy clutches. As a side note, to give an idea of the complexity involved in Wright's company and trust dealings over the years, here's how he described the ownership of this particular bitcoin haul when questioned about it during the *Kleiman v Wright* trial:

> *It belongs to different assignments, different companies, whatever else, so you would have to look through all the assignments in the corporate records to which bit owns where. Different companies, different groups own different amounts and still hold different amounts. I believe the Singaporean company still has rights to a certain amount, but I am not sure without going through accounts what the exact amounts that are owed, not owed etc.*

This explains why it's not always possible to follow the flow of funds in this story, especially when it keeps changing with every interview, blog post and court appearance. Once you strip away the lies, however, the path is absurdly simple to follow: there is no evidence that Satoshi Nakamoto was remotely interested in offshore trusts and Australian companies for wealth protection and tax efficiency purposes, and all the evidence Wright has produced surrounding such claims has been proven to be fraudulent.

The staggering collapse in the value of Wright's bitcoin holdings throughout 2013 didn't seem to impact him; he allegedly managed to spend all but 100,000 of his stash on his companies, a claim we will look at in more detail later. It's worth noting, however, that in court for the *Kleiman v Wright* trial, Wright distanced himself from the actual transfer of the coins or anything to do with their expenditure, saying that he never played any part in their movement and all the paperwork had been retained by High Secured. The remaining 100,000 were supposedly left out of Wright's reach when the person managing his bitcoins, the exotically-named Ritzela De Gracia, fled with them following the alleged arrest of High Secured's top brass on money laundering charges, after which, according to Wright, 'the other people disappeared'. Wright didn't specify when this police action supposedly happened, but he did remember that a 'Mark' from High Secured, who was one of those arrested, had been prominent in their dealings. Wright elaborated on this a little during the *Kleiman v Wright* trial in a frosty encounter with the opposition's counsel:

> COUNSEL: *Do you have any way of contacting Mark from High Secured?*
>
> WRIGHT: *He is in a federal penitentiary in the USA.*
>
> COUNSEL: *Which federal penitentiary?*
>
> WRIGHT: *I do not know. I did not follow his case.*
>
> COUNSEL: *Is there a way you can determine his last name and let us know what it is later?*
>
> WRIGHT: *You can do searches on High Secured. There is this thing called Google. You go into this taskbar, you type in 'High Secured,' and search.*

For all his sarcasm, Wright is incorrect: there is no online record of a 'Mark' of High Secured being arrested, but Wright could have been referring to an incident in July 2015 when High Secured's offshore legal services division manager, Michael Dodd, was arrested in New York on suspicion of agreeing to launder about US$2 million in an FBI sting. Dodd pleaded guilty in January 2016 and was sentenced to thirty-three months in prison, but there is no indication that further action was taken against High Secured or its employees in relation to the incident. There was also no mention of Ritzela De Gracia in the stories covering Dodd's arrest; in fact, she has no online presence whatsoever.

Wright claims that in June 2011, he took the first steps towards moving his Bitcoin IP offshore to prevent the ATO from getting its hands on it as part of its campaign to bankrupt him. The idea, Wright stated in a 2020 blog post, was that years later, he would be able to 'bring things back to Australia and repatriate some of the things that I had been working on before', including IP, bitcoins and money earned from his and Dave Kleiman's gambling work out of Costa Rica, which encompassed his spurious Liberty Reserve funds. Wright claimed that his first attempt to do this had been through WII, but this claim is connected to his 2008/09 tax return, which we know had nothing to do with Bitcoin. His second attempt, Wright said in the same post, was through another Seychelles-registered entity, Tulip Trading Ltd (TTL), incorporated on 21 July 2011 with one purpose:

> *I wanted to bring my inventions back into Australia, but I also needed to do so without shooting myself in the head. I wanted to remain as secret as I could and also repatriate funds to Australia.*

Wright's Seychelles-incorporated companies form the genesis of an infamous entity that runs throughout his story from this point onwards like a seam of coal through a Welsh hillside. It is, therefore, time to take a break in the narrative and discuss the entity in question, which sums up the worst and most ludicrous parts of Craig Wright's chequered past: the Tulip Trust.

Chapter 10 – Planting Tulips

The Tulip Trust first came to the public's attention with the *WIRED* and *Gizmodo* 'doxxings' of 2015, where the mention of approximately 1.1 million bitcoins transferred from Craig Wright to Dave Kleiman was seen as a key piece of evidence that Wright was Satoshi Nakamoto. This is the sum that Satoshi was thought to have mined between 2009 and 2010, but insiders were immediately sceptical of Wright's claim to the haul. The document published by *WIRED* and *Gizmodo* detailing the supposed custody of Satoshi's bitcoins saw Kleiman take hold of the coins on 9 June 2011, noting that Wright was allowed to use the fund for loans for his businesses and that the remainder would be returned to Wright on 1 January 2020. This fact became acutely important when Ira Kleiman sued Wright in February 2018, demanding half the contents of the Tulip Trust. This act saw the trust thrust back into the public consciousness and brought to the fore all of Wright's dealings with the ATO over his Bitcoin holdings, leading to the agency alleging that he had embarked on a monstrous tax fraud.

Wright's convoluted, ever-changing explanations of what the Tulip Trust is, how it was constructed, what it holds and who owns it is something even he himself no longer seems to be sure of, which is extraordinary given that the premise had previously been so simple: a man mining a million bitcoins and hiding them offshore for tax reasons. Instead, the Tulip Trust has become a sprawling mass of contradictory statements, its contents and purpose morphing over time as Wright has added confusing and complex details, with different interpretations, sister trusts and amalgamations popping up along the way. We will leave these shifts in the narrative to later books in this series and will focus here on the time period with which we are concerned, which relates to the trust's formation and its initial alleged purpose.

Wright says that the Tulip Trust has its roots in his entanglements with the ATO and that its creation dates back to 2011, linking his actions during the *Granath v Wright* trial to the ATO's alleged desire to force his companies into dissolution:

> *I implemented a corporate structure because of the Australian Tax Office wanting to bankrupt me. If they bankrupted me, that means they would be able to take my assets. To protect my intellectual property, I took all control away from myself...and then in 2020 I regained control of my intellectual property in full in a way that doesn't allow the tax office to take it.*

Ramona Watts's recollection is different, however, as she told her deponent for the *Kleiman v Wright* case in March 2020:

> *So he said that...we're going to have this trust, and we are going to make sure that the purpose of the trust and the rules of the trust are such that Bitcoin is used in a legal manner. And we are going to use it to continue research in Bitcoin, to possibly fund companies they are doing work that can...continue on the peer-to-peer research and do things that are legal, without the illegal nature of Bitcoin.*

Nowhere in Ramona's deposition was there any mention of the ATO having a part to play in the Tulip Trust, despite her claim that she and Wright 'really...had spoken about the trust quite a bit' at the time.

According to the document *WIRED* and *Gizmodo* saw, Wright supposedly put the 'software and keys used to manage bitcoin' into the Tulip Trust and sent them overseas to protect them from the ATO, with the intention that it would all be unlocked for him at a later date. This was the result of Dave Kleiman's entreaties to Wright that, rather than destroying all his connections to Bitcoin and the name 'Satoshi', Wright should package up all the software, IP and related Bitcoin paraphernalia and lock it away, including over a million bitcoins Wright had mined between 2009 and 2010. Kleiman was put in charge of 'holding documents' on behalf of the trust and overseeing the security around it by handing out 'keys' to the trust to carefully selected holders. Wright added an extra rationale to his decision not to be a trustee in a 2020 interview where he claimed to have been 'smart enough' to avoid being a trustee because if he were, 'people could force me to actually move coins.'

Central to the Tulip Trust is TTL, a company Wright says was created for him in the Seychelles by offshore company specialists Abacus on 21 July 2011, right around the time of the bitcoin and software transfer. In 2022, Wright claimed that TTL had existed in an unofficial capacity since 2009, but the evidence supporting this was found to have been manipulated. Wright says that the Tulip Trust was formally executed in 2012 with a number of trustees overseeing the holdings, from which Wright was allowed to request loans for his businesses. Anything left by 1 January 2020 would come back to Wright, by which time Bitcoin would, theoretically, be a more accepted commodity and repatriating it to Australia would not be so burdensome on him from a tax perspective.

This is the simple version of the story, but the real history of the Tulip Trust is, as we have alluded to, immeasurably more complicated. The first known mention of Wright supposedly moving bitcoins overseas didn't come in 2011 when he says it happened, or in 2012 or 2013, but in a February 2014 interview with the ATO, when his tax lawyer Andrew Sommer explained how Wright had been moving large numbers of bitcoins between his companies in the form of loans and payments for services rendered. The reason Wright's representatives were speaking to the ATO about his Bitcoin affairs in February 2014 was due to the agency's scepticism about Wright's claim that he paid for tens of millions of dollars in software from a company called MJF Mining. We'll come to this particular story later on, but for now, it's important to note that Wright's representatives were trying to explain his Bitcoin dealings to the ATO in an attempt to clear him of suspicion and aid in the release of tax rebates. These rebates were the lifeblood of Wright's companies at the time, but the ATO was withholding them while it investigated their legitimacy.

Wright told the ATO in that February 2014 interview that he began mining bitcoins in 2009, making no mention of doing so through Integyrs or Information Defense. This changed the following month, however, when he told the ATO that he had indeed mined the bitcoins through these companies. The story changed again in 2019 when, in a sworn declaration for the *Kleiman v Wright* case, Wright said that he had mined bitcoins personally into a trust in Panama, which, as we know, he later denied. Wright also told the ATO about the sale of the 1.1 million mined bitcoins and Bitcoin software/IP to Dave Kleiman for $5,000, using a blog post where he discussed the sale as evidence of it having taken place (see chapter six). Wright's accountant, John Chesher, summarised Wright's early activities in a 26 February 2014 interview with the ATO:

> *Craig Wright had mined a lot of Bitcoins. Craig then took the Bitcoins and put them into a Seychelles Trust. A bit of it was also put into Singapore. This was run out of an entity from the UK.*

In his March 2020 deposition for the *Kleiman v Wright* case, Wright was asked why Chesher had also told the ATO in this meeting that 'W&K was an entity created for the purpose of mining Bitcoins' when Wright had argued the prior year that W&K had not been set up for this purpose. Wright's response was typical:

> *...I had conversations with my Australian lawyers where we had pointed out many, many errors in this [transcript]. The errata for this document was too large and the document is not admissible even in Australian processes because it is completely inaccurate.*

Wright added that when the ATO asked him on 6 March 2014 to confirm the accuracy of the transcripts for the 26 February meeting, he 'told them where to go', but this isn't true; email records show that he had only one complaint – a mistranscribing of the word 'chords' for 'cores'. Wright also held to Chesher's version of events in an email to Ramona Watts in 2015, showing that, even a year later, he still hadn't detected any serious errors in the transcription.

The mention by Chesher of a UK entity refers to British company C01N Ltd (C01N), which will come to play an important part in the Tulip Trust. No further information on the Singapore entity has ever seen the light of day, however, throwing serious question marks over its existence. Wright's claim to have moved all these coins overseas came at a suspiciously propitious time for him: he could refuse the ATO's recent requests to cryptographically prove ownership of Bitcoin addresses by claiming that he no longer had the right to do so; it would open up the possibility of assigning rights to these bitcoins instead of physically moving them around for payment purposes; and it would negate him having to pay taxes on them. It's worth pausing here to note something else that Chesher told the ATO and which Wright did not correct him on: there was a point in time when Wright, through his mining, owned 'around 10 per cent of all the bitcoins out there' and Dave Kleiman 'would have had a similar amount'.

This equates to around 20% of all the bitcoins in circulation, which, when added to the coins Wright said he bought from his Liberty Reserve funds, means that Wright would like us to believe that, in mid-2011, he and Dave Kleiman temporarily owned almost a third of all the bitcoins in the world. As we will see, this suggestion is backed up by nothing close to legitimate evidence.

Following the February 2014 meeting between Chesher and the ATO, the agency asked Wright for further information on the Tulip Trust. This was provided the following month when Wright forwarded Chesher an email supposedly sent by Dave Kleiman in October 2012, referencing keys for seventeen addresses held by 'the trust'. The email said that these keys were contained within one wallet, with Kleiman adding that he had created a paper wallet for 'a couple of the holdings', an act that, were it true, eviscerates Wright's claim made during the *Kleiman v Wright* case that Dave Kleiman's involvement never stretched to the actual coins. The addresses in this paper wallet included the 1Feex address and another beginning 12ib7, both of which Wright would use as the basis of the *Tulip Trading Ltd v Bitcoin Association for BSV & Ors* case in 2022. The wallet also supposedly contained an address beginning 1933p, the owner of which MtGox records show was one Marc Lowe, a doctor involved in an early Bitcoin-related lawsuit in the U.S. in 2016. A further email introduced into the *Kleiman v Wright* proceedings saw Dave Kleiman tell Wright that 'Most of these [addresses] go back to 2010 and 2011 when you first transferred them', but this cannot be legitimate.

The ATO had its doubts over the addresses supposedly owned by the Tulip Trust, having already seen many of the addresses listed in Dave Kleiman's email to Wright used elsewhere in Wright's tax filings. It may also have known that, while it wasn't impossible to create a paper wallet for more than one address, it was very difficult and dangerous from a security point of view, something that Wright should have known. However, it wasn't until forensics expert Dr Edman got his hands on the emails for the *Kleiman v Wright* case in 2019 that the whole truth came out: the October 2012 email from Kleiman was never sent and was fraudulently created 'on or about 2 March 2014', around a week before Wright forwarded it to Chesher. Wright testified during the trial that he didn't recognise the email he had sent to Kleiman that had sparked Kleiman's reply, excusing this by saying, 'I hate to say it, but I was drunk.' This is not the last role that alcohol will have to play in the Tulip Trust.

In a 2016 report into one of Wright's companies, Zuhl Ltd (Zuhl), the ATO laid out Wright's contention over the purpose and function of the Tulip Trust:

> *Entities related to the taxpayer contend that Mr Kleiman then arranged for these Bitcoin to be held by the 'Tulip Trust'. The Trust was settled in 2010 and has 17 'members', including a Seychelles company related to Dr Wright. Dr Wright knows the identities of only five of the members. Under the terms of the trust Dr Wright was to have control and access to the trust deed after 2015. Dr Wright was unable to identify the beneficiaries of the trust.*

This wasn't strictly true: in his 18 August 2014 interview with the ATO, Wright had, rather unhelpfully, claimed that the beneficiaries of the trust were 'The world. Every single person, apart from government, and in a way government because it will stop debt financing.' Wright also used the opportunity of this interview to offer up the names of those behind its creation: himself, Dave Kleiman, Uyen Nguyen and a Playboy Gaming employee called Tim, whose surname Wright couldn't remember.

Wright tried to back up his Tulip Trust story with a variety of documents, two of which ended up with *WIRED* and *Gizmodo* for their 2015 'outing'. We have already alluded to the first of these, a contract between Kleiman and Wright dated 9 June 2011, which laid out the terms of the asset transfer and their return. As we have said, the unsigned document, which was emailed to Wright from Kleiman, saw Wright sign over 1.1 million bitcoins to Kleiman's care, as well as 'full control of all software and the keys used to manage bitcoin'. In doing so, Kleiman became 'the trustee for the transfer of the satoshi I have received from Craig Wright' ('satoshis', or 'sats', are the name for fractions of a bitcoin), although Wright later denied that a transfer of coins ever took place. The contract also contained some important and frankly extraordinary clauses that revealed Wright's hand in its creation. The document stated that Kleiman would form a trust 'to be managed by at least three people but not more than seven at any time' and that the value of the bitcoins handed to him was US$100,000, giving each bitcoin a price of $0.09. However, the true price of Bitcoin on the date the contract was supposedly executed was vastly higher at $29, suggesting that Wright still hadn't got the hang of properly valuing his assets. The contract also stated a timeframe for the return of the coins to Wright, cutting off a line halfway through:

> *All Bitcoin will be returned to Dr Wright on Jan 01ˢᵗ 2020. The return will be in the form of a return of control of a company to Dr Wright. The company and trust will be managed and held in Seychelles. This will be designated by 'Tulips' and the trading that was noted to have not been a bubble but*

This sentence decapitation and the spelling mistakes that also featured prominently in the contract were somehow supposedly missed by both Dave Kleiman and Craig Wright, although the former has an excuse, seeing as he was in hospital as part of his mega stay at the time. Wright has no excuse, however, and it is extraordinary to think that he tried to pass this off as a genuine document with the ATO. Wright explained during both the *Kleiman v Wright* and *Granath v Wright* trials that the timeframe chosen to return the coins to him, January 2020, supposedly allowed enough time for Bitcoin to become a more mainstream and accepted asset, with Wright working on the assumption that the rules regarding its taxation had been relaxed by that point.

The document stated that Wright 'MAY requested a loan of Bitcoin' for research purposes, with the trust being accessible through a multi-key identity system (identified later by Wright as a Shamir Sharing Scheme he had devised called, of all things, Tulip Trust). A series of conditions then followed, including that the 'entire minus an amount noted below value and trust holdings' should go to Ramona Watts in the event of Wright's death. This was quite a show of faith in the strength of their relationship, given that Wright's account is that the pair didn't start dating until after the agreement was drawn up. Even if we take Lynn Wright's more reliable version of history, Craig was still making quite a sizeable bequest just six months after he and Ramona began dating. Sometimes, you just know.

Another condition stipulated that if Kleiman passed away, Wright was to be 'returned shares in the Tulip trust and company' fifteen months after his death, at his discretion. This window opened up in July 2014, at which point the bitcoins alone would have been worth some $697 million. However, Wright chose not to take advantage of the windfall even though it landed just when his tax lawyers were begging the ATO to process GST rebates for fractions of this amount. There then followed a truly extraordinary condition:

> *The amount not included to be sent to Ramona Watts will be used to show the 'lies and fraud perpetrated by Adam Westwood of the Australian Tax Office against Dr Wright' The last condition is listed as a direct quote of Dr Wright who has specified against my advice that he requires this line to be included.*

This comment about Adam Westwood, which is typical of Wright's petty, combative nature, is the only public reference to this individual in relation to Craig Wright. Dr Edman did analyse a June 2011 email allegedly sent from Wright to Dave Kleiman about Westwood for the *Kleiman v Wright* case, in which Wright, in the words of Dr Edman, 'makes several allegations' against the ATO man, but he found it to be a forgery made in April 2014.

The contract also included a line about Lynn Wright, who, as we already know, knew nothing about Bitcoin:

> *Dr Wright has noted that he had agreed to forgo other assets to maintain these assets and has agreed with his wife, Ms Lynn Wright that they he [sic] will maintain the Bitcoin at the expense of all other assets he may have a right to.*

Of course, no such agreement was made with Lynn, while the inclusion of both 'they' and 'he' in terms of maintaining Bitcoin is extremely problematic from a contractual standpoint.

The contract ended with a stipulation that access to the trust required at least two of five keys, with the contract listing four PGP 'fingerprints' (strings of unique numbers) connected to keyholders with another keyholder to be 'selected without Dr Wright's knowledge'. The ATO's forensics agents found that the four PGP keys (the 'fingerprints') in the document were, according to the MIT server on which they had been created, attributed to Dave Kleiman, Craig Wright and Satoshi Nakamoto (twice). The agents discovered that it was child's play to create and backdate a PGP key and that no proof of identity was needed to do so, meaning that anyone could have created a PGP key in anyone else's name and backdated it to whenever they liked. The agency proved this by locating another key on the same key server also tied to Dave Kleiman, with a creation date of 26 February 2014, almost a year after his death. This, notably, was the very day of the ATO meeting where John Chesher had advised that Wright had taken his approximately 1.1 million bitcoins and 'put them into a Seychelles Trust'. This means that mere hours after Wright shared his story of sending 1.1 million bitcoins offshore with the ATO, someone created and backdated PGP keys for use in a document used by Craig Wright to back up this story.

Among much that was missing from the contract, including a handwritten signature from Wright, Kleiman or any witnesses, was any mention of who the trustees of the Tulip Trust were. Andrew O'Hagan noted that when he asked Wright and Ramona Watts about this in 2016, they 'went quiet', an enigmatic response that could be taken any number of ways.

The ATO, unsurprisingly, was not convinced of the merits of the document or the Tulip Trust, as this line from the 2016 report into Zuhl shows:

> *While we do not accept the Tulip Trust document, we further note that it contains contradictory information about whether the trust has been created or whether it will be created in the future.*

In truth, the ATO's doubts over the existence of the Tulip Trust had begun almost as soon as Wright had first tried to prove its existence, with all the evidence he put forward found wanting. This led to Wright enlisting the services of his own forensic analyst, Dr Alan Batey, to back up his story. In 2015, Batey affirmed that the Tulip Trust document had been cryptographically signed by Dave Kleiman (or an individual who had access to his PGP key) and that the public key was available on the MIT PGP keyserver, adding that if anyone else had access to the private PGP key, then that person would also need to know the passphrase associated with it. However, the ATO was careful to state that Dr Batey had failed to provide a copy of the document he had analysed for his report, meaning that it was unable to replicate his results. The inference was clear: Craig Wright could have handed Batey a document different from the one the ATO had received, with the problematic elements taken care of.

When the document was made public by *WIRED* and *Gizmodo* in December 2015, it didn't take long for the public to smell a rat. The odd clauses, the spelling errors, the aborted sentence about tulips, its entirely unprofessional nature and the fact that it was unsigned led to many calling it out as a forgery. Others picked up on the fact that the contents of the trust (theoretically what

Satoshi Nakamoto mined between 2009 and 2010) should, according to the document, have been moved from Wright to Kleiman in June 2011 as stipulated in the contract. There was, however, no sign of this taking place on the blockchain. Wright expanded on the June 2011 document in a 2019 deposition for the *Kleiman v Wright* case:

> COUNSEL: And it was written on or about June 24th, 2011?
>
> WRIGHT: *I had actually sent the original version to Dave a little bit before that. And after badgering Dave, he sent it back on that date. When I wrote it, I had drunk four bottles of wine.*

The suggestion, then, is that Wright got blind drunk, typed up the contract and sent it to Kleiman earlier in 2011, with Kleiman finally sending it back on 24 June but backdating it to the ninth. It's worth pointing out here that four bottles of wine contain around forty units of alcohol, getting on for three times the amount that the UK's National Health Service (NHS) says can lead to alcohol poisoning, a life-threatening illness. Symptoms of alcohol poisoning include confusion, lack of physical coordination, seizures and loss of consciousness, and the NHS says that hospitalisation is essential for anyone suspected of having it. It doesn't say whether or not the typing up and emailing of contracts is another of the symptoms of alcohol poisoning, but Wright is suggesting that he consumed the equivalent of a litre of vodka and then bashed out a contract, which he managed to send over to Dave Kleiman. If this had happened, it would have been incredible if Kleiman had been able to decipher any of it at all.

Wright muddied the waters of the formation of the Tulip Trust during a deposition for the *Kleiman v Wright* case in 2019 when he revealed that some of the legal documentation, which hadn't been presented as evidence, was drawn up by lawyers, saying, 'Some were initially done [by lawyers], but I couldn't keep paying them—I was running out of money in 2011—and other lawyers were brought in later.' Wright never indicated which documents were drawn up by lawyers and which weren't, but Ramona Watts clearly got the memo about the change in story, with her March 2020 deposition for the same case building on this new version:

> *So we had a trust document in 2011 and then we firmed it up again in 2012. In 2014 we changed a few things and I really cannot remember*

what it was. It was not purpose or rules of the trust, but we might have added a few things to it, I cannot remember.

Ramona Watts said that she and Wright had disagreements over the structure of the Tulip Trust, saying, 'We did have several conversations in 2012 that he put me straight, and I understood things,' adding, 'He just explained to me how it was structured, because my understanding was apparently all incorrect, all wrong.' Ramona and Wright may have been discussing *a* trust in 2012, but, as we will see, it cannot have been the Tulip Trust.

Wright addressed the formation of the Tulip Trust during the *Kleiman v Wright* trial, denying that there was anything complex about it:

Craig Wright sets up a trust in 1998, changes the name of the trust in 2011. That trust owns Wright International Investment. The Australian companies mine into the foreign company. I think that's simple.

Throughout three days of testimony, Wright failed to back up this new story of an annually updated Tulip Trust and the 2014 changes, sticking resolutely to the now outdated 2011-2012 formation version. He did, however, reveal in a supporting statement for the case how he and Ramona were able to get hold of trust documents in January 2020:

I asked my wife, who is the primary trustee of the trust, to obtain a copy of the trust agreement.

Wright seemed to have forgotten this slice of history by the time the *Granath v Wright* trial rolled around two years later when he said that, due to him not being a trustee, he was excluded from access to trust documents before January 2020 and didn't know how to request them if he had wanted to. This was despite the trust having been supposedly reformulated by him and Ramona in 2017, as she had claimed in her *Kleiman v Wright* deposition. They had both apparently forgotten that, as trustee, Ramona could simply ask for a copy of the documents at any time.

Wright eventually fell in line with Ramona's story over the trust for the *Granath v Wright* trial in 2022, choosing to dismiss the 2011 Tulip Trust incorporation document entirely despite having hired a forensics expert to authenticate it seven years earlier. Wright's new story was that the day after Dave Kleiman had supposedly emailed him with the Tulip Trust document, Wright scrapped it and engaged corporate lawyers to draw up the real thing. Wright was challenged over this new version of events during the *COPA v Wright* trial in 2024, where he offered up further details to support the changed story, and this time, he had a name: one Dianne Pinder of Lloyds Solicitors in Brisbane had been responsible for setting up the Tulip Trust in 2011, a claim trotted out in the witness box for the very first time and not supported by even a shred of evidence. Wright may have thought he was digging himself out of a hole with his change in narrative, but, of course, he was simply creating more: why did he use a knowingly erroneous document as proof for the ATO in 2014? Why did he hire a forensic analyst to authenticate it only to declare it a fake in 2019? Why did he only remember that Lloyds Solicitors created the real documents in 2024? Justice Mellor summarised that Wright's account of the Tulip Trust 'appears to have been refashioned successively in the ATO proceedings, in Kleiman, in Granath and in this action [COPA]' and noted that Wright had a penchant for augmenting and then undermining evidence at will depending on what the situation demanded.

When Wright handed over his Tulip Trust evidence to the ATO in 2014, it wasn't just the odd document that concerned them; its investigators also found fault with the email from Kleiman which contained it (or, as it turned out, email*s*):

> ...*the taxpayer has provided two versions of the email from Mr Kleiman to which the Tulip Trust document was purportedly attached. The emails are identical except one is dated 24 June 2011 and the other 17 October 2014. Mr Kleiman died in April 2013.*

This date of 17 October 2014 is telling as it is the date on which Wright bought TTL, adding more weight to his direct involvement. These emails were next analysed by Dr Edman for the *Kleiman v Wright* case after Wright had sworn in a June 2019 deposition that he remembered receiving the email in question from Dave Kleiman. Dr Edman found that the 17 October email contained a sender and recipient address of 'craig@panopticrypt.com' in its header and that when it had arrived, the recipient had exported it to a PDF and 'modified [it] to appear as if Dave Kleiman had sent the email to Craig Wright'. Dr Edman also noted that the email was created on Microsoft Outlook 15, which wasn't released until eighteen months after Kleiman allegedly sent the email.

These findings were echoed by Patrick Madden for the *COPA v Wright* case in 2023, leaving us with a debunk hat trick spanning almost a decade. As for the 2011 email itself, this, Dr Edman said, was simply an amended copy of the 2014 email with the arrival date modified. A third identical email was also obtained during the discovery process for the *Kleiman v Wright* case, which Dr Edman said was a forgery also created from the first email on 17 October 2014 and modified to make it appear as if it arrived on 24 June 2011. This meant that someone with access to Craig Wright's computer and email account created three forgeries of the same email to back up Wright's Tulip Trust story, one of which was made on the very day Wright bought TTL.

Dr Edman's discoveries were put to Wright during a June 2019 deposition for the *Kleiman v Wright* case, where Wright argued that, because they were PDFs of emails rather than raw emails, they didn't count as evidence. He also argued that the 2014 metadata date stamp was due to someone printing the email on that date. Wright went as far as claiming that Ira Kleiman's lawyer, Vel Freedman, was 'provably misleading the Court' by introducing such evidence and almost earned himself a night in the cells with a show of petulance:

> WRIGHT: *You are committing perjury by falsely putting in a document. That is not real evidence. You have created something.*
>
> JUDGE: *Dr. Wright, you throw another document in my courtroom, you will be in handcuffs so fast your head will spin.*

Wright also claimed that the craig@panopticrypt.com email address in the metadata was not in operation in 2014 when Dave Kleiman's email was sent, saying he 'stopped using it about 2013', but could not produce any corroborative evidence. Freedman also pointed out that the date on the email was Thursday, 24 June 2011, which was, in fact, a Friday. When challenged on this, Wright offered his first of many similar rebuttals:

> COUNSEL: *Dr. Wright, do computers often mistake the day of the week?*

WRIGHT: When someone has modified a file on a compromised server that was hacked, and is known to be hacked, then all sorts of funny things happen.

COUNSEL: Did you edit the metadata on this PDF, on this e-mail?

WRIGHT: No. And you're collecting data from a known compromised server.

Wright addressed these emails again in a witness statement for the *Tulip Trading Ltd v Bitcoin Association for BSV & Ors* case some four years later, where he expanded on his theory: the duplication was caused by a 'reimport [of] a number of files' into a new system at DeMorgan following the need to rebuild the servers after a hack, which included the email in question. Wright said that the later date of 17 October 2014 was, therefore, the date that the file was reimported, steamrolling his prior argument that this was the printout date and adding that it 'simply reflects that the metadata was updated at that point.' Wright added, somewhat brazenly, that 'There should therefore be no dispute over the veracity of that document.' In 2024, Wright was back on the hacking trail, telling the court in the *COPA v Wright* trial that Ira Kleiman had fabricated the emails and sent them to the ATO 'to throw mud at everything', despite the ATO stating that the documents had come from Wright and Kleiman having no role with the company on whose behalf the documents were sent.

Wright's Tulip Trust contract may have been discredited, but he had supplied other documents to the ATO that he hoped would convince them of its existence. One of these was a Deed of Trust, supposedly between WII and TTL, which was signed by multiple parties on 23 October 2012. The deed, formed as a 'Declairation of Trust' (one of a number of telltale Wright typos) and intended to formalise the transfer of 'Bitcoin and associated ledger assets' in June 2011, was the 'legal solution' to the 'technical solution' of the bitcoin and software move. Among the assets to be moved were 'All Assets held in Liberty Reserve (Costa Rica) under the company Wright International Investments Ltd' and 'All Assets held in Liberty Reserve (Costa Rica) by Craig Steven Wright for and under the company Tulip Trading Ltd'. These items were listed separately from the '1,100,111 Bitcoin held under that former arrangement and the attached conditions', suggesting that the Tulip Trust contained assets held in Liberty Reserve in addition to the mined bitcoins. Access to the trust was divided up into 'slices' with one slice going to each trustee and three going to Wright, although no reference was made as to what these slices pertained to.

The Deed of Trust also revealed the trustees who would guard over the Tulip Trust and lend out the coins to Wright if the request was appropriate. This had been arranged, Ramona Watts told Andrew O'Hagan, as 'a guarantee that you can't flood the market...we can't use it to pay the bills, no matter how desperate things get.' The Deed of Trust featured seven trustees, three of whom were one Uyen Nguyen (no relation to Jimmy), Dave Kleiman and Seychelles outfit Savanah Ltd (or 'Savannah'; Wright seems to have used the spelling interchangeably), one of Wright's companies. This is particularly notable given that, according to his testimony for the *Kleiman v Wright* case, the then-teenaged Nguyen only entered Wright's orbit in 2011-2012, having ingratiated herself by 'cyberstalking' him (an email purportedly from Nguyen to Gavin Andresen in 2016 puts the date at 2010, but this email was almost certainly a forgery). Despite this, Wright apparently felt comfortable naming Nguyen as a trustee for the Tulip Trust and appointing her to various high-powered positions within his companies over the years (as we will see, many of these appointments turned out to be fraudulent).

The other four trustees made interesting reading to those who were aware of Wright's later claim that he had asked Dave Kleiman to make sure Wright was not connected to the Tulip Trust in any way. Two companies were listed: Panopticrypt and 'The company in the UK registered by 08248988', both of which Wright served as director of (this latter company was the UK variant of C01N, whose omission by name will become clear later when we cover its history and role within the Tulip Trust). The final two trustees made even more of a mockery of Wright's claim that the Tulip Trust had nothing to do with him: 'Craig Wright' and 'The holder of PGP key IDs 0x4ff1cfebc941fe6d, 0x491f9bdf0f7bd4ad, 0x18c09e865ec948a1'. Those PGP keys were later confirmed as being associated with 'Satoshi Nakamoto, i.e. Craig Wright' on the MIT server. This meant that, far from Wright being distanced from the Tulip Trust as he had asked, he was either named as or directly connected to four of the seven trustees.

Unlike the 2011 Tulip Trust document, the Deed of Trust was at least signed, although it was hardly convincing: indistinct squiggles represented the names of the people signing on behalf of Savanah and Abacus, with their names not printed underneath, making identification impossible (Wright would later say in a 2019 declaration for the *Kleiman v Wright* case that his contact at Savanah was Seychelles-based lawyer Denis Mayaka). The beneficiaries of the Tulip Trust were listed as WII and TTL, with Wright saying in a deposition for the same case that he was the point of contact for both trusts. Wright's stated wish had been to divest himself of everything that could connect him to Bitcoin through the Tulip Trust, and yet the creator of the trust, supposedly Dave Kleiman, had fitted it with a giant flashing arrow that pointed to Wright as being front and centre of the whole thing.

Before we deal with the analysis of this document, we need to look at the formation of the Tulip Trust and the entities connected to it. We have already discussed how Patrick Madden found that Wright purchased WII on 17 October 2014 and backdated it to 4 August 2009, and the story concerning TTL is almost identical. Wright's story was that he formed TTL, the company that he said held some of the assets that would eventually go into the Tulip Trust, through Abacus in July 2011, a year before the trust was formally executed. However, emails taken from Wright's system for the *Kleiman v Wright* case reveal the truth of the matter, while other documentation offers us a likely motive for his actions. By October 2014, the ATO was confident that what Wright was still calling the 'Seychelles Trust' did not exist, as it noted in an interim audit ruling on Coin-Exch:

> *We do not accept that the Seychelles Trust existed as a matter of law or fact during the relevant tax period.*

This need to prove the ATO wrong seems to have been the catalyst for what happened next: on 16 October 2014, Wright emailed Abacus asking to buy an 'aged shelf company'. An Abacus agent – none other than Denis Mayaka – responded by presenting Wright with a list of companies to choose from, with Wright selecting Tulip Trading Ltd, a company incorporated by Abacus on 21 July 2011. Wright's rationale for his selection was probably twofold: he needed a company founded in 2011, and he could pass the name off as a pun based on Bitcoin's unkind comparison to the Tulip Mania of the 1600s (hence the aborted reference in the Tulip Trust contract). Wright was billed accordingly, with the cost coming in at US$3,650, the first instalment of which he paid on 17 October, the day he also purchased WII.

With TTL now secured, Wright seemingly sprang into action, with several other events taking place later that day:

- Someone created and backdated three identical emails purporting to be from Dave Kleiman to Wright regarding the Tulip Trust's inception.
- Someone registered the web domain tuliptrading.net.
- Someone took the October 2014 invoice from Abacus to Wright concerning the purchase of TTL and used it to create a fake invoice dated July 2011. This document was edited on 18 October 2014 'in a time zone consistent with Australia', according to Dr Edman, and left on Wright's computer.
- Someone amended the TTL incorporation certificate, listing Wright as the beneficial owner and making other changes to reflect his involvement in 2011.

Wright exchanged emails with Mayaka and several other Abacus employees over the following week in order to finalise the purchase, during which Abacus pointed out a problem: Signia Enterprises Corp, the company Wright had asked to be appointed as an initial director of TTL, was founded nine months after TTL's incorporation date, rendering its position impossible. This, of course, was the Panamanian company supposedly behind High Secured, the alleged custodians of the Tulip Trust's bitcoin stash, although whether the company's directors were aware that their outfit was almost used by Wright in this way is unknown. Wright eventually plumped for Panopticrypt as TTL's director, presumably because of its June 2011 formation date, which is where the backdated ASIC registration certificate for Panopticrypt found on Wright's system can be explained: Dr Edman found that the certificate was created using a modified copy of Coin-Exch's certificate on 23 October 2014, the date of the emails between Wright and Abacus confirming the appointment of Panopticrypt as director. It doesn't take an ATO investigative division to work out why the dates match.

Wright tried his best to hit back at this criticism of his evidence when faced with it during the *Kleiman v Wright* trial, denying that the invoices showed the payments they clearly did and arguing that he couldn't have bought TTL from Abacus because someone else would have had to sign off on the purchase. He also tried to argue that the bank transfer to Abacus was 'not a real bank transfer, because it has a company that doesn't deal with the U.S.' before claiming that his opposition's counsel had put in front of him 'documents I don't recognise' because they came from machines associated, again, with his supposedly malicious ex-staff. When questioned as to why he couldn't produce any emails between himself and Denis Mayaka from 2011, Wright claimed that he no longer had access to the email account in question, with no mention of why he couldn't ask Mayaka or Abacus for their copies.

The issue of the Tulip Trust and TTL reared its head again during the *COPA v Wright* trial, where Wright tried to prove the existence of TTL in 2009, two years before it was registered. Wright also submitted evidence which, on its face, suggested that Abacus had indeed been looking after TTL since 2011, including four invoices from Abacus to Wright's company for various services. However, each invoice contained the same spelling mistake ('Invoive' for 'Invoice') despite them supposedly being created and sent years apart, while Patrick Madden found that one invoice was a doctored version of the 2014 TTL purchase invoice with the text edited to remove the purchase of the company and replace it with ongoing management and accounting services for TTL. Worse, the document this forgery was based on was itself a forgery in the form of an email from Abacus to Wright on 17 October 2014, confirming the purchase of TTL more than three years after Wright said it happened.

Faced with even his own forensics experts in the *COPA v Wright* case finding that everything he had submitted to back up his TTL formation claims was fraudulent in some way, Wright was forced to pivot; he acknowledged for the first time that they were indeed forgeries but claimed that he hadn't created them, alleging once more that the documents had come from compromised company machines where they had been planted ahead of discovery for the *Kleiman v Wright* case. Wright once more turned the blame cannon on Ira Kleiman before shifting it to target former nChain CEO Christen Ager-Hanssen, who had fired Wright in September 2023, a few days before he himself was let go. Wright claimed that Ager-Hanssen had faked the documents and planted them on his computer, but Justice Mellor didn't buy this spurious tale, finding that 'this alleged conspiracy was another lie from Dr Wright in his attempts to deflect responsibility from his own forgeries.' Justice Mellor also found, unsurprisingly, that the key emails were 'not genuine and were sent by Dr Wright to himself'.

Four years earlier, Dr Edman had analysed the Deed of Trust for the *Kleiman v Wright* case and found that someone with access to Wright's computer had created multiple versions of it, which they backdated to 21 July 2011 and left on Wright's machine. One of these was then modified in mid-2015 on the same machine by someone in an Australian timezone. The version supplied to Dr Edman also had fonts with a 2015 copyright notice and timestamped digital signatures from 22 May 2015, meaning it couldn't have been created before this date. When faced with this, Wright doubled down, claiming that this was merely the date on which the document had been last opened, with the software used to read it replacing the old fonts with new ones. Wright maintained his story over the legitimacy of the Deed up until the *Granath v Wright* trial in 2022, when he slammed the car into reverse and outed it as a forgery, calling it 'a number of documents put together', something he was able to verify having supposedly gotten his hands on the originals.

Wright explained that starting in 2020, he had begun to get access to the real trust documents, which had allowed him to compare them to ones from his systems and play a game of spot the difference. Only when he was able to compare them side by side did Wright deduce that the version he sent to the ATO was a fake, a quite stunning revelation for a self-proclaimed document forensics expert. One of the decisive differences, Wright told the *Granath v Wright* judge, was that his signature was missing from the fake, which constituted a red flag for him. Of course, Wright would have been aware of this omission the first time he clapped eyes on the imposter document, yet he only apparently realised that it was missing his signature when he was able to compare it to the real version years later, despite having looked at it multiple times in the intervening years. Quite aside from this, a question that needs to be asked in relation to this matter is why a document setting up a blind trust on behalf of someone who was supposed to know nothing about it would require that person's signature.

Having admitted during the *Granath v Wright* trial that the Deed of Trust he had submitted as evidence was a forgery, Wright's defence was a familiar one: employees with a grudge against him had used their access to his servers to manipulate the Deed of Trust before he could send it over to the ATO. This ploy would have been a risky one, however, as it required Wright to abstain from looking at the document at any time after sending it, lest he spot the fakery (although given that he didn't spot the lack of a signature for years, this might not have been too hard). It was also doomed to failure, given that the ATO would inevitably flag up the errors that it did indeed find, at which point Wright would have known something was wrong with the document. There is no sign, however, that he ever queried the ATO over its findings. Wright also claimed in his June 2019 deposition for the *Kleiman v Wright* case that he had used the Deed of Trust in a battle with the ATO in 2012 over the existence of the Tulip Trust, a statement we know to be false because Wright didn't start supplying the ATO with documents pertaining to the Tulip Trust by name until October 2014.

The most glaring issue over Wright's Deed of Trust story comes when we analyse the source. During the *Kleiman v Wright* case, Wright voiced his concern that the copy of the Deed of Trust analysed for the case came from his systems, which he believed had been compromised. Given that Abacus supposedly drew up the document, Wright's natural response should have been to go straight to Denis Mayaka for a legitimate copy. This, he said in 2019, was exactly what he did:

> So I've been given it by the people at Abacus, and I can only say I received a document from the people at Abacus. Whether they updated it at any point, I don't know.

This claim throws Wright's story entirely on its head and undermines at a stroke any complaints about compromised documents. What's important to note here is that only one version of the Deed of Trust was presented for the *Kleiman v Wright* case, the fraudulent one, which, as of June 2019, apparently had two sources: Wright's compromised servers and Abacus. If there was anyone Wright should have been investigating over his allegations of compromised material, therefore, it should have been Denis Mayaka. Wright has never been challenged on this discrepancy, but he was asked during the *COPA v Wright* trial why the documents he had received since 2020 hadn't been presented as evidence at the trials that had taken place since then. Wright replied that legal restrictions surrounding the trust prevented him from submitting them as evidence, but was not pressed on how hard he had tried to overcome this hurdle, given the importance of the case.

The ATO, having received these and other documents pertaining to the Tulip Trust throughout 2014 and 2015, analysed them and delivered its succinct verdict in its report on Zuhl in April 2016:

We do not accept the existence of the 'Tulip Trust'...due to the anomalies, inconsistencies and gaps in the taxpayer's contentions.

This report was published just as Wright was gearing up for the public exhibition of his Satoshiness via his signing sessions, which we will cover in Volume II, meaning that, at the precise moment the ATO was dismissing the existence of the Tulip Trust, Wright's backers were trying to obtain permission from its trustees to sign early blocks and, later, send coins from addresses supposedly held by the trust. Seeing as Wright had already signed away ownership of his companies by that point, he likely wouldn't have received the ATO letters denouncing the Tulip Trust. Someone in Wright's camp would have seen them, however, and potentially decided that it was not the time to throw that particular hand grenade into the mix.

Four years after the ATO dismissed the Tulip Trust, it was the turn of the magistrate judge in the *Kleiman v Wright* case, Bruce Reinhart, to offer his thoughts. Judge Reinhart accused Wright of 'knowingly producing a fraudulent trust document and giving perjurious testimony' over the matter, echoing the ATO's conclusion that the Tulip Trust was a fiction. Justice Mellor also joined the bandwagon in May 2024 when he found that the Tulip Trust was 'a fabrication designed to shield Dr Wright's assets against possible bankruptcy.'

As we have alluded to, the Tulip Trust has gained a myth of its own in the years since the ATO debunked it in 2016, with Wright changing the narrative over the contents, the timeline, the trustees and more. For these and further reasons, which we will explain later in this series, we can dismiss the existence of the Tulip Trust, at least the one dated by Wright to 2011. There is no concrete evidence to support the notion that Craig Wright, Dave Kleiman or anyone else created a Tulip Trust or did anything with TTL before 2014; the only authentic documentation shows Craig Wright creating it in October of that year, having bought an aged Seychelles company right when the ATO was demanding evidence of his Seychelles trust. Every single piece of evidence surrounding the creation of the Tulip Trust and its contents has been proven by multiple forensic experts to have been created and modified between October 2014 and mid-2015, and to believe the alternative means casting aside logic and this glut of independent expert testimony in favour of an ever-changing story and unproven conspiracy theories.

As we have outlined, Craig Wright has stuck rigidly to his story that the Tulip Trust was created in 2009 and formalised in 2012 ever since he first proffered it in 2014, blaming the usual cast of characters for forging and backdating documents while resolutely failing to provide any untampered evidence from the 2009-2011 period to back up his claim. However, the odds of someone else creating the documents just in time for Wright to send them to the ATO are simply laughable, as is the idea that it took him years to spot the forgeries and that someone else provided the manipulated documents to the ATO behind his back. To believe Wright's story, you also have to believe that he had no idea that someone was infiltrating his systems to plant fake invoices, incorporation documents, emails and more, all of which they sent to the ATO at precisely the right time and then, for some reason, left on his system. Equally, this theory assumes that Wright failed to send the ATO the real evidence once the forgeries were identified. All of this played into Justice Mellor's finding that Wright's Tulip Trust story was 'very confused and contradictory and parts were incredible', commenting on the Deed of Trust in particular:

> *Dr Wright's evidence about this document, and the Tulip Trust more generally, has been confused and internally inconsistent. In particular, he has invented the excuse of having been precluded from seeing the document to explain away his having sworn to its authenticity in the Kleiman proceedings and made a sworn declaration based on its terms, but then having denied its authenticity in the Granath proceedings.*

The three court cases that have involved examination of the Tulip Trust have shown that there is not one unvarnished document or email that supports Wright's story about the existence of the Tulip Trust, and there are dozens that defy it. This leaves its existence in league with the likes of the Loch Ness Monster and Bigfoot, only perhaps less feasible.

As stated at the outset, this chapter has only covered the genesis of the Tulip Trust and Wright's first attempt to utilise it. The *Kleiman v Wright* case saw the trust take on a life of its own, with Bitcoin address algorithms, encrypted files, key slices, destroyed hard drives, bonded couriers, spinoff Tulip Trusts and a plethora of other factors being introduced on an almost monthly basis as Wright tried to dodge a contempt of court conviction over his claims of its existence. These stories are for another time, but it's important at this juncture to know what Wright was telling the ATO with regard to the Tulip Trust: that it was holding over a million bitcoins on which Wright could call for use in his companies, plus Bitcoin-related IP and software. It's also worth noting what Wright told Justice Mellor during the *COPA v Wright* trial: he felt comfortable putting all the IP out of reach because it was all in his head, and, were he ever to be bankrupted, he could regurgitate it and start working on it again. Wright made this outlandish claim during a trial in which he frequently forgot important names, incidents and communications, suggesting that he wouldn't have gotten far in this endeavour.

With the genesis and purpose of the Tulip Trust understood, we'll now examine how Craig Wright used it to peddle what ATO reports suggest were some of his most illuminating and egregious attempts to defraud the Australian government between 2011 and 2015.

Chapter 11 – The Professor Rees Affair

The same day that Craig Wright falsely says he incorporated TTL, 21 July 2011, he was legitimately incorporating Strasan, which became C01N Pty Ltd (C01N Pty) in 2014 (Strasan is sometimes misspelt as 'Strassen' because it is named after the algorithm of the same name). Wright said in 2019 that he started Strasan 'with other people who were friends at the time' but then complained that 'the other people in the company wanted something different than I wanted'. One of these was Shoaib Yousuf, who must have patched up any differences with Wright between this fallout in 2011 and the *Granath v Wright* trial in 2022, given that Yousuf was called as a witness for Wright, a role he undertook again for the *COPA v Wright* trial two years later. Aside from Yousuf, the shareholders were Panopticrypt (owned by Wright and Ramona Watts) and two companies: EA Professionals Pty Ltd and Deuba Pty Ltd. EA Professionals would fold less than a year after its first involvement in Strasan, while Deuba was sold to nChain in June 2015 as part of Wright's bailout deal.

Strasan, according to court and ATO transcripts, recruited one Professor David Rees as a contractor, a simple statement that belies the complex manner of the alleged relationship between the professor and Craig Wright, a relationship that is, at times, hard to comprehend on both a human and technical level. Wright's story over Professor Rees's level of involvement in his life and work changed so much during the course of the ATO's investigation into Strasan that it's hard to wrap one's head around the various shifts in the narrative regarding the work supposedly done, the agreements put in place, the method of payment and more, but we will endeavour to do it justice. The Professor Rees affair is one of a number of tales Craig Wright spun the ATO in order to try and obtain tax deductions or multi-million-dollar rebates, but the reason why we have chosen to go into detail with this story is because it offers a great example of three things that provide a fuller understanding of Craig Wright's methods: the lengths he was willing to go to in order to achieve his goals, the bodies he was prepared to step over on the way and the slipshod manner in which he went about it.

Professor Rees was a renowned mathematician who, Wright says, was one of the influences behind Bitcoin, going as far as stating in an August 2018 WeChat message that 'Satoshi was me, Dave Klieman [sic] and Prof David Rees'. Wright expanded on this in a 2019 blog post (in which he perpetually spelt Professor Rees's name as 'Reese') that the mathematician 'gave me some pointers' towards the calculations involved in Bitcoin's design. This was because Professor Rees allegedly worked with Wright's grandfather, Ronald Lynam, doing codebreaking work during World War II. This mention of World War II should ring alarm bells over Professor Rees's supposed involvement in Bitcoin, and with good reason: in 2009, when Bitcoin was launched, he was ninety years old and was, in the words of his family, 'mentally confused', 'very frail' and suspected by doctors of suffering from senile dementia. Clearly, there was no way that Professor Rees could have had any direct input into Bitcoin at this stage of his life, and, as we shall see, his family denied that Professor Rees had any kind of relationship with Craig Wright whatsoever.

We'll start with the work that Wright says Professor Rees did for him in 2011-12, for which Rees allegedly charged a staggering $2.25 million. This was remarkable for a number of reasons, not least because at the time he was supposedly doing this work, Professor Rees was ninety-five years old and had moved into a nursing home. Wright asked for Professor Rees's payment to be deducted from his 2012-13 tax bill, saying that the nonagenarian had been contracted to create an e-learning 'pathway outline' for Strasan, which inclued providing a 'statistical algorithmic library, a project plan and a budget.' Strasan then sold this to another of Wright's companies, Hotwire Pre-Emptive Intelligence Pty Ltd (Hotwire), which made its own claim for a tax rebate on the purchase. In February 2015, Wright told the ATO that Professor Rees had provided source code, small algorithms and other notes and had answered a number of questions for Wright, particularly around algebra and the Otway-Rees protocol. This work supposedly demanded the astronomical sum Wright paid Professor Rees, despite the ATO noting that the Otway-Rees protocol was developed by a different Professor Rees than the man in question.

A month later, Wright told the ATO that he had acquired some software and a library of unpublished papers from Professor Rees, suggesting that some may have come from his daughter, Sarah, herself a professor, adding that her father had been paid for consulting services. Wright also revised the timeframe in which he had worked with the professor, claiming that they had been introduced in 1996 and that Wright had received the assistance and advice between 2003 and 2011. However, as late as 26 October 2012, Wright allegedly told Dave Kleiman in an email, 'David [Rees] is becoming a little vague, but the guy is in his 90's,' suggesting a continuing working relationship at this time. Wright's shifting timeline led the ATO to point out that Professor Rees had now supposedly carried out work for Strasan up to twelve years before the company existed, leading its agents to dig further into the story. In April 2015, they paid a visit to Strasan to see for themselves what Professor Rees had provided in return for his bumper payout. Wright was given a week's notice of the visit and was told that he would be required to provide the library of unpublished work that he had allegedly paid Professor Rees for, but when the two ATO agents got there, Wright claimed he had left it at home. Wright later said that he would not provide the documents to the ATO but that an 'agreed expert' could review them if the authority was amenable. It wasn't.

Wright was also asked to run the software he claimed that Rees had written for him, but again, he refused, claiming that it consisted of mathematical calculations that had already been solved, so there was nothing to demonstrate. This was important because Sarah had claimed that her father didn't write software, so the idea that he decided to branch out at the tender age of ninety five when he had dementia and no access to a computer was somewhat startlin The ATO also noted that the software Wright claimed that Professor R provided was similar to software publicly available online, with Wright argu that what was valuable to him was the software's 'variables and configurat They can't have been that valuable, however, because Strasan director S Yousuf stated during the *COPA v Wright* trial that he had never he Professor Rees or his work.

It wasn't long after this visit that the ATO learnt about Professo condition, after which Wright changed his story again; in November claimed that Professor Rees had been assisting him between 1999 and that by 2005, the pair barely spoke. He added that in 2010, they alleg that Professor Rees should get paid for his years of assistance, with Wright, for some reason, delaying this payment until mid-2013. This neatly addressed the issue that Professor Rees's family had raised over his mental health after 2011, although it thoroughly undermined Wright's initial claims over the e-learning work Professor Rees had done for Strasan, which was what he had claimed the deduction for in the first place.

It wasn't just the work that Professor Rees did (or didn't do) for Strasan that troubled the ATO: the payment story had taken on a life of its own, too. In fact, Craig Wright's changing story over this element of the tale gives us a great insight into the murky, convoluted waters into which Wright was to sink over the coming years. Strasan initially recorded a payment of $2.25 million to Professor Rees in the form of 19,470.12 bitcoins sent on 30 June 2013, with Professor Rees's family telling the ATO that both the amount and the form of the payment were so unlikely as to be borderline impossible. Blockchain records show that the receiving address already contained 29,569.57 bitcoins two days before the transfer was allegedly conducted and that there was, in fact, no transfer made on 30 June. The next activity in the receiving address came on 13 August when the 29,569.57 bitcoins were sent from it to another address, starting 1LXc, where ey were joined by an additional 4,943 bitcoins from an address starting 1M7c.

led the ATO to believe that Strasan had set aside a total of 34,512.57 ns for Professor Rees, getting on for double the amount agreed.

n challenged on this, Wright said that the coins were still under his 'though he seemingly forgot this attestation a year later when he ave used the same coins to pay for unrelated software purportedly ember 2013. This, of course, meant that the coins couldn't have ol the following month to pay Professor Rees, which, the ATO tended, 'casts further doubt on the taxpayer's assertion that s.' Wright didn't give up, however, claiming in May 2015 011, he had told Professor Rees that he would give him ins in recognition of his contributions, with the as an interim payment. This would have been a fine dn't found issues with the only invoice associated , which didn't reference an interim payment, was n Strasan's, with Wright claiming that this was o adapt to a new accounting system. At the

A month later, Wright told the ATO that he had acquired some software and a library of unpublished papers from Professor Rees, suggesting that some may have come from his daughter, Sarah, herself a professor, adding that her father had been paid for consulting services. Wright also revised the timeframe in which he had worked with the professor, claiming that they had been introduced in 1996 and that Wright had received the assistance and advice between 2003 and 2011. However, as late as 26 October 2012, Wright allegedly told Dave Kleiman in an email, 'David [Rees] is becoming a little vague, but the guy is in his 90's,' suggesting a continuing working relationship at this time. Wright's shifting timeline led the ATO to point out that Professor Rees had now supposedly carried out work for Strasan up to twelve years before the company existed, leading its agents to dig further into the story. In April 2015, they paid a visit to Strasan to see for themselves what Professor Rees had provided in return for his bumper payout. Wright was given a week's notice of the visit and was told that he would be required to provide the library of unpublished work that he had allegedly paid Professor Rees for, but when the two ATO agents got there, Wright claimed he had left it at home. Wright later said that he would not provide the documents to the ATO but that an 'agreed expert' could review them if the authority was amenable. It wasn't.

Wright was also asked to run the software he claimed that Rees had written for him, but again, he refused, claiming that it consisted of mathematical calculations that had already been solved, so there was nothing to demonstrate. This was important because Sarah had claimed that her father didn't write software, so the idea that he decided to branch out at the tender age of ninety-five when he had dementia and no access to a computer was somewhat startling. The ATO also noted that the software Wright claimed that Professor Rees provided was similar to software publicly available online, with Wright arguing that what was valuable to him was the software's 'variables and configuration'. They can't have been that valuable, however, because Strasan director Shoaib Yousuf stated during the *COPA v Wright* trial that he had never heard of Professor Rees or his work.

It wasn't long after this visit that the ATO learnt about Professor Rees's condition, after which Wright changed his story again; in November 2015, he claimed that Professor Rees had been assisting him between 1999 and 2008 and that by 2005, the pair barely spoke. He added that in 2010, they allegedly agreed that Professor Rees should get paid for his years of assistance, with Wright, for some reason, delaying this payment until mid-2013. This neatly addressed the issue that Professor Rees's family had raised over his mental health after 2011, although it thoroughly undermined Wright's initial claims over the e-learning work Professor Rees had done for Strasan, which was what he had claimed the deduction for in the first place.

It wasn't just the work that Professor Rees did (or didn't do) for Strasan that troubled the ATO: the payment story had taken on a life of its own, too. In fact, Craig Wright's changing story over this element of the tale gives us a great insight into the murky, convoluted waters into which Wright was to sink over the coming years. Strasan initially recorded a payment of $2.25 million to Professor Rees in the form of 19,470.12 bitcoins sent on 30 June 2013, with Professor Rees's family telling the ATO that both the amount and the form of the payment were so unlikely as to be borderline impossible. Blockchain records show that the receiving address already contained 29,569.57 bitcoins two days before the transfer was allegedly conducted and that there was, in fact, no transfer made on 30 June. The next activity in the receiving address came on 13 August when the 29,569.57 bitcoins were sent from it to another address, starting 1LXc, where they were joined by an additional 4,943 bitcoins from an address starting 1M7c. This led the ATO to believe that Strasan had set aside a total of 34,512.57 bitcoins for Professor Rees, getting on for double the amount agreed.

When challenged on this, Wright said that the coins were still under his control, although he seemingly forgot this attestation a year later when he claimed to have used the same coins to pay for unrelated software purportedly bought in September 2013. This, of course, meant that the coins couldn't have been in his control the following month to pay Professor Rees, which, the ATO understandably contended, 'casts further doubt on the taxpayer's assertion that it paid Professor Rees.' Wright didn't give up, however, claiming in May 2015 that at some point in 2011, he had told Professor Rees that he would give him exactly 34,512.57 bitcoins in recognition of his contributions, with the 19,470.12 bitcoins offered as an interim payment. This would have been a fine get-out clause if the ATO hadn't found issues with the only invoice associated with Professor Rees: the invoice, which didn't reference an interim payment, was on Hotwire's accounts rather than Strasan's, with Wright claiming that this was down to his companies struggling to adapt to a new accounting system. At the same time, Wright argued that the bitcoin payment had been made to Professor Rees in June 2013, when Hotwire had been founded.

There was a very good reason why an invoice related to Professor Rees had been found on the Hotwire system: it had supposedly purchased the Professor Rees material from Strasan and was claiming its own deduction on it. In October 2013, Hotwire advised the ATO that it had sent bitcoins to Strasan as payment for the Professor Rees material on 18 June 2013 using a Bitcoin address starting 1MyG, an address Wright had told the ATO was at that time the property of the Seychelles trust. One may think that by 'Seychelles Trust', Wright meant the Tulip Trust, but he was instead referring to WII, despite the fact that it should by this time have been subsumed into the Tulip Trust. This is another sign that the Tulip Trust wasn't conceived, or TTL and WII purchased, until 2014, following those meetings between Wright's accountants and the ATO. One of these meetings took place on 18 February 2014, marking the first known mention of a Seychelles trust to the ATO.

On that same day, Hotwire changed its story over its Professor Rees dealings, producing a Deed of Assignment, which purported to show that it had transferred the private keys to eleven Bitcoin addresses over to Strasan on 30 June 2013, the date that Strasan said it had paid Professor Rees. Four days later, it updated the Deed of Assignment to scrub all mention of these eleven addresses and instead claimed that it wasn't Bitcoin addresses that had been transferred at all, but equitable interests in Bitcoin. Why the change? This may have something to do with the fact that the ATO had found several issues with the original version: one of the addresses in the list had been repeated no less than three times, while another contained no bitcoins whatsoever at the time of the purported transfer. In addition, the original 1MyG address was not even mentioned. The ATO also noted that the cumulative value of the bitcoins supposedly used to pay Professor Rees was $2.7 million, around $450,000 higher than the sum stated. This prompted Wright to switch to the equitable interests gambit, but in his rush to do so, he made more mistakes: the Deed of Assignment had an incorrect Australian business number for Strasan and stated that Strasan was getting the 'entire right, title and interest in and to' the bitcoins rather than an equitable interest in them. It was also signed by Uyen Nguyen as director of Strasan, despite her not holding that position. Wright later contended that Nguyen signed in her capacity as CEO, but no evidence supporting this appointment was ever provided.

This episode over the payments leads us to ask a very pertinent question: where was Wright finding these Bitcoin addresses? The answer could be absurdly simple and, for Wright, absurdly dangerous, with his probable method best described by Kim Nilsson, the man who helped untangle the MtGox mess following its collapse:

> ...it's some guy browsing a 'blockchain rich list', picking out a couple of addresses at random and saying 'I own those' for whatever reasons, while offering no evidence except for some clumsy document backdating. These claims would never have gotten past an actual specialist.

It really would be that simple: Wright could browse the public blockchain for Bitcoin addresses that suited his needs and pretend they were his, knowing that the ATO would have no way of disproving him. This, however, conveys as much ownership as standing next to a Ferrari in a car park and claiming it is yours. In these early years, of course, the ATO didn't know this, and Wright was happy to show its agents how to verify his holdings with the blockchain equivalent of the Ferrari-car park trick by sending them hyperlinks to block explorers with the public addresses already plugged in.

Hotwire's 2012-13 tax return saw it try and claim an offset against the $2.96 million it said it had paid Strasan for the Professor Rees material, but the ATO was still nowhere close to approving it. The agency tried to iron out Wright's changing story in a February 2015 phone call where it asked him to clarify, among other things, where the bitcoins to pay Professor Rees had initially come from. During the call, Wright suddenly remembered that the funds hadn't come from WII at all but had instead come from the Tulip Trust (created just three months earlier), with Dave Kleiman ringfencing the bitcoins for him. Wright also had the audacity to claim that he assumed the coins were still sitting in trust for Professor Rees, with the executor of his estate unaware of their existence. If this were true, it is staggering that Wright didn't once think to tell the family of their huge windfall. As we know, however, Wright has form for this.

In the same February 2015 phone call, Wright changed his story yet again over not just the source of the funds to pay Professor Rees but the payment method, too. Rather than paying the professor in actual bitcoins on 30 June

2013, Wright said, Strasan had instead paid him on 28 June by giving him the private keys to seven Bitcoin addresses containing 19,470.12 bitcoins, made up of the eleven previously cited addresses revised down to remove the problematic ones. The ATO, however, noted that Wright's new story undermined his previous comments that the bitcoins were held in trust for Professor Rees, an accusation Wright denied, saying that the bitcoins would have been held in trust until the keys were released. The ATO also pointed out the frankly ludicrous suggestion that not only was the dementia-ridden professor happy to get paid in bitcoins, but he knew perfectly well what to do with private keys to Bitcoin wallets, how to extract the coins, how to protect the keys and potentially how to sell them too. Wright's story also suggested that the ninety-five-year-old dementia sufferer, who was just weeks away from death, did the deal behind his family's back, despite Sarah having looked after her father's financial affairs since 2011. Someone would also have had to prepare and send an invoice for $2.25 million without anyone other than Professor Rees knowing. No such invoice was ever shown by Hotwire or Strasan to have been received; it just appeared in their accounts.

In its March 2016 assessment of Strasan's claim, the ATO was clear on its view of Wright's involvement with Professor Rees:

> ...the taxpayer provided documents including an invoice and contract, in addition to the same documents relating to the Professor Rees deduction. We consider this to be the provision of documents that are false or misleading. On this basis we consider that the taxpayer took steps to prevent or obstruct the Commissioner from finding out about the false or misleading statement with respect to the purported Hotwire income.

The fact that Wright filed a false invoice on behalf of someone he was supposed to revere is bad enough, but the invoice itself contained something worse: a note saying, 'For memory of Ron Lynam'. This shows a disgusting abuse of the relationship between Wright's grandfather – for whom he had tremendous respect – and a fellow World War II veteran. Wright argued during the *Kleiman v Wright* trial that the document that made up the ATO's accusations was the 'equivalent of a charge sheet' and that 'the companies were closed down with both auditors finding no fraud.' Crucially, we have no documentary evidence to support or rebuke this claim, but the fact remains that the ATO still found enough evidence to accuse Wright of such crimes across multiple companies.

Wright had tried to support the sale of the Professor Rees material with BitMessages and emails purportedly between himself and Dave Kleiman discussing the importance of the software and the Bitcoin payments. The ATO noted in its exhaustive report on Strasan's activities that some emails had been tampered with after receipt to insert comments favourable to Wright, while others had never been sent but were presented as if they had been. They also noted that blog posts supporting Wright's arguments appeared to have been manipulated post-publication to include the pertinent information, noting that similar treatment had been meted out to the BitMessages, too. Wright argued that this wasn't true but never backed up his claim with evidence, such as the originals.

Needless to say, Strasan's $2.26 million deduction claim for the Professor Rees material was denied, with the ATO ruling that Wright had provided no evidence of any communication with Professor Rees, whose ill health 'indicates he was incapable of communicating during the later stages of his life.' It also criticised Wright's 'conflicting and inconsistent contentions' regarding the payment to Professor Rees, while the testimony from the late professor's family indicated that there was 'no relationship' between Professor Rees and Strasan. The ATO's summary of Wright's actions pulled no punches:

> *Taken together, these facts indicate that the taxpayer's claim was based on a transaction that did not take place. Given Dr Wright contends to have communicated with Professor Rees about their agreement, received the material from Professor Rees and instructed that payment be made to Professor Rees, we conclude that Dr Wright knew that the amount had not been incurred by the taxpayer and that the taxpayer dishonestly included the amount as a deduction. We infer that a number of documents have been dishonestly created and submitted to the ATO in an attempt to substantiate the taxpayer's claim.*

Wright discussed his behaviour surrounding Professor Rees in an April 2019 blog post, completely missing the point in the process:

> *I told the Australian tax office about David Rees in 2009. I was discussing some of his role as I moved assets into other companies again in 2013.*

This entirely insubstantial summary of course misses out several crucial elements of the story. During the *COPA v Wright* trial, Wright denied the ATO's allegations afresh:

> *They were told that he was transferred bitcoin at a particular time and they were initially told one year before this. They then chose to do the audit after he died on his stuff saying that he couldn't prove anything.*

If this had happened, it would have been done informally, with the first official notification coming in Strasan's 2012/13 filing, which would have been filed right around Professor Rees's death, if not after. Wright claimed in the same blog post, 'The problem is, I don't know who will die in advance of their death.' The ATO would no doubt argue that it wasn't to know who had invoiced Wright in advance of his tax returns. Wright also claimed in the blog post that the Professor Rees issue was another example of his perceived persecution by the tax office:

> *We are all mortal, and if you need something verified, do it when the person is alive. Then, the Australian government never really sought to prove anything. They just wanted me gone.*

A different 2019 blog post, written as the *Kleiman v Wright* case was just finding its feet, saw Wright trying to blame the kinds of issues the ATO would discover with virtually all his company and personal tax affairs between 2008 and 2015 on simple misunderstandings:

> *When there are errors in files, it isn't because of some malicious construction, but rather errors happen in files and filing... The funny thing is, we have documents that are being compiled wrong and it is easy to determine as being an error, yet the truth of the matter is that people do not want to look and see the discrepancies that are clear but seek to find something to discredit me in error as doing so is what protects their false idea of what Bitcoin is about.*

As we have seen with the Professor Rees affair, and as we will see as we look at further such contrived examples, this explanation is about as watertight as a submarine made from Victoria sponge.

Chapter 12 – Welcome to Bitcoin

Having taken a slight chronological detour to discuss the Tulip Trust and the Professor Rees affairs, we will return to August 2011, a crucial period where we see Craig Wright talk publicly about Bitcoin for the first time. This inaugural comment came through the news and opinion website The Conversation, which Wright joined as a contributor that month, offering opinions on current affairs from a tech and computing perspective. On 29 July 2011, Wright wrote an article entitled 'Are Anonymous and LulzSec about to hack PayPal for WikiLeaks?' in response to that December 2010 episode when the payment processor locked WikiLeaks's account. In the comments section a few days later, Wright briefly touched on PayPal's lack of Bitcoin adoption:

Basically, I know of over 50 alternatives to PayPal. Some are close to PayPal in size and we also have to remember that WikiLeaks was the site that selected PayPal and not one of the alternatives. WL could have selected BitCoin, but it did not.

Wright discussed the WikiLeaks issue in response to a comment on another piece for The Conversation a week later:

WikiLeaks can get payments from other sources. It CAN get money transfers. It can get bit coins it can do many things if it wants. There are MANY options that allow people to send money to WL.

Here, we see Wright discussing his future archnemesis, but notably absent is the lip-frothing bellicosity that would accompany references to WikiLeaks and its founder, Julian Assange, in later years. In fact, Wright barely mentioned WikiLeaks and never mentioned Assange in the rather heated thread that developed in the wake of this post, straying onto other subjects such as capitalism and the rudeness associated with writing in all caps. One respondent wasn't too keen on Wright's conduct and offered a rather pointed insight into his character:

> *I come here for the high standard of respectful and intellectual exchange and, while I don't always agree with what I read, I (and, in my experience, the other authors and readers of this site) try to maintain a level of respect and dignity in disagreement. You might think you're right and everyone else is wrong, but here's a newsflash: *everyone* thinks they're right. Thinking you're right isn't a license to be rude.*

Wright's failure to criticise WikiLeaks in his discussions on The Conversation, despite being given an adequate pedestal from which to air his views, is another indication that he only thought of blaming the organisation and its founder years later when it suited him. If Wright had had negative feelings about WikiLeaks at this point, he would have grasped the opportunity to berate and belittle Assange, and the fact that he didn't speaks volumes. In addition to passing up this opportunity, Wright actively advocated for WikiLeaks using Bitcoin, taking the opposite stance that Satoshi had taken months earlier. When faced with this during the *COPA v Wright* trial, Wright claimed that his concerns rested on WikiLeaks being Bitcoin's first use case, saying that he didn't want it to be a 'WikiLeaks thing'.

Elsewhere in the comments section underneath Wright's pieces, we see him showing a very limited understanding of Bitcoin:

> *Bit Coin (Bit Coin) is a digital currency. Bit Coin offers a full peer-to-peer currency solution. P2P transfer of funds is available using methods that can even be untraceable. [There are ways of] using this technology to transfer funds that cannot be intercepted or stopped.*

As those with even the rudest understanding of Bitcoin will know, and as Wright made abundantly clear in his post-2018 Satoshi crusade, Bitcoin is not untraceable but instead, as the whitepaper states, contains an acceptable level of privacy through pseudonymity rather than complete anonymity.

We should also note Wright's spelling of 'Bitcoin' in these 2011 posts. Satoshi wrote the word 'Bitcoin' hundreds of times across messageboards, forums, and emails, and in virtually every instance, he spelt it 'Bitcoin' or 'bitcoin'. On one occasion, in January 2009, he wrote 'BitCoin' in a text file, only to later correct himself and change it back to 'Bitcoin'. Wright, in contrast, spelt it 'BitCoin', 'bit coin' and, curiously, 'Bit Coin (Bit Coin)' in his responses to comments on his 2011 pieces. Wright addressed these discrepancies in court in 2022, claiming that Satoshi Nakamoto used 'all different types of capitalisation and more than once' without offering examples, and added that some discrepancies were down to his speech-to-text software not knowing how to spell 'Bitcoin' properly. He then absolved himself of all responsibility by dropping in the old chestnut that he didn't manage his online accounts 'even back then'. This raises the suggestion that Wright was either paying someone to pretend to be him in the comments section, which is bizarre, or he *wasn't* paying them, which is worse. Fortunately for the slave trade, however, we can kill this suggestion off by noting that Wright admitted to having written the comments during the *COPA v Wright* trial two years later.

Unlike his emails and blog posts, Wright hasn't been able to expunge or otherwise amend these discussions, and it is telling that he displays a very limited knowledge of Bitcoin and espoused views that oppose Satoshi's. Wright claimed during the *COPA v Wright* trial that these comments on The Conversation weren't his only public discussions of Bitcoin at the time, but he fell short when asked to prove this:

> COUNSEL: You say you have earlier public writings related to Bitcoin?
>
> WRIGHT: Yes. Are they all available anymore after fifteen years? No.

In his ruling, Justice Mellor agreed that Satoshi 'would not have used two words or capitalised the C' and added that there was 'no reason to believe that Satoshi would have reversed his original view' on the WikiLeaks affair just months after airing it, ending with an illuminating conclusion:

> ...these posts show that Dr Wright had no significant familiarity with Bitcoin in July 2011, and that it is reasonable to suppose that all his familiarity was gained subsequently by careful study of the materials which had been made public.

Wright had an amusing discussion with another respondent to his pieces on The Conversation, which ended with him petulantly listing the fourteen books he had supposedly written as an author or co-author. Of the six books Wright provided the links to, five listed him as one of up to seven contributors, meaning that 'co-author' was something of a stretch, while the only one in the list that was solely under his name, *IT Regulatory and Standards Compliance Handbook*, was hardly a hit: one reviewer labelled the writing 'Absolutely incoherent' and the editing 'SO BAD that it makes it impossible to read more than a paragraph'. Similarly, another reviewer said that the book was 'not very well written or edited' and called the writing 'disjointed', noting that it was riddled with spelling and grammatical errors. Plus ça change.

Worse was to come for Wright in 2012 regarding this book, however, when he was publicly accused of plagiarising huge parts of it. The accusations came via an organisation called Attrition, a 'computer security website dedicated to the collection, dissemination and distribution of information about the security industry for anyone interested in the subject.' The members of Attrition were very interested in a certain aspect of Wright's book, discovering a pattern that Wright would repeat over the years:

> *While the quantity of stolen text does not comprise a majority of the book, there is enough to demonstrate systematic plagiarism, typically in the frequent bulleted lists throughout the book. The more interesting (and confusing) thing is that the author properly cites some sources, but not others. In fact, the level or lack of citation could lead one to think that three people contributed to the material.*

In dissecting the plagiarised material, the reviewers noted that 'the author(s) went through considerable effort to generate original content, but got lazy when providing supporting lists', noting several cases where 'attempts were made to obscure the plagiarised content'. This, they said, 'shows willful infringement of copyright and inexcusable plagiarism.' Another giveaway was an instance where Wright had changed domain names from the source text but forgot to change the code, which still matched an old domain.

In their totality, the accusations were so plentiful that Wright needed three blog posts to tackle them all, but he still managed to be 'surprised' by how much plagiarism Attrition had detected. He claimed, ironically, that he was 'strongly opposed to the unauthorized and unattributed use of other's works' before going into great detail to cite the pressure of deadlines, the merging of chapters but not footnotes, working with groups of people, his plagiarism software and plagiarism of his own work among the litany of reasons as to why so much of the book contained copied or unattributed content. Wright said that he 'trusted too much in technology' and that he was 'not too happy...right now' with the tools he had used, although he acknowledged that he 'screwed up' and was 'humbled by my stupid error'. He even tried to claim that the author whose work he had stolen had given him permission to use it, but this is unlikely given that the author in question, Robert Auger, said on Twitter in 2020 that he hadn't heard of Wright until he 'found my content in his book'. In the interests of balance, we must note that a more recent reviewer believed the book to be of 'excellent quality'.

Wright claims an interesting coda to these posts on The Conversation. In a 2019 blog post, he said that the few pieces he wrote about the hacking groups Anonymous and LulzSec led him to receive unwanted attention:

In 2011 I wrote extensively about numerous hacker groups including anonymous and Lulz. Unfortunately, amongst other things this made me a target. My companies were broken into, my personal email and much more was accessed by hackers. I had accounts created using my information and I had people targeting my family.

Wright never mentioned such hacks to the police or even the ATO, an excuse he most certainly would have used to help cover up any indiscretions with his supporting evidence, as he has in the years since. He also never mentioned anything like it to Andrew O'Hagan, at least not that O'Hagan reported, despite the pair discussing Wright's career as a hacker in some detail during their months together. Similarly, Wright gave no details of these hacks to Mark Eglinton for *Hero/Villain*. In fact, the alleged attention of these world-famous hacking groups garners little more than a side note in this lone blog post, with Wright never offering up anything more in the form of evidence or corroborating reports. It's also highly unlikely that Wright's fairly tame discussions about their merits riled these feared hacking gangs enough for them to take retaliatory action against him, not least because they had bigger fish to fry: in early-mid 2011, Anonymous was spreading its time and talents between the likes of Sony, Bank of America, the Spanish police force, Facebook and the Arab Spring movement, while LulzSec, which only operated between May and June 2011, targeted the likes of Fox News, PBS, Nintendo and multiple U.S. authorities including the CIA. It is, therefore, highly improbable that Anonymous or LulzSec had the time or inclination to divert its resources away from these high-profile targets and onto Craig Wright after his handful of articles for The Conversation.

While it would be churlish to criticise Wright if he genuinely had been hacked by LulzSec or Anonymous, which theoretically could happen to any of us, it's worth looking at the reason *why* he apparently fell victim: he was playing cyber-Batman:

> *Importantly, if I had [publicised their activities] any other way, I wouldn't have managed to patent and protect my inventions and this would have allowed those who seek crime in the lower aspects of society's sewers to come forth and take over.*

This baffling connection between hackers and Wright's patents is given no further explanation, for which we should probably be thankful.

While protecting the good people of Lisarow from sewer-dwelling criminals and making himself a target for the world's most feared hacking groups as a reward, Wright was also busy working on Panopticrypt and Strasan during the second half of 2011. On 10 September, months after he had been allegedly booted out of Bitcoin, Wright emailed Dave Kleiman about his legacy:

> *It is recorded. I cannot do the Satoshi bit any more. They no longer listen. I am better as a myth. Back to my lectures and rants that everyone ignores as me. I hate this Dave, my pseudonym is more popular than I can ever hope to be.*

This email, taken from Wright's system, was analysed as part of the *COPA v Wright* case, where it was found to have been created on 1 March 2014, a year after its recipient had died. Even without this analysis, it is curious that Wright should send this message having already 'left' Bitcoin months before, which Kleiman would have known all too well, having supposedly helped him do so. The motive behind this forged email and the manner in which it was attempted are both so clumsy that they land with a 'clunk' that could be heard from space. Indeed, in its summary of the email, COPA claimed, 'The effect of the tampering is to make the document appear to be supportive of Dr Wright's claim to be Satoshi Nakamoto (i.e. as an email to an associate indicating that Dr Wright had been using the Satoshi persona, supposedly well before Dr Wright made a public claim to be Satoshi), contrary to fact.' This email, one of the few that Wright forwarded to Andrew O'Hagan for 'The Satoshi Affair', backs up the oft-aired allegation that, rather than being a genius inventor, Wright is nothing more than a sloppy forger looking to capitalise on the work of others for his own gain.

Other than using it to defend himself from plagiarism over his IT handbook, Wright's blog was comparatively quiet in 2012, with only 105 posts throughout the year, almost half that of the previous year. This could be because he was tied up in ATO matters, as he referenced in a possibly genuine email to Dave Kleiman in May of that year when he accused the agency of trying to 'get a result through attrition rather than honesty', adding that the agency would 'drain all I have if they can'. He then made his opinions on the ATO as clear as the night sky in the Antarctic:

> *FUCKING DICKS. Bloody lying ATO cock sucking bastards! They lost evidence and use my temper against me. I hate their lies. I did everything right and I am STILL punished.*

This email has not been forensically analysed, so we cannot say for sure that it is fabricated, but the allegation that the ATO lost Wright's evidence (which he has never backed up with proof) and still saw fit to accuse him of fraud plays neatly into his claim of being victimised. With regard to Wright's statement that he had done 'everything right' over his ATO investigations, as we have seen and as we will continue to see, his version of doing everything right is very different to other people's.

2012 appears to have been a quiet year for Wright all round, apart from earning some more degrees in computer science, taking him up to fifteen by the end of June, but his activity began to pick up towards the end of the year, not least when he and Ramona Watts moved into a rented house in Gordon, a suburb of Sydney. The house's owner told *Guardian Australia* that this move took place in November, but Wright says that the move happened no later than October. The couple could scarcely have believed that the building would be besieged by news crews and combed through by ATO officers and police some three years later. A neighbour referred to Wright as 'Cold-shoulder Craig', while Andrew O'Hagan said that Wright had 'what appeared to be a whole room full of generators' at the rear of the property. These generators fed a rack of computers that Wright called his 'toys', which were presumably a reincarnation of his server rooms from 2008 for use by his companies. Wright's pride and joy, however, which he told O'Hagan was 'nearly nine thousand miles away in

Panama', was one of his supercomputers. This particular supercomputer, whose existence Wright used to try and claim millions in R&D tax rebates, mysteriously went missing at the conclusion of the ATO's investigation, with Wright claiming during the *Kleiman v Wright* trial that he had no idea what happened to it, despite it supposedly having cost him tens of millions of dollars.

Shortly after moving into his new pad, Wright convened a meeting with some associates regarding his plans to reinvent Bitcoin. The meeting, which Wright called an 'eye-opener', was attended by 'people that I had known in late 2012', including Steven McLaughlin, who Wright knew from his time at Charles Sturt University; Jamie Wilson, an accountant and cybersecurity developer; Robert Urquhart, a forensic analyst; Wright's lawyers; and Dave Kleiman, who would still have been forced to attend this meeting from his hospital bed at the tail end of his marathon 850-day stay. Wright says he told the gang he was forming a group of companies using the IP bound up in his existing companies to create what he hoped would become 'a global financial conglomerate'. The head of this multi-company snake would be the previously mentioned Hotwire, a name the ATO would become all too familiar with in the years ahead.

Despite supposedly believing that his new company would take Bitcoin where he always intended it to go, as 2012 made way for 2013, Wright still had no designs on slipping into the Satoshi Nakamoto costume. The reason for this was very simple: none of his tax rebate claims up to then had mentioned Bitcoin. Lynn Wright confirmed as much during her deposition for the *Kleiman v Wright* case when she said that the ATO issues at this time were concerned with 'the farm stuff', adding that they were 'all to do with the – the [business development] grant and transfer – the transfer of businesses' and had 'nothing to do with Bitcoin'. This was all about to change, however.

On 2 April 2013, two weeks after his victory over the ATO concerning his 2008/09 tax filing, Wright purportedly discussed the imminent formation of Coin-Exch with Dave Kleiman over email, with Kleiman accepting a directorship of the nascent company. However, in a sign of things to come, this email was later revealed to have been a forgery based on a different email from Kleiman to Wright, created around 23 October 2014. Wright told the ATO that the startup money had come from Craig Wright R&D, about which he was quizzed during an April 2019 deposition for the *Kleiman v Wright* case:

COUNSEL: *How did Craig Wright R&D provide the $30 million in capital to Coin-Exchange?*

WRIGHT: *You would need to go to the financial records and accounts of the companies.*

COUNSEL: *Which companies?*

WRIGHT: *Coin-Exch for a start.*

COUNSEL: *Who has access to Coin-Exchange records?*

WRIGHT: *I do not know.*

[Cut]

COUNSEL: *Are you sitting here today able to recollect anything about how Craig Wright R&D transferred $30 million in capital to Coin-Exchange?*

WRIGHT: *I instruct people to do things. Things happened.*

Coin-Exch would soon be put under the Hotwire umbrella, as would some of Wright's other companies, as Wright sought, on paper at least, to expand his Bitcoin-related corporate empire. It would also come to play an important role in Wright's fraudulent attempt to accrue massive wealth almost overnight.

Soon after the founding of Coin-Exch came a somewhat seminal moment in Craig Wright's history: he fell in love with Bitcoin. Over the period of just a few days in late April 2013, Wright bought and sold his first bitcoins on MtGox, penned four blog posts extolling its virtues and even became a paid-up member of the Bitcoin Foundation, whose board members included Gavin Andresen, a supposed member of the cabal that had turfed him out of Bitcoin in 2011. His blog posts referenced the thrust of the message espoused by Satoshi Nakamoto – that Bitcoin was to be prized because of its trustless and decentralised nature – with Wright failing to mention his apparently burning desire for Bitcoin to be used for good rather than evil, that the people in charge of it were distorting its purpose or that WikiLeaks and Julian Assange were a bunch of bastards. Instead, he was all for it:

Hold fast to your beliefs if you wish and I will place my bet is you did yours. For this is what it is. You may bet on currency controlled by state player and I will bet on something that is decentralized and which cannot be devalued at a whim. A currency that can be trusted by all.

It isn't a stretch to believe that these are the writings of a man excited by a new discovery rather than the actions of an embittered creator out to set the world straight on his creation's proper purpose. Wright also referenced the all-important micropayment function that he would later say was the sole rationale behind his ambitions for Bitcoin, although he only mentioned it once across all four posts, with the focus being on trustlessness and decentralisation, rather undermining his later claims.

With his newfound love of Bitcoin and his plans for Hotwire taking shape, things seemed to be looking up for Wright in early 2013. He got a nasty shock on 30 April, however, when he found out that Dave Kleiman had tragically died. Kleiman, who had been severely ill due to complications with a long-standing MRSA infection, had checked himself out of the West Palm Beach Veterans Affairs Medical Center weeks earlier under the guise of having some disability equipment fitted in his home, with a *Kleiman v Wright* filing noting that he was 'unstable and nearing death' at the time. The circumstances surrounding his passing are unclear, including the exact date, but his partially decomposed body was found on 26 April, with the cause of death stated as the impact of the infections that had plagued his final years.

When it was revealed in the *WIRED* and *Gizmodo* pieces that, according to Wright, Kleiman had died with around 300,000 bitcoins to his name, many asked why he hadn't used them to better his circumstances rather than dying in poverty. Wright told Ira Kleiman that most of his brother's wealth had been tied up in Liberty Reserve, making it now unreachable, while the subject of Dave's bitcoin holdings came up in a discussion in early 2016 between Wright and Stefan Matthews. This was retold by Andrew O'Hagan in 'The Satoshi Affair', where Matthews told the author that Dave Kleiman had 350,000 bitcoins in wallets 'encrypted on his hard drive, with three or four keys to his trust.' Matthews also explained why Kleiman hadn't sold a single coin:

> *Because bitcoins weren't worth that much when Dave died. They skyrocketed around that time and in the weeks thereafter. But he was a man of principle apparently and wouldn't spend those coins unless Craig told him to.*

There are several points amiss with this claim, most notably that no Bitcoin wallets, key slices or references to his own trusts were ever found in Dave Kleiman's possession, and he never mentioned their existence to anyone (Wright would later put this down to Ira wiping Dave's computer disks). Additionally, far from not being worth much, Dave Kleiman's haul would have been worth a staggering US$45 million at the time of his death, but he would have been wise to have cashed out when he could; far from skyrocketing after his passing as Matthews claimed, Bitcoin's price dipped by 50% over the next three months. During the *Kleiman v Wright* case, it came to light that Dave Kleiman owed loan providers US$560,000 at the time of his death, equating to just 1.2% of his alleged bitcoin holdings. It is, therefore, inconceivable that he refrained from covering his debts in this manner all because Craig Wright hadn't given him permission to sell the coins.

Wright posted a video tribute to Dave Kleiman shortly after learning about his death, referring to Kleiman as a 'special man' who 'gave far, far more than he ever took'. It is sadly fitting, therefore, that Dave Kleiman's passing would see Wright try to take from his deceased friend far, far more than he was entitled to.

Chapter 13 – The $57 Million Swindle

In May 2013, as Jamie Wilson settled into his role as Hotwire's Chief Financial Officer, he began to notice a change in Wright, which he explained in his deposition for the *Kleiman v Wright* case in 2020:

> *Once Dave had passed away and things started to get kicked off with these new companies...all of a sudden he had to dress in flash suits, you know, wear the best watches, shoes, [a] fascination with socks. Even down to vehicles. He moved from his normal Subaru which was beaten up and went and got a brand new car. It was just a massive change in lifestyle. It wasn't the Craig I originally met.*

This sudden change – and the apparent desire to leave his old self behind – may explain why Wright has been so quick to denounce anyone who says he used to live and dress in this manner; it shows that there was indeed a huge shift at this time. Wilson added that he also witnessed a change in Wright's personality:

> *...the confidence went through the roof. It was a matter of 'I'm the man, I'm going to do this, this is the way I'm going to go about it'. Whereas [he was] a lot more humble prior to Dave's passing.*

CoinGeek interpreted this, with an almighty stretch, into Wilson resenting that Wright was 'looking like he has money'. Whether it was envy or something else that piqued Wilson's interest, he couldn't ignore what he was seeing: Wright was suddenly acting like a millionaire. In one universe, the one where Wright possessed, at the very least, hundreds of thousands of bitcoins, the reason for his sudden wealth was evident, given that Bitcoin's price had increased from $20 at the start of the year to $140 by the end of April. As we have discussed, however, there is no evidence that Wright held enough bitcoins for such an increase in value to make an appreciable difference to his level of wealth, and the real reason for his change in attitude is far less palatable.

In June 2013, Wright sent Wilson an email that explained his new trajectory following Dave Kleiman's tragic passing:

> *This is where this started. All has started to move much faster now. Dave passed a couple of months ago, so I am no longer waiting for him to get better.*

Wright elucidated on this point a few weeks later, telling Wilson on 2 July about 'assets to come in from the US' in the form of IP and asking him to prepare invoices on behalf of the various companies in his stable which would procure the IP when it arrived. Wright also referenced 'NSW Supreme court action' in relation to the IP, but it wasn't immediately clear to Wilson how Wright planned to obtain this IP or what this court action might be. All became clear just three weeks later when, on 25 July 2013, Craig Wright, in the form of Craig Steven Wright Pty Ltd (Craig Steven Wright), a company established back in 2007, sued W&K in the Supreme Court of New South Wales for a staggering $28.5 million:

> *Between 2011 and 2013 the plaintiff provided contract labour services to the defendant. The plaintiff loaned money to the defendant...at a set interest rate with a commercial expectation that the said monies would be repaid in full when a project was completed.*

As filings lodged with the court and later with the ATO would show, Wright claimed that the Panama branch of Craig Wright R&D had signed a deal with W&K to allow the latter to mine bitcoins and develop related software. The agreement came in the form of an 'Intellectual Property License Funding Agreement', which stipulated that Craig Wright R&D would loan W&K 215,140 bitcoins in two tranches in 2011 for development work as well as two supercomputers that W&K would use to mine bitcoins, with the contract stating that W&K expected to net 12,000 bitcoins per month from the enterprise. The total cost to W&K would be 300,000 bitcoins, not payable until June 2013 (250,000 bitcoins) and December 2013 (50,000 bitcoins). Given that Dave Kleiman died, of course, these repayments were never made.

The contract noted that the value of the loan to be repaid by W&K was $40 million, but given that Bitcoin's price on the day the contract was allegedly signed was just $1.22, Wright clearly valued the computers extremely highly. The manufacturer of the computers, Silicon Graphics Incorporated (SGI), was bought out in 2009, so we can't enquire as to the value of the SGI XE310 512-core 2011 model stated in the contract, but given that most supercomputers were priced at the hundreds of thousands to the low millions at the time, the chances of Wright owning two computers worth $20 million each are slim to none. During a deposition for the *Kleiman v Wright* case, Wright claimed that 'All of my machines ended up costing around 60 million', which is a ludicrous figure not borne out by reliable evidence.

When questioned about these machines during an April 2019 deposition for the same case, Wright said that W&K 'did not expect to earn anything' from Bitcoin mining, mainly because it would have been 'totally stupidly foolish' to even attempt the activity given the proliferation of specialist ASIC mining hardware that was coming out at the time. Wright confirmed that 'There was no mining at all in any way that I know of on those machines, ever', which rather begs the question of why it formed such an important part of the deal. Wright had an answer for this:

> *Those machines were running enhanced versions of Bitcoin that I was creating, the node software, so that I could see how far I could scale Bitcoin as a blockchain. Any other side use, while not being used, was originally envisioned that others could mine Bitcoin with.*

Here, then, we see Wright denying that the two computers would ever have been capable of mining the 12,000 bitcoins per month that W&K had expected to bring in through their use. This presents the argument that, far from W&K breaching the terms of the contract by virtue of Kleiman's death, Craig Wright had been the one to breach them by knowingly sending computers that couldn't fulfil the contract. The reason for Wright's change in story between the purported contracts of 2011-2013 and his testimony of 2019 is simple to comprehend: in the 2011-2013 period, it was in his financial interest to claim that W&K had carried out Bitcoin mining and that Dave Kleiman had joined him in various ways, while in 2019 he was being sued over these very claims and so had to create a retrospective distance. In the former case, he was hoping to secure a hefty tax rebate; in the latter, he was hoping to avoid a multi-billion-dollar penalty.

Wright added during this deposition that he didn't know if the two Bitcoin payments from Craig Wright R&D went to W&K because he wasn't involved in the process, explaining that he 'told people what to do' and they 'told me they had done it'. When asked what the process was for getting the bitcoins from Craig Wright R&D to W&K, Wright perpetually gave evasive answers, offering lengthy technical descriptions of how any bitcoins moved anywhere, before eventually claiming that he had requested High Secured and Liberty Reserve to send the coins over to 'Dave's company in Panama'. This answer, given after many minutes of prevarication and belligerence, conveniently allowed no further follow-up, given Liberty Reserve's extinction and the lack of access to High Secured's files. However, Wright's claim that Liberty Reserve owned 'quite a number of bitcoin' is not a view shared by anyone else with experience of the company, and, indeed, there have never been any claims that Liberty Reserve ever held any bitcoins for customers or touched it at all. Wright used the same tactic to explain how the bitcoins had gotten to Craig Wright R&D in Panama in the first place, although this was far from straightforward: the agreement stated that a Bitcoin address starting 1933p, owned by Craig Wright R&D, would remain in escrow and revert to Wright if W&K defaulted. The other two documents in Wright's evidence pack, however, attributed different functions to it.

On the subject of Bitcoin addresses, the Intellectual Property License Funding Agreement between Craig Wright R&D and W&K listed two addresses as being the source of the loans, one beginning 12C9c and one beginning 12hRm. Kim Nilsson's analysis of MtGox's records revealed that 12C9c belonged to MtGox co-founder Jed McCaleb, while 12hRm belonged to MtGox itself, as evidenced by the fact that it connected directly to a public transfer of 424,242 bitcoins that MtGox CEO Mark Karpelès conducted in June 2011. This brings the number of Bitcoin addresses used in the Craig Wright R&D-W&K deal that were knowingly owned by other people to three, and it is a near certainty that the others were also picked from the Bitcoin rich list.

In the Intellectual Property License Funding Agreement, Wright also referenced the 'Bitcoin and Exchange Software in C/C++/C#/R code' that W&K was supposed to be developing, saying that it wasn't just for an eventual Bitcoin exchange:

> *There were certain things that were to do with a Bitcoin exchange, and some other aspects of poker software, other aspects of the software I have mentioned before, and the other stuff, intellectual property, under the unawarded DHS projects.*

These were the DHS projects that Wright had told the ATO were 'used by the U.S. Military, DHS and other associated parties', something he had also told Ira Kleiman to explain the work that W&K had been engaged in. A couple of years later, Wright told Andrew O'Hagan that the departments had, in fact, 'ripped off' the software from himself and Kleiman, but in 2020, he told the court in *Kleiman v Wright* that the software was 'all given freely' and that it had been open source since 2012. Ira Kleiman's legal team lodged a Freedom of Information request with the DHS over the software, discovering that all four projects had been rejected just weeks after they had been submitted in 2011. Under questioning, Wright was forced to backtrack:

> *My indication was that [Dave Kleiman] had filed for the DHS plan, that all the information was in, that it was progressing and I have nothing else saying that he didn't go down that path.*

Wright's new story, therefore, was that because he had heard nothing to the contrary, he believed the projects to have been green-lit and the funding awarded. To believe this, we have to believe that Wright never once thought to confirm with Dave Kleiman the awarding of the contracts or the US$5 million-plus that came with them, despite them being the sole reason for the formation of the company. Equally, we have to believe that Kleiman never told Wright that the projects had been approved either. Ira Kleiman's counsel also took issue with the terms of the funding agreement, labelling them 'nonsensical' and arguing that the prospect of a company financing its operations with bitcoins between 2011 and 2013 was impossible because 'there was essentially nothing that could be purchased with bitcoins at that time'. They also noted that the contractual terms were 'extremely convenient for Craig', adding that the agreement provided complete confidentiality 'even from family members' and that a date in the document had been manually corrected from 2013 to 2011. This, they argued, was 'likely because it was written in 2013', the year Wright filed his lawsuit against W&K.

Ira Kleiman's team also had issues with the digital signatures used on the documents, which were simply Dave Kleiman's name written in the Otto font, labelling them 'fraudulent' and arguing that they didn't match any known handwritten signature attributed to him. This issue had already come up between Wright and Ira in 2014, with Wright saying that the nature of the signature didn't matter because the PGP key made it an authentic and unique signature. During the *Kleiman v Wright* trial, Wright was asked if the representation of Dave Kleiman's name on the contract genuinely reflected his signature. This should have been a simple yes or no answer for Wright, but he responded with a minute-long ramble about the legal definition of signatures before stating that he did not give 'a rat's rectum' where the signature had come from. Wright's counsel was no doubt surprised, and perhaps a little disheartened, that their client didn't just offer a simple 'yes'.

An important question the ATO had for Wright (one of many) when it assessed the W&K-Craig Wright R&D deal was where Craig Wright R&D got the 215,140 bitcoins to lend W&K. Wright explained this with a document that was to have far-reaching consequences in his dealings with the ATO and beyond: a 'Deed of Loan' purportedly drawn up between Craig Wright R&D, Denariuz Seychelles Trust and Design by Human Ltd (Design by Human). Design by Human was one of three companies founded by CFS Secretaries Ltd, a now dormant organisation based in Doncaster, England, that earned its money by creating and selling shelf companies, much like Abacus in the Seychelles. While investigating Wright's Tulip Trust claims, the ATO was tipped off that Design by Human was a trustee for the Tulip Trust and dug into the public records of the company, where it found some fascinating details.

Design by Human was incorporated on 11 October 2012, but having failed to sell it, CFS Secretaries changed the company's name to Moving Forward in Business a year later. Craig Wright bought Moving Forward in Business on 3 January 2014, picking up two more companies from CFS Secretaries at the same time: Permanent Success Ltd, founded on 18 October 2012, and Achieve & Succeed Ltd, founded on 22 October 2012. The last of these had been formed just the day before the Declaration of Trust and Deed of Trust were allegedly signed, increasing their significance dramatically. Within a matter of days of his purchases, Wright had appointed himself as director and secretary of Moving Forward in Business and renamed the company to C01N, which we came across earlier (he would later claim to have bought Design by Human in 2012, hence why its name featured in his purported activities of the era, but he actually bought it after its 2013 name change). Wright also appointed himself as director and secretary of Permanent Success, which he changed to Denariuz Ltd (Denariuz UK), while Achieve & Succeed was also confusingly changed to Denariuz, but no director was immediately added. The big question for the ATO, of course, was: what on earth did Craig Wright want with these British companies?

Here's where we turn to the Deed of Loan, a document purportedly drawn up on 23 October 2012, the same date as the Declairation of Trust and twelve days after Design by Human had been founded by CFS Secretaries. Produced for the ATO, it showed Craig Wright R&D accepting a loan of 650,000 bitcoins from Design by Human and promising to return it in June 2020. The deed had a handwritten note scribbled across its appendix:

As agreed, all wallets to be held in UK in trust until all regulatory issues solved and Group Company formed with Dave K and CSW.

Design by Human's role, then, was to look after the 650,000 bitcoins, while the 'Group Company' refers to Coin-Exch. Design by Human's purpose was solidified by an email Dave Kleiman supposedly sent to Wright on 7 September 2012, which read, in part:

The trust is set up in the Seychelles. I will arrange a shelf company to manage it in the UK, as we discuss later. There is no rush there.

The Seychelles trust in question was the Tulip Trust, a connection that pokes a rather large hole in Wright's claim that Dave Kleiman did nothing but hold some papers in relation to it, while the shelf company mentioned was Design by Human. There is, of course, a massive problem here: Wright bought Design by Human in 2014 after its name changed to Moving Forward in Business, so it couldn't have been used in the legal formation of the Tulip Trust in 2012. It also, therefore, couldn't have accepted the mined bitcoins on behalf of the 'Seychelles trust', as Wright's accountant, John Chesher, told the ATO in February 2014. It is likely not a coincidence that Ira Kleiman's forensic examiner, Dr Edman, found the digital signature in Kleiman's email to have been created on 28 February 2014, just two days after Chesher had been instructed to spin this story to the ATO and almost a year after Kleiman died.

Wright's initial court filing over his $28.5 million claim stated that an agreement had been in place between Craig Steven Wright and W&K since 8 January 2009. The deal saw Craig Steven Wright provide 'property and consulting services to complete research' to W&K, as well as funding 'a project for the development of a Bitcoin SDK and exchange.' This funding allegedly took the form of $20 million in bitcoins, gold bonds and Bitcoin mining hardware, the latter of which had a value of $8.8 million. Repayment had been due on 30 June 2013, but due to Dave Kleiman's death two months earlier, it had naturally been missed, resulting in a breach of contract. This meant that, by the terms of the contract, all the IP and systems should be returned to Craig Steven Wright. When Wright was asked during a deposition for the *Kleiman v Wright* case about the nature of the work he had undertaken for W&K, his answer was less than convincing:

> COUNSEL: *What were the labour services you provided?*
>
> WRIGHT: *The document is badly drafted.*
>
> COUNSEL: *Who drafted this document?*
>
> WRIGHT: *Myself.*
>
> COUNSEL: *What does it mean to say, or why is it badly drafted?*
>
> WRIGHT: *Because some of the things were in error, it was rushed, I was trying to get through a document so that I could simply just state the intellectual property that I had and start moving forward.*

The reason why Wright was in such a rush would become clear later, but here we have a rare example of him taking the blame for something rather than planting it on someone else. Wright claimed that W&K was developing 'software and code used in the creation of a Bitcoin system' as well as mining bitcoins, with Wright submitting evidence to the court in the form of invoices and contracts to back up his suggestion that this was what the company had been doing alongside working on those DHS projects. The claim left Jamie Wilson in no doubt as to why Wright was discussing GST rebates for material coming in from America and why he was suddenly acting as if he was the cat that had inherited a creamery. It seems that $28.5 million wasn't enough for Wright, either – three weeks later, he made an almost identical filing, this time for $28.2 million. The premise was the same, with Wright suing over yet more unpaid work and loans he had seemingly forgotten to add to the first filing. He was now claiming that W&K owed him a grand total of almost $57 million worth of back pay and loan repayments despite the company never producing anything. Given its lack of cash, Wright magnanimously said he would take his money in the form of company IP.

Wright was clearly confident of victory with these two cases, given that they were months away from conclusion, and yet he was already telling Jamie Wilson to prepare invoices regarding their transfer onwards to Wright's various companies, invoices which would result in GST rebates for the taxed amounts. The rush to get the GST rebates banked accounted for several glaring errors, including the contracts between Wright and W&K stating that the company was formed in September 2009 or September 2008, depending on which contract you read. When challenged over these impossible formation dates during an interview with the ATO, Wright claimed, 'I'm not professional[y] qualified as a barrister and I don't do good pleadings all the time.'

To aid the smooth transition of the court case, Uyen Nguyen was installed as W&K director in the U.S. on 1 July 2013 following an agreement made with Dave Kleiman the prior December, and eight days after this appointment, she transferred all the software and related algorithms from W&K to Craig Wright R&D in exchange for the release of W&K from its existing debts. On 23 August, Wright incorporated W&K Company Pty Ltd (W&K Company) in Australia, an act that kicked off a business incorporation marathon that saw five more Australian companies established over the next three days. As we will see, these companies were all supposed to receive a slice of the W&K pie once it was in Wright's possession, with tax rebates planned for all individual acquisitions.

On 28 August 2013, a consent order was entered for Wright's first claim against W&K, which stated that Jamie Wilson, who had been appointed director of W&K, had acquiesced to Wright's IP request on the company's behalf, with Wright claiming during the *Kleiman v Wright* trial that Wilson had signed in person at the courtroom. Wright added at the same trial that the non-appearance of any defendants at the following 30 October hearing was due to Wilson having been fired and Lynn Wright choosing not to appear. At that hearing, Wright shared an important update:

> ...there's been a shareholders meeting held and resolution to pass the matter has been obtained and the company will be wound down straight after the matter.

Wright asked for 'the orders that we did by consent in the past' to be approved, but the registrar stated that they were not prepared to sign over $28.5 million in IP without first seeing some 'detailed affidavit evidence' and other evidence relating to the authority of Jamie Wilson to sign off on W&K's behalf. Wright was given a week to provide these documents, and on 5 November, he submitted his affidavit which stated that he had lent W&K 215,140 bitcoins and had wanted 300,000 bitcoins in return as well as 'a series of software projects'; that W&K had mined bitcoins using two computers Wright had lent the company; that the work linked back to what Integyrs had been doing in 2009; and that Dave Kleiman had died just days before he was supposed to be added as a shareholder and director of Coin-Exch. Wright also reiterated Con-Exch's alleged purpose: it was the vehicle for the pair's long-term plans over Bitcoin and had been slated to receive all the IP created by W&K in relation to it as well as any 'remaining capital' and a further injection of capital later in 2013. Kleiman's death, however, had also been the death knell for these plans, leaving the IP in limbo.

The affidavit also stated that the Bitcoin addresses used in connection with the loans had been 'independently validated by NSW Solicitors under oath', notably one Stephen D'Emilio, but, as we will see, Wright invalidated this through an ill-advised post to his followers years later. Also included in the affidavit was an allusion that 'Work and research was conducted under the U.S. Dept. of Homeland Security DHS BAA', which we know it wasn't, with Dave Kleiman arranging for everything to be sent to W&K in April 2013 on the first leg of its journey to Australia, where Coin-Exch was waiting to receive it. Unfortunately, Kleiman's tragic passing interrupted the process, leaving Craig Wright with no option but to take legal action to get it over the line and fulfil the pair's ambitions.

Wright's evidence over the appointment of Jamie Wilson took the form of notes from a 16 August 2013 meeting where Wilson had agreed to be appointed as director of W&K 'for the purposes of consenting to orders and the company to be wound down.' This, together with Uyen Nguyen signing everything over from W&K to Craig Wright R&D, made the matter a fait accompli for the registrar: with both sides having agreed to the deal, on 6 November 2013, Craig Steven Wright was granted a combined $57 million in IP from W&K.

Those who have become inured to the modus operandi of Craig Wright by this point might be more than a little sceptical over the legitimacy of this deal and how it sailed so smoothly through the court. Was W&K really mining bitcoins? Why did Jamie Wilson agree to ease the lawsuit's passage by becoming a director of W&K? How much did Craig Wright charge per hour to be owed tens of millions of dollars in consulting fees for a company that never recorded earnings? The ATO would ask all these questions and many more once Wright's companies began submitting their GST rebates, and the answers they uncovered shone an unforgiving light on Wright's skulduggery and his use of both the living and the deceased in his pursuit of riches.

Wright may have felt that he had stumbled across a surefire way to make himself a multi-millionaire with minimal effort, but he was about to find out that while he could fool some of the people some of the time, he couldn't fool all the people all the time.

Especially if those people are tax inspectors.

Chapter 14 – A Miner Issue

In March 2013, a month before Dave Kleiman's passing, Craig Wright was allegedly attending a conference on mining and security (physical mining rather than Bitcoin mining), having been invited as a speaker. Wright's connection with the mining industry may not seem too obvious at first glance, but he says that during this period, he was asked to speak at 'up to 16 conferences a year as a result of my research and publications' on the possible use of blockchain technology in the mining contract process. This, it is needless to say, is an entirely evidence-free claim. Wright says that during a break following the talk, he was approached by one Mark Ferrier, who said he was 'heavily involved in mining and finance of mining' and wanted to talk about Wright's blockchain research. This led to further discussions about Wright's plan to set up a Bitcoin bank called Denariuz. Despite Ferrier knowing nothing about blockchain and labelling Bitcoin 'funny money', Wright seems to have been impressed by him, not least because of the large number of contacts Ferrier possessed in the pornography industry, as Wright told the ATO.

Ferrier told Wright that he would be able to source software from tech giant Siemens and Saudi Arabian conglomerate Dallah Al Baraka Group that could be useful for Wright's plans and that he could find vendors who would accept Bitcoin. Ferrier added that his company, MJF Mining, was also working with gold miner Paynes Find Gold over a deal that would see MJF supply machinery for gold exploration in exchange for a 50% claim of future discoveries. The pair thrashed out a deal, signed on 3 June 2013, which included Wright taking part in the same gold deal that Ferrier claimed to have with Paynes. Wright agreed to pay $5 million for the Siemens mining automation software, $11.5 million for microfinance software and accounting packages developed by Al Baraka and $18.75 million for the gold options from Paynes. MJF issued two tax invoices pertaining to the deal, with the total cost coming to a hefty $59.1 million, including GST. Wright handed over 380,000 bitcoins and received the software, splitting it up and selling it to the relevant companies in his Hotwire group, filing Input Tax Credit claims (essentially GST rebates) at every step. The ATO was perhaps unsurprisingly suspicious of many elements of Wright's deal and was already looking into it when Mark Ferrier was arrested for fraud on 25 September 2013. Ferrier's arrest wasn't connected to the Hotwire deal; in 2011, he was on parole following a conviction on dishonesty charges when he breached his conditions by skipping the state, whereupon he embarked on what *ABC News* called a $500,000 'fraud spree'.

It soon emerged that rather than being a well-connected mining broker, Ferrier was nothing but a confidence trickster who had spent the past two years scamming hotels, aviation companies, mining contractors, lawyers and more by claiming to offer services he had no intention of carrying out. One can only imagine how Craig Wright must have felt upon hearing the news of Ferrier's arrest, having handed over one hundred and twenty times more money to Ferrier than all his other victims combined. His biggest concern, of course, would have been over the software and the gold claims; if Ferrier was nothing but a scammer, the odds of him having delivered the real thing were a million to one. Not so, as Wright told ATO's Des McMaster in his 18 February 2014 interview:

> MCMASTER: And [the software] worked...okay?
>
> WRIGHT: It does...
>
> MCMASTER: I accept what you're saying. It's just given Mark's prior history I'm a little bit surprised.
>
> WRIGHT: We were very careful with the software. When I did the software stuff I made sure...the payments happened as I got the software.

Wright was suggesting that serial fraudster Ferrier had, for some reason, decided not to scam him and had secured legitimate software, breaking a two-year pattern of behaviour. Of course, $59 million is enough to turn any criminal straight, at least for a one-off. The gold claims, on the other hand, had gone up in smelting smoke, with Paynes cancelling the contract it had with Ferrier five days after his arrest.

Wright, naturally, intended to claim back the tax he was due to pay over the purchase of the software, for which it needed to be genuine. As Andrew Sommer made clear in the same interview, Wright was desperate for the money:

> *The real refund that the guys need is in relation to the MJF transactions...these things are the things where we have paid GST-inclusive amounts to our supplier and they're considerable and we need those, you know...to try and get those refunds back so they continue funding activities in Australia.*

Wright also told the ATO that his team had spent 'an inordinate amount of time' combing through the software 'after finding out what Mark Ferrier is actually like' before giving it the green light and implementing it into their operations. Their checks, however, didn't include verifying the software's legitimacy, as we will soon discover. While Ferrier may have diddled him over the gold claims, Wright could think himself sensationally lucky that the man who made a living from defrauding everyone, including his own brother, decided not to take the money and run but had, contrary to all his other activities at the time, managed to obtain banking software from vendors who were happy to accept Bitcoin for it in 2013.

What the ATO may not have known at the time was that two months prior to this interview, Wright had filed a lawsuit against MJF in the Federal Court of Australia, claiming the sum of $84.4 million based on the contemporaneous value of the 380,000 bitcoins used to buy the software (there is no mention of the lawsuit in the ATO interview transcript). Wright discontinued this case in March 2014 but had more luck with the Supreme Court of New South Wales, where the company Craig Steven Wright picked up an award of $59.1 million on 4 February 2014 over the fraudulent deal. This might imply that the court believed Wright's story over the software, but, once again, Wright might have gotten away with a lack of examination: there is no evidence that Ferrier engaged with the lawsuit at all, suggesting that Wright was awarded a default judgment. Despite the high award, it is unlikely that Wright saw any of this money, and he couldn't simply ask for IP in its place this time around.

We have already noted that the ATO was sceptical about the MJF deal, partly because the bumper figure paid by Wright never featured in any documentation surrounding the case or any reporting on it and also because of the suggestion that Wright had encountered Dr Jekyll whereas everyone else had been screwed over by Mr Hyde. McMaster and co. became even more suspicious during their interview with Wright and Sommer when the latter explained how MJF had been paid:

> ...there is in fact a physical transfer of bitcoin out of those trusts to those third-party suppliers...things are moving out of the Seychelles' trusts to...the wallets designated by the relevant contractual counter party. There's nothing that touches Australia. The only thing that happens in Australia is the grant of that right to have the bitcoin transferred out of the trust. Bitcoin didn't move, except in relation to the Al Baraka transactions and the MJF transactions.

The transfers in question were 245,000 bitcoins sent on 30 August 2013 and 135,000 bitcoins sent two weeks later on 15 September, with Sommer adding that 'Bitcoin was transferred for a trust, the trustee of which I believe is the entity by the name of [Design by Human] Limited.' Here, then, we have Craig Wright's tax lawyer stating that the bitcoins for MJF were held in trust by Design by Human on behalf of the Tulip Trust, which, of course, we know cannot be true for all the reasons detailed earlier. A follow-up meeting took place eight days later between Wright's accountant, John Chesher, his bookkeeper and Andrew Miller of the ATO, with Wright's suspicions over the agency's motives laid bare in the opening exchanges:

> CHESHER: *I am uncomfortable with the fact that Des McMaster is looking after these audits. We have had past dealings with him in the previous audits.*
>
> MILLER: *That is why I'm coming in with a fresh pair of eyes.*
>
> CHESHER: *Des' judgment is tainted due to his involvement with the old audits. We don't want the current audits to be tainted by the past audits.*
>
> MILLER: *Yes, I understand.*

Wright had asked for his case to be reassigned following the 18 February interview with McMaster, who Chesher thought a 'really nasty piece of work', although seeing as no derogatory statements about McMaster appear on any of

Wright's Tulip Trust paperwork, we can assume he was not a patch on Adam Westwood. Wright claimed during his March 2020 deposition for the *Kleiman v Wright* case that McMaster was 'sent to Papua New Guinea as punishment' for his poor work on Wright's case, including his actions during and around these meetings, has proved impossible to verify.

The question of MJF came up early in the conversation between Miller and Wright's representatives, with the ATO man wanting clarity on how MJF had been paid for the software and gold claims:

MILLER: I have a question to ask. Were actual Bitcoins physically paid to MJF Consulting or Mark Ferrier?

CHESHER: Yes. We paid Bitcoins to him. We paid the Bitcoins to where he directed for the Bitcoins to be paid into.

MILLER: Just to confirm, was it actual physical Bitcoins that was paid?

CHESHER: Yes.

Chesher then clarified how the deal had gone down:

> ...the Bitcoins left Doncaster in UK and was transferred to West Africa. Craig Wright obtained the automation and banking software through Mark Ferrier. The software first goes to Craig Wright and then he transfers them into the trustee for the Wright Family Trust (DeMorgan) for distribution. The banking software was transferred into Coin-Exch as this company is acting as the banking front. The automation and exchange software was transferred to Hotwire. Basically, everything goes through Craig Wright and then into the trust.

As we know, Doncaster was the home of CFS Secretaries, which at that time owned Design by Human (already renamed to Moving Forward in Business). This is a sign that Wright was well aware of the potential problems associated with the purchases of the UK companies, made just weeks before this meeting, and was looking for some means of suggesting that he was involved with them in 2013. Where West Africa fits into the narrative is not clear; the only known African connection, Denis Mayaka, was based in Kenya on the east of the continent, so it cannot be related to him.

Chesher confirmed with Miller that Wright personally owed $4.2 million in GST for the Al Bakara deal but added that, when the other companies' activities were taken into consideration, Hotwire was expecting a $5 million GST rebate, which, he said, it needed fast:

> *There is an amount coming our way...we want it released immediately. We have spent a lot of money during this process and we need the funds to ease our cash flow. The Bitcoin industry is very volatile and there is no clear picture as to the future. Our bank options are limited. Everything we have been doing is legitimate. If you were able to come out to our premise[s] today to hold the meeting, you would have seen 40 to 50 people working out there. We have lots of activity happening at the moment. $5 million does make a difference. We need to recover the money already spent.*

This paints a picture of the perilous situation Wright's companies were in by early 2014 and shows that he was already relying on tax rebates to keep the Hotwire ship afloat. It's also worth noting at this juncture that Wright was financing his businesses with an asset that was so volatile its value could jump or fall by double digits in a single day; between the time Wright allegedly locked away the 1.1 million bitcoins in June 2011 to the day of this meeting, Bitcoin had dropped 93%, risen 50,000% and dropped 50% again. The idea that anyone could budget for the operation of not just one company but half a dozen using a form of money accepted by barely any suppliers and which appreciated and depreciated so rapidly is utterly implausible. The ATO raised the issue of Bitcoin's volatility in a later interview, where Wright tried to argue that it was no more volatile than some fiat currencies:

> WRIGHT: One Zimbabwe dollar can't even buy you a grain of sand at the moment. I believe the typical currency note is now in the hundred trillion dollars in Zimbabwe dollars...Equally, one ounce of gold in the US was a dollar just a hundred years ago.
>
> ATO: Okay. But I'm talking more day-to-day, week-to-week, month-to-month volatility...Do you accept that bitcoin does have a volatility that is quite extreme relative to most currencies?

> WRIGHT: No. Actually, most currencies would be - I mean, there's over 120 different currencies in the world, and bitcoin is probably about 30th on volatility.

Shortly after the second February 2014 meeting, Chesher emailed the ATO to confirm Wright's story that the bitcoins used to buy the software and gold claims were from his mining operations in 2009-2010 and had been locked away in a Seychelles trust in 2011, with Wright able to call on the bitcoins when he needed loans for his businesses. This was the 650,000-bitcoin loan, with the Deed of Loan clearly stating that the funds were to be held in trust by Design by Human until needed, which they finally were when Mark Ferrier and Professor Rees supposedly came knocking. Unsurprisingly, the ATO wanted more than just vague stories of Seychelles trusts to verify that Wright had actually spent $59 million on the software and gold claims from MJF and asked for a list of addresses from which the bitcoins had come. Wright responded to this request through John Chesher on 2 April 2014, at which point the narrative changed: as with Professor Rees, these transactions had not been conducted on-chain as initially stated but had instead been done 'off blockchain', with private keys to nine Bitcoin addresses being the method of payment. If it is hard to believe that a ninety-five-year-old dementia patient would readily accept Bitcoin private keys as payment, it is frankly absurd to suggest that Al Baraka, Siemens and their intermediaries all felt comfortable accepting $59 million in the same manner. Convincing Siemens and Al Baraka to take payment in bitcoins would have been a tough enough sell for Ferrier, so for him to then have to switch to private keys and still facilitate the deal is simply laughable. Remember, Bitcoin had only been around for four years by this point, and those who actually used it as a currency spent it on just one thing – drugs – as Wright supposedly knew all too well.

If things were looking bleak for Wright's claim that he had paid a known scammer $59 million through private keys to Bitcoin addresses, behind the scenes, they were going pitch black. What neither Wright nor the ATO knew at this time was that the coins in five of Wright's nine addresses were in the process of being emptied by the trustee for the recently collapsed MtGox. The addresses and the 180,000 coins they held all belonged to the exchange, and the trustee, Nobuaki Kobayashi, had ordered that all remaining assets be moved into addresses under his control shortly after his appointment in March 2014. This meant that at the very moment Wright was giving the ATO a list of Bitcoin addresses from which the MJF payments had allegedly come, 4,850 miles away, MtGox CEO Mark Karpelès was moving the coins out of those addresses and into Kobayashi's care. This lends validity to the suggestion that Wright was simply picking addresses from the Bitcoin rich list and passing them off as his own without considering the implications.

Even without this knowledge, the change of story over the payment method understandably disconcerted the ATO, which wanted proof more than ever that the software existed. In an April 2014 interim ruling on Coin-Exch, the ATO cast doubt on the validity of the software and Wright's licenses to use it. This resulted in Andrew Sommer criticising the agency the following month over its assertions regarding the software:

> ...it is absurd for the ATO to state that there must have been an agreement with Siemens in order for Dr Wright to have obtained the "Siemens Software". The agreement entered between Dr Wright and MJF required MJF to supply the Siemens software. It is assumed that MJF had arrangements with Siemens that enabled MJF in return to supply that software. However, such arrangements are outside the knowledge and control of Dr Wright and outside the knowledge and control of Coin-Ex.

Seeking reassurances, Andrew Miller and Stuart Coulson of the ATO attended the Sydney offices of Wright's solicitors, Clayton Utz, that June, where Wright demonstrated the software in action. In a rare show of deference to others in the field, Wright noted in an August 2014 interview with the agency that Coulson, a forensic auditor, 'has got a really good reputation for this sort of stuff', suggesting that he would accept Coulson's findings. This must have made it all the more galling when Coulson told Miller the following day that he had managed to download all the Siemens software that had cost Wright $5 million for free through a torrent site, with pirated keys available for a few dollars. This was alluded to in that August 2014 interview, where Wright appeared to suggest that he didn't mind if he had been sold a $5 million fake:

ATO: And you're satisfied that it is legally licensed software?

WRIGHT: I'm satisfied that it's working, that there's a licence and I can log into the site and download.

Wright confirmed that at no stage, either before the deal or since Ferrier's arrest, had he taken any steps to verify the legitimacy of the software, saying, 'If some sort of nefarious deal was done between an employee of Siemens, for instance, and Mr Ferrier, that didn't involve Siemens, then that's not my problem, I don't really give a rat's.'

Wright had also provided Miller and Coulson with communications between himself and Al Baraka customer service staff to support his claim that the software was legitimate. Coulson had even more reservations about this software, however, telling Miller that he was 'not confident' that it was genuine, adding that the system, if run on the code he had witnessed, would be of 'Low quality, bordering on a childish (immature – as though the coder had only written a web page once or twice before, not professional) attempt to develop a webpage/interface.' When asked by Miller whether it was worth the $11 million Wright had paid, Coulson noted, 'It does appear strange to me to spend 11 million for code that you aren't going to use...you're only going to rip out snippets that you can utilise in a webpage.' Coulson also found issues with Wright's Al Baraka support emails, discovering that they came from a domain that wasn't registered until January 2014, six months after the emails were purportedly exchanged. Worse, the domain had been registered by a virtual office in Istanbul, with Wright's credit card records showing a purchase to that same virtual office shortly before the domain was established. When questioned over this by the ATO, Wright played dumb, claiming 'I don't know half my [credit card] accounts' and added that he had spoken to 'people who I believe worked for AlBaraka' since receiving his software, again showing a staggering lack of interest in their legitimacy. Wright eventually blamed the virtual office purchase on an unnamed Al Baraka middleman, who allegedly stole Wright's card and made the purchase; no motive was given as to why they raced off to buy a random web domain, which Wright then used, compared to, say, buying a pair of Gucci loafers or the latest iPhone. This, of course, isn't too dissimilar to the story of the anonymous Redditor providing Wright's attorney with the Bitcoin.org bank records. The stolen credit card theory, which was put forward by an unnamed 'related entity', was given equally short shrift by the ATO.

With the ATO now having evidence that the software was illegitimate, Wright was faced with two options: admit that he must have been duped after all and lose the potential rebate or double down and try to prove the software's authenticity. Perhaps unsurprisingly, Wright chose the latter, persisting with his story on the origins and credibility of the software through a fifteen-page 'draft prepared for the purposes of legal proceedings' against Mark Ferrier over the gold claims. In the document, Wright claimed that it was 'not in dispute' that he had received the Siemens software, stating in bold for extra emphasis that he received the keys to unlock it in August 2013. Wright also explained the lengths he allegedly went to in order to authenticate the software and Ferrier's integrity, recalling small details with a clarity that would be entirely absent when he was faced with contradictory evidence during the *Kleiman v Wright* trial. Wright also provided the ATO with emails and BitMessages between himself and Ferrier and the MJF accounts department to bolster his case, including one dated 15 August 2013, which stated that MJF had 'accepted and verified the private keys' to the nine Bitcoin addresses, including the five that belonged to MtGox.

If Wright was under any illusions over the potency of his evidence regarding the MJF affair, the ATO dispelled it in October 2014 in an audit report on Coin-Exch:

> ...we do not accept that you acquired software from MJF...as Siemens and Al Baraka have confirmed that they did not transact with any of MJF...and it is from these entities that you purport to have acquired Siemens and Al Baraka software.

This categorical dismissal of Wright's claims was followed by an equally withering assessment of his evidence:

> ...it follows that these documents (including any related purported invoices or tax invoices) can be considered a nullity based on sham.

The ATO pointed out that Wright was claiming tax relief on the purchase of software he said was legitimate while simultaneously seeking legal recourse against Ferrier based on the suggestion that it was never delivered. Wright was challenged on this during the *Kleiman v Wright* trial:

> COUNSEL: Dr. Wright, would it be accurate to say you filed a police report because you paid Mark Ferrier or companies associated with him for something he never delivered?

WRIGHT: *I filed a police report acting for corporations. The corporation, in capacity, had a police report filed where I acted as the corporate representative.*

COUNSEL: *Because those corporations paid Mark Ferrier for something that he never delivered?*

WRIGHT: *His organisation would have had to deliver but, yes, Mark Ferrier was a con man.*

A con man he may have been, but Wright, eight years after the fact, still maintained that Ferrier had delivered two-thirds of what he had paid for, claiming that Ferrier 'acted as an agent for other parties who gave me source code to Islamic banking software' and that 'We were given a complete set of all Siemens software, all control software and all management software, including for power plants and other global operations.'

When it came to the gold claims, Wright and the ATO finally found common ground, although Wright was still trying to pull a fast one, as the agency noted:

It is noted that you advised that the Gold Options and Valuation services were never provided to you and you are taking legal action against MJF in relation to this. Regardless of the supply not occurring, you claimed an input tax credit for these acquisitions in your BAS for the relevant tax period.

The ATO also dismissed Wright's effort to avoid GST via the use of private keys rather than actual bitcoins, ruling that it amounted to the same thing and hitting him with a provisional $1.65 million GST bill over the transfer. It also noted that there would anyway have been 'insufficient amounts of bitcoin available under the [650,000 bitcoin] loan to support all of the relevant transactions.' Indeed, it turned out that not only had Wright created a fictitious 650,000 bitcoin loan from a fictitious trust, but he had been so sloppy with the maths that his fictitious invoices and fictitious acquisitions used up more coins than the fictitious loan allowed him.

The ATO was equally scathing about the way Wright had supposedly conducted the deal:

> *The manner in which you negotiated the acquisition of the MJF software lacks any apparent due diligence or commercial prudence. For example all correspondence regarding the acquisition was said to have been undertaken by Skype between you and Mark Ferrier directly. This is highly unusual and added to the contrivance of the scheme taking into account the large values involved. It does not appear that you had sought any legal or commercial advice on the transaction, despite it being valued in the millions.*

During their conversations with Wright about the value and importance of the software, ATO agents had queried the high price that Ferrier had demanded. In response, Wright compared the $16.5 million outlay to the hundreds of millions of dollars that other banks spent on their IT upgrades. This might have washed had Denariuz been in the same league as these multi-billion-dollar financial behemoths, but it wasn't lost on the ATO that Denariuz was instead an unproven startup run by a man they were investigating for potential tax fraud. Wright had tried to emphasise the importance of the deal by adding, memorably, that he would have 'sold my mother to get that software', so at least someone in the Wright family would have been glad that the whole thing appeared to be an invention rather than a genuine deal.

The *Kleiman v Wright* case also saw the plot thicken over the payment to MJF, with an email from Wright to Ira Kleiman and Andrew Sommer dated 23 April 2014 making it abundantly clear how much Wright had budgeted for the software:

> *I have sold all the BTC that I plan to sell for now. In doing what we wanted to do, Dave and I arranged for the sale of around 500,000 BTC so that we could have access to Core Banking software.*

This, of course, presented a problem for Wright, given the vastly different figures touted compared to his previous submissions to the ATO and to the court. His solution was all too predictable: he claimed that he 'did not send a single email that day' due to his presence in various meetings and laid the blame at the feet of a familiar foe:

> *...this is a fraudulently fabricated document involving Ira and other people that I was not involved in the sending of.*

Incidentally, the email in question was a beast, clocking in at almost 2,000 words and covering a wide range of issues, including Wright and Dave Kleiman's history, their plans for the future, details about Wright's trusts and his companies, financial projections for the following years, how much his code was worth and more. It is highly unlikely that Ira Kleiman would have had the inclination, resolve or resources to be able to fake a 2,000-word email covering such minutiae, even with help from others. It's also worth noting that the email was sent at 6.14 p.m. in Australia when Wright's meetings could easily have concluded. Wright was also challenged over the payment during a March 2020 deposition for the *Kleiman v Wright* case, where he claimed, falsely, that he had paid MJF Mining in 'a combination of bitcoin directly to them and as a direct assignment with them as an agent.'

Wright discussed the MJF Mining deal in *Hero/Villain* (in which Mark Ferrier is erroneously called 'Michael'), where he told Mark Eglinton, 'I got the damn software, but I never got the bank launched.' This, as we know, undermines the purpose of Wright's lawsuit against Ferrier, while his claim over the reason why Denariuz failed to launch is also erroneous: Wright blamed this on Silk Road tarring the Bitcoin industry with the 'crime' brush, but it was lack of funds due to frozen rebates that really killed the company.

We will cover the financial impact of Wright's failed attempts over his MJF Mining tax rebates later in the book, but the question we have to ask at this point is: how much of Wright's story is actually true? We know that Wright never paid Ferrier because at least five of the Bitcoin addresses never belonged to him, with the whole lot almost certainly taken from the Bitcoin rich list. We also know that the ATO found all the documentation surrounding the contracts to be fraudulent. If Wright never paid Ferrier, then did the deal actually happen? The notion that Wright, on the verge of bankruptcy, would hand over $59 million to a man he met at a conference, $20 million of which was for gold speculating, is frankly ludicrous. This, when combined with Wright's fraudulent evidence and the knowledge that Mark Ferrier was a confidence trickster, leads us to conclude that there was almost certainly no deal between him and Craig Wright, unless it was for some dirty magazines.

In the absence of a deal, we next need to ask if there was even a relationship between the two. The story of Ferrier and Wright meeting at a mining conference at which Wright was speaking is hard to swallow, especially as Wright couldn't remember in his heavily detailed account of their interactions which conference it was, meaning we can't check. We do have an account of sorts from Ferrier, who was approached by *The Australian* newspaper following the *WIRED* and *Gizmodo* pieces in 2015; Ferrier said that he had 'never met' Wright and had not been paid 'one cent' by him. This is the extent of the comment from Ferrier on their alleged relationship, leaving us with the unpalatable decision of which of the two fraudsters to trust.

If we are to believe that Wright's deal with MJF is nothing but fantasy, how and why did he land on Mark Ferrier and his gold contracts at all? The answer could be as simple as sheer opportunism. The details regarding Ferrier's deal with Paynes all made it into the public domain following his arrest, and, perhaps buoyed by the success (at the time) of his $57 million W&K gambit, Wright simply implanted himself into the story as one of Ferrier's victims, using the gold scam to try and make it more believable. Wright might have gotten away with it had the claim been for a smaller amount, but the ATO was never going to wave through a rebate on $16 million worth of software bought in bitcoins from a fraudster, which was conducted over Skype and BitMessage.

Assuming this is the real story, Wright's decision to also use Ferrier for the software ploy was his biggest mistake; there was nothing in Ferrier's background that even hinted at any knowledge of banking software, and so for Wright to install him as a broker who could facilitate multi-million dollar Bitcoin deals will have stretched the ATO's credulity to breaking point. It also asks several questions of Wright, who, so the story would go, was taken in by Ferrier's outlandish promises and paid him handsomely to supply products he had no history of handling. Even those with lower IQs than Wright, such as Albert Einstein and Stephen Hawking, certainly would have asked a question or two. As we have seen, however, such instances are typical of Wright, with multiple examples abounding throughout his career where he has made a blunder so obvious it is inconceivable that he thought he could get away with it. This is due either to his misplaced belief that he is smarter than those who seek to hold him to account or because he is so desperate to achieve certain goals that he fails to keep an objective viewpoint over crucial matters. The pattern of behaviour we see throughout the MJF story, from the unverifiable historical details treated as fact to the changing story and the forged evidence, all with the aim of achieving a backdoor to wealth, is something we have witnessed many times in this story to date and which we will continue to see over the next decade of Wright's life.

The MJF affair played a big part in the ATO's assessment of Wright's companies and the penalties it eventually issued to him, sitting alongside and indeed intermingling with the Professor Rees affair, the W&K IP grab and more. These stories, and Wright's actions concerning them, provide us with a level of hypocrisy that is staggering in its audaciousness: the man who would in later years rail against Bitcoin's use as a 'crime coin', used by the worst kind of people to exact their terrible crimes, had been accused by the ATO of utilising the exact same medium to try and defraud the Australian taxpayer out of more than $10 million.

The software Wright claimed to have obtained through Mark Ferrier formed the bedrock of the operations within his Hotwire group, a group that Wright had envisioned would, on paper at least, cater for all the applications one could think of on the Bitcoin blockchain. It didn't take long, however, for the ATO to smell a rat over Hotwire, helped in no small measure by the droppings Wright left in his wake through episodes such as the Professor Rees and MFJ affairs. Once they got the scent, it didn't take them long to locate the nest, leaving Wright staring down the barrel of the exterminator's gun.

Chapter 15 – Failure to Launch

The formation of Hotwire on 2 June 2013 should have been the spark that lit the rocket of Craig Wright's Bitcoin dreams. The blockchain technology that underpinned Bitcoin was gaining traction, and there was already an appetite to see what it could achieve. The stage was set for a company to take the lead in developing applications that would accelerate the adoption of blockchain technology and Bitcoin itself. With the potent combination of his recently gained interest in Bitcoin and his computing talents, Wright was in a prime position to lead this charge, and his Hotwire group of companies seemed poised to be that driving force. Instead, according to the ATO, Wright chose to use his advantage to create what the agency alleged was a Bitcoin laundrette, which operated with one goal: to advance his ever-evolving tax fraud.

The official announcement of Hotwire's launch came on 15 September 2013, three months after its formation, with Wright breaking the news through his blog. Hotwire, he said, was the result of fifteen years of planning, four years of development and a 'five-year, $x million development budget', with Wright declaring that the group's multi-faceted mission was to 'make the world wiser and better', 'inspire enduring optimism and trust' and 'create value and make a difference'. The word 'Bitcoin' was not mentioned once in the post, with Wright adding that further details would be 'slowly revealed' over time. Wright alluded to this period during a talk in 2019, claiming, 'In the days when no one knew about Bitcoin, I had forty-five staff in Australia working on Bitcoin projects, basically secretly under the radar.' The ATO, however, was more interested in how Hotwire had been funded, especially given that the companies in the group were theoretically reliant on the software sourced by Mark Ferrier, the material provided by Professor Rees and the IP from W&K, all of which was already, or soon would be, in the ATO's crosshairs. Leading internet security blogger and

Craig Wright critic Nik Cubrilovic explained in his May 2016 piece, 'Craig Wright is Not Satoshi Nakamoto', how Hotwire had been funded:

> *What Wright did was establish [Hotwire] for the purpose of carrying out research and development on e-learning software it had acquired from Wright's own trust. Wright would inject $30 million in Bitcoin to fund the company, $29 million of which would be paid to Wright's trust to acquire the software and $1 million of which would fund operational costs – including an office in Sydney and 40 employees.*

Wright's initial claim to the ATO was that he transferred an 'initial bitcoin wallet' worth nearly $33 million to Hotwire as a capital subscription, confirming in December 2013 that this was paid for with bitcoins. Eight months later, however, when the investigation into his companies and their use of bitcoins was ramping up, Wright told them the subscription had, in fact, been funded by rights to call on bitcoins held by a trust in the Seychelles (the as-yet-unnamed Tulip Trust).

Despite Hotwire's grand ambitions, the first thing it did post-formation had nothing to do with Bitcoin; it filed two batches of GST rebates, one relating to $8.25 million in capital purchases and another regarding $3.2 million in non-capital purchases. These, Wright said in emails to Jamie Wilson and others, had been 'processed and accepted' by the ATO and noted that they were 'contingent of the NSW Supreme court action', proving that they were directly related to the action against W&K, which had only just begun. Conscious of the fact that he was submitting these rebates as part of the 2012-13 tax year in order to get them sooner, Wright noted, 'We just need to ensure that the Court judgement is completed by August 30.' Tellingly, Wright also noted, 'As the assets to come in from the US are not [Australia], there is not GST on supply.' It's not clear how Wright came to this understanding, but it proved to be expensively incorrect.

The official launch of Hotwire came at an already troubling time for Craig Wright. Just a month prior, he had been hauled in by the ATO on two occasions a week apart to explain his justification for millions of dollars in tax rebates and deductions by his companies in the 2012/13 tax year. These included Coin-Exch, with Wright telling the ATO that the company had been funded from a trust in Panama, having told its agents several times up to that point that the trust was located in the Seychelles. Wright also admitted in these interviews that there was, as the ATO reported it, 'no business plan for Coin-Exch', adding that the company didn't expect to have any incomings for the 'foreseeable future' but that it would be spending millions to establish itself. Wright would, naturally, be claiming these costs back. Wright also admitted to having backdated invoices to ensure they qualified for the prior tax year, specifically the deals concerning the IP from W&K, which the ATO had expressly told him not to do, something he later denied, claiming that it is 'legally permissible to engage in transactions and purchases on behalf of a company before the official registration of that company has taken place'. He changed tack in an October 2023 filing for the *Tulip Trading Ltd v Bitcoin Association for BSV & Ors* case, however, claiming that the invoices were 'sent to the ATO by Ira Kleiman, who believed that if he could force the company into liquidation it would provide him with money.'

Perhaps unsurprisingly, Jamie Wilson was kept at arm's length from the W&K claims as they made their way through the court system, telling his deponent for the *Kleiman v Wright* case that getting hold of updates from Wright was a 'very slow feed' because 'Craig is not forthcoming with information.' Eventually, however, Wilson got the background on the W&K situation as well as some documentation that supposedly backed up Wright's position in the lawsuits pertaining to it. Wright did not elucidate on the level of Dave Kleiman's involvement or exactly what the pair had supposedly been up to with W&K, but Wilson's enquiries, combined with the analysis of the income from Wright's other Hotwire companies, were starting to concern him:

> *I only understood later on, when I was going through the paperwork to do the R&D, that all of the material of the break up of the money that Dave Kleiman was actually on all of these applications, all of the grants for the…U.S. government. So, that is how I started to become aware of it…the longer I was there, the more I started to realize that this is not the correct way of doing business.*

Wilson, of course, was already aware of Wright's plan to split the IP into portions that he thought best suited the different Hotwire companies, claiming GST rebates for each inter-company transfer. And Wilson wasn't the only one. Wright sought a private ruling from the ATO in August 2013 over the tax status of intellectual property brought in from abroad, tax that Wright had told his associates would not be levied and, therefore, had not been included in the Coin-

Exch accounts for 2012/13. In filing for his private ruling, Wright told the ATO about the $57 million worth of IP coming in from W&K and his plan to divide it up, backing up his case over its taxation with three agreements between Hotwire, Coin-Exch and Cloudcroft. The ATO noted, however, that the agreements conflicted with similar arrangements Wright had already submitted for the same companies, to which Wright responded by saying that the first round of invoices were erroneous. The ATO considered his request and, in September, ruled on it:

> There are no provisions in the GST law that would make your proposed supplies GST-free or input taxed. While there is provision in the GST law for the GST-free supply of rights either for use outside Australia or in limited circumstances to an entity outside Australia, this is not contemplated in your contracted arrangements.

This ruling meant that Wright now not only owed GST on all the IP that had come in from W&K, but he had also alerted the ATO as to what was coming down the pipeline; in early October, it informed Wright that Hotwire was under audit, just two weeks after Wright had announced its launch. This would prove to be the striking of the match that would eventually burn down Wright's Potemkin village and, following that, his descent into the Satoshi Nakamoto fraud that would eventually ruin him.

This was all still at least two years away, but Wright's activities in this field did have an immediate impact: as Jamie Wilson filed more and more invoices concerning the as-yet undelivered IP, he became so concerned with what he saw that he no longer wanted to be a part of it. Wilson resigned from Wright's group of companies on 23 October 2013, expanding on his rationale and his feelings at the time during his testimony for the *Kleiman v Wright* case:

> ...I didn't agree on the employment of the staff and the buildup of these companies without understanding, the full understanding, of where the funding was coming from. So, I know there was a lot of Bitcoin there. However, when I started to have a look at the R&D and the claiming of the R&D...for the Australia Federal Government I didn't feel comfortable when I noticed that these amounts were from the U.S....and I am still not aware if the money actually was funded by the U.S. government. And I thought, well hang on, the Supreme Court of Australia

has turned around and brought this IP into Australia, and now Craig is turning around and claiming the R&D on this money, that was paid by the U.S. government. And I thought, this to me looks fraud. And, I want nothing to do with it.

This shows that Wright had told Wilson that the DHS had funded the W&K projects, a lie he would repeat to Ira Kleiman in February 2014, telling the latter that he and Dave Kleiman had secured US$5.85 million in 'Dept of Homeland Security and Australian government' funding. However, this clashes with Wright's claim to the ATO that he had never confirmed the funding with Dave Kleiman, once again illustrating his propensity to change a story when it suits him.

As we can expect concerning someone whom he perceived to have wronged him, Craig Wright has a different version of events concerning the actions of Jamie Wilson. In a 2019 blog post, Wright claimed he had fired Wilson because his CFO 'fabricated documents…and then left me without even giving me access to all of the documents he had been working on.' Wright used this latter complaint as a reason behind the company's accounting mess that eventually led to a six-figure penalty from the ATO. Wright's allegations over Wilson relate to the Cryptoloc data encryption software that he and Wilson were working on at the time. Wilson began developing Cryptoloc on his own in 2010, eventually turning it into his life's work, bringing Wright on board in 2012 to tap into his technical expertise. Wright disputes this, telling his followers in June 2019 that Cryptoloc was 'a broken implementation of my patent' that Wilson 'fraudulantly assigned away'. Wright added during the *Kleiman v Wright* trial that the patent belonged to him and that Wilson had tried to secretly sell Cryptoloc to Google in 2013, hypocritically accusing Wilson of forging his signature to do so. Wilson was not cross-examined over these allegations by Wright's lawyers, which is reflective of their legitimacy. Wright's claim that Wilson was fired is also provably false: when his legal team engaged a forensic analyst to try and prove that it was Wilson who signed the W&K Consent Order, they used the signature on Wilson's resignation letter as the control sample. Nevertheless, Craig Wright continues to state as fact that Wilson tried to steal Cryptoloc from him and sell it and that he fired him as a result.

The ATO's first port of call concerning its investigation of Hotwire was to ask Wright where the $30 million in seed money had come from. Wright argued that discussions over Hotwire were, at that time, 'an area of utmost secrecy', adding that the company 'controls 5% of the global Bitcoin market', a boast that might have been true had the company actually owned any of the addresses Wright had told the ATO that it did. Wright doubled down on the covert nature of his plans for Hotwire, and in particular his Bitcoin bank, Denariuz, by saying that it was 'beyond secret' but promised more information in due course. This he eventually offered, explaining that his companies controlled $230 million in funds, $165 million of which was formed of bitcoins held in a series of addresses. However, as the ATO was to later note, the coins in these addresses were only worth $70 million at the time.

Wright's attempts to prove the sources of Hotwire's wealth went down like a concrete zeppelin, and the ATO informed him on 9 October, just five days into its audit, that it was retaining a $3.1 million GST refund. This left Hotwire in dire straits right from the off, with Wright responding to the ATO three days later to inform it that he planned to provide evidence to counter its arguments that his deals with companies, including Al Baraka, were not genuine and that he could call on the capital he said Hotwire owned. Wright promised to supply contracts and evidence of bitcoin holdings and transfers, including a 'letter of support' from Saleh Abdullah Kamel, the billionaire chairman and founder of the Dallah al Baraka Group. The very idea that Wright was hoping to obtain a personal letter from the founder and chairman of the entire Dallah al Baraka group over a single deal conducted by a third party who had been arrested for fraud two weeks prior is one of the more outlandish of Wright's many tall tales. It would almost certainly have been inauthentic had it ever been attempted, and in some ways, it is a shame the letter was never produced.

Wright also provided the ATO with the statutory declaration from New South Wales solicitor Stephen D'Emilio, initially used for the W&K IP grab. In it, D'Emilio declared that he had viewed five Bitcoin addresses on Wright's phone over which it appeared Wright had control, but the ATO didn't buy the story. Their suspicions were proved right in May 2019 when Wright produced an updated version of the declaration to his online followers, which was almost identical to its predecessor, except for the rather crucial difference that all five addresses had been swapped out for alternatives. Two of the expunged addresses were the troublesome 1Feex and 1933p addresses, while a third, beginning 16cou, had, just two days earlier, been cryptographically signed by its owner:

Address 16cou7Ht6WjTzuFyDBnht9hmvXytg6XdVT does not belong to Satoshi or to Craig Wright. Craig is a liar and a fraud.

The message, which was verified by third parties, was later attributed to Craig Wright's business partner-turned-nemesis, Roger Ver. Wright's supporters claimed that the new version of the declaration was the real one and that the copy obtained by the ATO was a fake used to implicate him. All would become clear, they said, when Wright submitted the replacement as evidence in the *Kleiman v Wright* case. Indeed, Wright was questioned about the declaration in his March 2020 deposition for the *Kleiman v Wright* case, where he claimed, 'I cannot tell you from memory which Bitcoin addresses will or will not be correct.' This, of course, would have been the perfect opportunity to produce his 'genuine' document, but Wright failed to do so, likely having seen how quickly it had been torn apart by his critics. It has never been referenced since.

Following the ATO's scepticism over his alleged ownership of the Bitcoin addresses, Wright provided screenshots of a Bitcoin wallet containing the addresses the company supposedly controlled. However, this only served to harm his case: further, the ATO noted that one address was 'written in a different font to the rest of the text within the software', which it said pointed to manipulation. In the email, Wright had the gall to discuss in glowing terms two of the men he had abused for financial gain:

David Reese and David Kleiman have both been central parts of this project. Both of these gentlemen, who I had the good fortune to call friends, passed away this year. David Reese was a friend of my grandfather before he died of Parkinson's. Dave Kleiman was my best friend.

We already know the extent of Dave Kleiman's activity with Wright's businesses, most of which involves Wright retrospectively placing Kleiman where he needed him following his death in April 2013, and it is worth noting that there is no suggestion anywhere that Professor Rees was ever diagnosed with Parkinson's.

Wright's attempt to get the ATO to refund him the GST on his $57 million IP grab from W&K appears to have been accompanied by a second request, possibly filed earlier, over the treatment of Bitcoin. Wright had argued that bitcoins should be treated as a form of currency rather than as a commodity, which would preclude GST charges on their movement. Such a ruling would have dramatically reduced the GST Wright would owe and would have made achieving future refunds much easier, so it is immediately clear why he attempted it. It would also have made Australia the first country in the world to formally acknowledge Bitcoin as a form of money, something that, as we can see from a 27 September 2013 email Wright sent to some of his staff, he believed was going to happen:

> *The ATO will be swarmed with press after this and we expect the quanta of the ruling to be global news. A five million dollar Bitcoin fund was world news and TV globally, we make this look like a mum and pop operation from the Winkly [Winklevoss] bros. That stated, we want this to be global news without our name being noted as yet. I do not know how many and how deep the journalists will be coming, but I know I have had Forbes and the WSJ already digging. Right now, we are sitting on one of the biggest stories globally and we are not going to talk.*

Wright may have been denigrating the Winklevoss brothers here, but he changed his tune a few months later when he tried to seek an introduction to Tyler Winklevoss through a former associate, Ben Wright. Craig Wright said that he had 'a few things that will interest them' given the twins' involvement in Bitcoin, but it seems that Tyler wasn't exactly won over by the approach: in 2020, he mockingly tweeted, 'Have you spoken to Craig Wright?' when former Mayor of Toronto, Norm Kelly, asked if anyone genuinely understood Bitcoin. Wright tried to distance himself from the message during the *Kleiman v Wright* trial the following year, saying that it 'wasn't written by me' and that the printout was 'a document from LinkedIn that I don't run, even now'.

Unfortunately for Wright, the ATO's press office remained resolutely unswarmed when, in December 2013, the agency dismissed Wright's request, ruling that it would not change its definition of Bitcoin. This dealt a further blow to Wright's attempt to obtain tax rebates for all his bitcoin transfers, but it came with more problems: the ruling arrived two days before Christmas *after* several of Wright's companies had submitted a batch of Business Activity Statements (BASs) which included hefty bitcoin transfers between them. The ATO's records stated that the ruling had been made on 30 September, before the BAS filings were made, meaning that Wright's companies, including Hotwire, were technically claiming tax rebates they weren't entitled to. Wright insisted that the

ATO had made the ruling on 29 November, backdated it to 30 September and only sent it to his representative, Andrew Sommer, on 23 December, by which time the filings had been assessed and rejected on the basis of the ruling. Wright stated in a February 2014 meeting with the ATO that a contact inside the Internal Fraud and Investigations department had told him of the backdating but declined to reveal the name of his source. In response, the ATO confirmed that it had sent the letter to the appropriate address at the appropriate time and never admitted fault over the matter, but this only served to fan the flames of Wright's allegations of a conspiracy against him. In the wake of the ATO's rejection of Wright's attempted reclassification of Bitcoin, he appealed to the government, pitching Bitcoin to Australia's Assistant Treasurer, Arthur Sinodinos, presenting himself as a 'leading international expert in cryptography' in his attempt to bring more firepower to bear against the ATO. However, his entreaties seem to have gained little traction with Mr. Sinodinos, who failed to join Wright's campaign.

Given how the year ended for him, we can infer that Craig Wright was in a bittersweet frame of mind as he saw out 2013; in November, he had been granted the $57 million in IP from W&K and married Ramona Watts, but the ATO was already digging into his funding of Hotwire and how it was making its money. He can't have been too concerned, however, given that in an email to Jamie Wilson, he joked that it was time to 'party' over the measly $14 GST bill he had calculated for the company for the 2012/13 tax year. This was based on his belief that he was going to receive GST rebates on the IP imported from W&K and his inter-company bitcoin transfers, but Wright was about to discover that his interpretation of the taxation rules was vastly different than those of the ATO, which was about to shut down Wright's party before he had even laid out the canapés.

Chapter 16 – The Hacker Hacked

Craig Wright began 2014 with a trip to Singapore, which he says he used to pull a 'little stunt' on the ATO to force its hand over its handling of Bitcoin taxation. In a May 2019 blog post, Wright said that he bought 31,000 bitcoins (worth $30 million at the time) from an overseas exchange, which led to a $3 million GST bill. He then sold the coins to himself and took them to Singapore in the form of a paper wallet, informing the customs officials at Sydney Airport that he was taking $30 million out of the country:

> *It was a rather surreal experience; the poor guy at the counter of the tourist refund centre did not know what to do. The computer had a field in the database that had a maximum value of $9,999,999.99, and he could not enter the amount that I was taking.*

An already tall tale grew taller two months later when Wright increased the number of bitcoins involved in the story to 55,000 for the benefit of his online followers. However, this pales into insignificance when we consider that, at the very moment he was blowing $30 million on bitcoins for a stunt, Wright was complaining that the ATO was putting Hotwire in jeopardy by withholding a comparatively paltry $3.1 million tax rebate.

Wright claimed that his Singapore jaunt was designed to put further pressure on the ATO to strip GST from Bitcoin transfers, but it didn't work; Wright's request was once again rejected, which he put down to him being a 'rather brash individual' who had mistakenly taken matters into his own hands rather than letting his lawyers handle discussions. Wright added that, despite rejecting his particular request over the treatment of Bitcoin, his efforts finally bore fruit:

In looking at it, the tax office quickly realised how easy it would be to abuse the GST system if GST was applied to Bitcoin. Which was of course the point I was trying to make.

While the ATO did eventually change its ruling over the treatment of Bitcoin with regard to GST, it certainly didn't do it 'quickly' or because of Wright's alleged stunt; it ruled in August 2014 that bitcoins should be considered a form of property, before it changed its mind in 2017 and ruled that, for GST purposes only, it equated to a form of currency. During the *Kleiman v Wright* trial in 2021, Wright claimed, naturally, that this change was 'my private ruling'.

Wright repurposed this story for the *Tulip Trading Ltd v Bitcoin Association for BSV & Ors* case in 2023, whereupon he suddenly remembered that one of the addresses within the wallet taken to Singapore was the 12ib7 address, an address central to the case. Having been pressed for months to explain how the 12ib7 address came into his possession in the first place, Wright eventually claimed that the coins had been deposited there having been purchased through WMIRK, the same Russian exchange allegedly used to buy the 1Feex coins. He could not, however, 'be certain as to the date or method of acquisition.' Wright seemed to have forgotten that, ten years earlier, he told the ATO that the 12ib7 address was one of a number that mysteriously came into his control through 'a matter of fate and other circumstances' rather than buying them from WMIRK.

While Wright was busy running his companies, handling the ATO investigations and bobbing off to Singapore for tax stunts, someone was taking advantage of his lack of attention by editing entries on his blog, 'Cracked, InSecure and Generally Broken'. Oddly, they weren't deleting entries or adding anything nefarious but were instead inserting subtle references to Bitcoin, cryptocurrencies, blockchain and the ATO. The amendments seeded these references at the relevant points in history to back up the idea that Wright was behind Bitcoin and had fought with the ATO over it, resulting in timely comments that were often totally out of context with the rest of the post. Seeing as Wright was never caught red-handed amending a blog post, we can't state categorically that it was he who made the changes, but any TV detective worth their salt would have recognised instantly that such was Wright's means, motive and opportunity when it came to the crime that the case would have been wrapped up before the first advert break. What the perpetrator didn't seem to realise, however, or was confident that they could explain away, was that Internet archives had taken snapshots of the blog posts in their original form before the changes had been made, allowing casual browsers an easy opportunity to put together a timeline of edits.

Some of the edited blog posts mentioned Bitcoin in an oblique way, while others were more blatant, with one from 10 January 2009 simply entitled 'Bitcoin' being a frequently cited example. The post discussed Wright's abandoned e-gold idea, saying that it had gone 'down the toilet', but added that something else had taken its place:

The Beta of Bitcoin is tomorrow. This is decentralized... We try it until it works. Some good coders on this.

The miscreant clearly hadn't done their homework: Satoshi didn't put Bitcoin into a Beta release until October 2009, but this wasn't the only error. The editor may have been trying to tie this post in with a famous tweet from early Bitcoin developer Hal Finney dated 11 January, which simply proclaimed, 'Running bitcoin'. This would have been the 'tomorrow' to which Wright's post referred, but this would have been wrong too; Bitcoin had been running, as Satoshi would have known, since 3 January 2009. A search of the Internet archives reveals that the post was published not in 2009 but in June 2014 and backdated to the earlier date. It was then re-edited in May 2015 to strip out all the content and change the title to 'Bitcoin – AKA bloody nosey you be...', using the less common spelling of 'nosey' seen in other communications from Wright. A later update, which the poster claims was made on 25 September 2015, adds the line, 'It does always surprise me how at times the best place to hide it right in the open.' This leaves us with two scenarios. The first is that a third party found a way into Wright's blog and amended his posts to seed incorrect Bitcoin references, possibly hoping that an experienced Bitcoiner might stumble across them, spot the inaccuracies and call him out over them. This included re-editing one of the posts a year later. Alternatively, they may not have realised that the information they were including was wrong, which might suggest they genuinely wanted Wright to be recognised as Satoshi. Setting aside the fact that this person managed to hack into the blog account of a self-professed global cybersecurity expert, all of this was carried out with the very real risk that Wright might one day come across the altered posts and remove them. Taking these factors into consideration, the idea that someone else was behind the backdating and editing of these posts leaves us with more questions than answers.

The second scenario is that Craig Wright wrote the posts and backdated them to 2009 in an attempt to back up his recently made claims that he was Satoshi Nakamoto, not realising at the time that what he was writing was incorrect. When he did realise this in May 2015, he edited a key post to leave just the title and stripped out the incriminating content. We'll leave the reader to decide which is the most likely turn of events, but it's worth noting that when Wright was accused of faking the Bitcoin Beta blog post on Reddit in 2017, he admitted to having written it, saying he had done so in order 'to throw Wired'.

As well as slipping in references to Bitcoin in Wright's blog posts, the editor was also careful to insert mentions of the very Bitcoin trusts the ATO had raised doubts over, which is where the previously mentioned 'small minded' blog post purportedly from March 2011 makes an appearance. This edit, too, was made around June 2014, some four months after Wright's decision to don the Satoshi mask. What's interesting to note is that these blog posts were being amended before Wright had even bought TTL from Abacus, and yet they were already being discussed by the ATO. Once again, we are being asked to believe that either a third party had intimate knowledge of Wright's plans and ATO entanglements months in advance and posted about them without his knowledge, or Wright edited and backdated the posts to back up his story with the ATO. It should be remembered that Wright used these backdated posts as evidence in his battle with the agency, where he claimed to have written them, only to disavow them during the *Kleiman v Wright* trial after they were used against him.

The blog editor wasn't just adding things to Wright's blog posts retrospectively; they were removing bits, too. One such example was on, of all things, Wright's post dedicated to the memory of Dave Kleiman, which included the line, 'It was Dave's Vistomail account that allowed me to start some of my more radical ideas.' This line was present in July 2013, three months after Kleiman's death, with Kleiman's ownership of the Vistomail account featuring in a February 2014 email from Wright to Ira Kleiman. By November 2015, however, it had been removed. Joseph Gardling believes that this removal reinforces the idea that Wright capitalised on Kleiman's death fairly soon after it:

> Given that he started his Bitcoin fraud shortly after Dave died, I think it's still true — he likely added [the line] between April and July [2013].

Wright was presented with this discrepancy during the *Kleiman v Wright* trial, where he claimed that the July 2013 version 'is not the original version either', suggesting that there had been skulduggery with the posting of the tribute:

> COUNSEL: But you wrote it, Dr. Wright?
>
> WRIGHT: I didn't write this one. I wrote a document. Many times the documents I have had have been edited and changed.

The blog amender wasn't just carrying out text edits, either. Gardling pointed out one notable example in 2021, which he describes as his favourite blog forgery: a November 2008 blog post on the subject of entropy which featured a long PGP key as its footer and a request from the author that readers 'use the public key below to discuss this and other crypto matters.' However, seeing as 'crypto' wasn't even a thing in November 2008, with Bitcoin being nothing more than a barely-read whitepaper, this request would have been futile. If that wasn't big enough a breadcrumb to leave behind, the writer had doubled down and inserted a PGP key linked to Satoshi Nakamoto. This was something that would not be obvious at first glance but would be spotted if researched by those in the know, allowing that person to make the link and 'unmask' Wright. However, as Gardling pointed out, it carried a critical mistake:

> *Just to be clear what happened here: Craig created a backdated 'Satoshi' PGP key in 2014 and uploaded it to the MIT keyserver. He then searched for an old blog post around the time the whitepaper was released. He then copied the PGP info from the key server into that old post. But he didn't realize that the MIT keyserver lists the version of its software in that PGP output. Here, it's 1.1.4, which was released in late 2012 and integrated into the MIT keyserver in late 2013.*

Wright's defence of these amended blog posts has, it will be no surprise to learn, changed over the years. When challenged on the backdated posts during a talk at the Oxford Union in June 2019, Wright claimed that the fact that the pages contained alterations didn't mean they had been backdated:

> *So the argument is: there are multiple different versions of web pages that have existed. Yes, things have been turned off and whatever else. That doesn't mean they were backdated.*

Wright then went down a familiar path, alleging that Greg Maxwell 'was sending documents that were stolen from my company' to *WIRED* and *Gizmodo*, which had nothing to do with the blog posts, before moving away from them altogether. Wright circled back to argue that the manipulated posts were not valid evidence because the original page had been deleted, so there was nothing to prove that the references hadn't been there in the first place. However, this theory meant that someone had to have removed the references at some point (not captured by Internet archives) and then re-added them years later, which made little to no sense.

Under questioning during the *Kleiman v Wright* trial two years later, Wright seemed to admit that the posts had been backdated but denied involvement, saying that his blog was 'run under my name and under my instruction' by staff. While he was responsible for the initial content, he said, he had nothing to do with the mechanics of the blog or future edits. These amended blog posts represent a handful of times when Wright's blog or email accounts have allegedly been compromised, resulting in the posting of content that has been used to inflict costly legal defeats against him over the years. The same goes for his social media accounts, as Wright relayed in a 2020 interview:

> *I don't actually manage any of my social media other than Slack, so I can't even say what was on anything like that...I don't run LinkedIn, I don't run Facebook, I don't have a Twitter account, so I won't vouch for anything that any of these things say because I don't run social media.*

Despite Wright's certainty over his subscriber-only Slack channel being his sole outlet, he was apparently unsure of one rather important aspect the following year during the *Kleiman v Wright* trial: when asked if 'CSW' was his handle on Slack, Wright responded, 'I don't actually know, but it could be, yes.' The year prior, during a March 2020 deposition for the case, Wright was asked if he ever let third parties comment under his name in his Slack group, to which he responded, 'No, I do not.' Four years later, however, in order to excuse the content of certain problematic posts, Wright claimed during the *COPA v Wright* trial that 'other people at nChain' had been writing on the platform in his name since 2018. This would have come as a shock to members of the Slack group, who paid a monthly subscription for the service, with one of the perks being that they got to chat directly with Craig Wright. Now, it seemed they might have been chatting with a surrogate, with Wright not even knowing the names of his impersonators.

In dismissing the personal management of his social media channels, Wright was clearly attempting to absolve himself of criticism over any social media post or comment that might come back to bite him. This theory comes with a caveat, however: Wright was apparently happy to entrust his blog and social media accounts to third parties for over a decade, in some cases to unknown individuals, despite believing he was a target for hackers during this entire period. This includes supposedly offloading a new Twitter account made after the original was lost to hackers who stole the credentials from Uyen Nguyen and continuing to entrust his Slack account to nChain staffers even after the Slack group itself suffered a security breach in May 2020. Wright was happy to do this even after telling Andrew O'Hagan that a 'disgruntled employee' was to blame for leaking the documents that led to the *WIRED* and *Gizmodo* stories in 2015. In addition, it's worth noting that Wright's contentment over his social media arrangements wasn't seemingly shaken by the alleged theft in February 2020 of over a billion dollars' worth of cryptocurrencies after his home network was compromised (a claim later found to have been completely without merit). If Wright had experienced all this and was still allowing strangers to look after his social media accounts, then one has to question the IT security qualifications he possesses.

Wright finally acknowledged the error of his ways in this regard in an August 2024 tweet, posted from a newly created account:

> *I generally have not managed any social media accounts. I shall be doing this here. The outsourcing of this has not resulted in any good results.*

This, of course, was an understatement of the size of Wright's ego.

As well as ne'er-do-wells fiddling with his blog posts, Wright claims that they were also busy inventing emails concerning him, despite them happening to back up certain of his claims at crucial points. We have already seen emails involving Wright and third parties that have been proven false, with the third parties in question often unaware of their supposed involvement in Wright's schemes until their names pop up in evidence. One example is an email exchange between Dave Kleiman and Uyen Nguyen, purportedly from December 2012. In the email, Kleiman offers Nguyen a directorship of W&K and then responds to her alleged acceptance, although her side of the discussion has never been published. This email was crucial in Wright obtaining that seven-figure sum in IP from W&K, so we can assume that, if false, it was written solely with this purpose in mind. Dr Edman analysed the email for the *Kleiman v Wright* case, where he found a plethora of issues and inconsistencies, including that the PGP key purportedly used by Dave Kleiman was created on 12 March 2014, nearly a year after his death, on a computer in an Australian time zone. Equally incriminating was an email on Wright's system which was sent from Wright to himself 'on or about' 16 April 2014, the content of which was identical to the content of the Dave Kleiman-Uyen Nguyen email, down to the backdated PGP key and misspelling of 'apppointment'.

Worse for Wright was that the source for the email he had sent himself was an email that Dave Kleiman had sent to a mailing list in October 2012, with the recipient's name changed to Uyen Nguyen and the contents altered to reflect her acceptance of the W&K directorship. This narrowed the list of potential forgers down to someone on that list of recipients, a list that just so happened to include Craig Wright. Dr Edman ruled, unsurprisingly, that the Kleiman-Nguyen email was a forgery, which also eviscerated the legitimacy of the other emails in the chain. Wright, naturally, blamed his various nemeses for creating the fake email once this was exposed, but if someone other than Craig Wright had been behind the forgery, they did it by accessing a legitimate email from Wright to himself and using it to forge an email conversation between two different people with the sole purpose of assisting Wright in obtaining $57 million in IP, just at the time the ATO was looking into the matter. The circumstantial evidence against Wright is already damning, but the idea of someone else creating the emails vanishes when we learn that Wright used this very email chain with the ATO as evidence to support his IP grab.

Wright seemingly took particular umbrage over the ATO's discovery of the dodgy PGP keys and hired digital forensic analysts Dr Nick Sharples and Dr Alan Batey to analyse it alongside other elements of the ATO's case against him. Unfortunately, the report hasn't been made public, but we get an idea of Batey's findings regarding the PGP key from the ATO's response to it:

> *We also reject the conclusion of Batey's PGP report. Given anyone can upload a key pair to the MIT key server with no proof of identity requirements, Batey is not in a position to state that the keys belonged to Mr Kleiman. We maintain that the creation dates of keys on the MIT*

key server and the time stamping of digital signatures can be easily manipulated by changing the time and date settings on the computer they are created on. The key purportedly used by Mr Kleiman...was created with an encryption algorithm that did not exist at the time it was purportedly created.

We end the examination of this particular set of emails by noting that the faked emails bringing Nguyen on board W&K were created just two weeks before W&K was reinstated in her name.

The ATO's investigation into Wright's companies led to it accusing Wright of faking contracts, bitcoin transactions, blog post entries, PGP keys, emails between third parties and more, all with the sole purpose of obtaining fraudulent tax rebates. One ATO report even hints that Wright might have faked a phone call to High Secured with ATO agents in attendance. Much of this activity is alleged to have taken place around February and March 2014, just as the ATO was ramping up its investigation into his tax rebate and deduction claims. This will be explained in more detail in the following chapter, but it's important to note that Wright has perpetually denied, in the face of overwhelming evidence and plain logic, that he was behind any of this fraudulent activity, even that which nobody else could have known about and which only benefited him.

If Craig Wright wasn't behind all this skulduggery, then who was? Here is where we can turn to another aspect of Craig Wright's history that is as indelibly connected to him as the Eiffel Tower is to Paris: hackers did it. According to Ramona Watts, in 2014, computers within Wright's organisations began getting 'very, very strange messages'. These messages, she claimed in her deposition for the *Kleiman v Wright* case, led to a realisation by Wright, Ramona and others that 'we had our computers hacked, our personal computers at home and the computers in the office.' According to Wright, their investigations led to the determination that 'certain individuals altered records within Hotwire' with the desire to 'cause me problems with the Australian government'. Wright expanded on this during the *Kleiman v Wright* trial:

> In altering records, they created a number of subverted files that were designed to keep the companies in audit and lead towards liquidation. Such was the goal...some of the same backdoors led to documents ending up

somehow with Mr Ira Kleiman, who is of course suing me through false pretences.

We will look at the accusations involving Ira Kleiman, the allegations of ATO collusion and the theory over certain files being doctored when we cover the trial in Volume II, but it's important to examine certain aspects of Wright's arguments when considering his claim to have been compromised.

We know that Wright says he was hacked by LulzSec and Anonymous in 2011, but he never mentioned anything about his systems and files being compromised in 2014 until the *Kleiman v Wright* case in 2018. In the four years in between, Wright had been shadowed by Andrew O'Hagan for 'The Satoshi Affair', conducted multiple interviews with journalists, discussed his company dealings with Ira Kleiman and supplied the ATO with reams of documents pertaining to their investigations of said companies. In all this correspondence, not once did Wright mention the discovery of nefarious activity on his systems that could have led to the tainting of certain documents. Even after he suspected this, he *still* sent documents to the ATO without saying a word, documents which turned out to be fraudulent. Had Wright genuinely been hacked in 2014, he would unhesitatingly have told the ATO what he has told every court and judge from the *Kleiman v Wright* trial onwards – that his systems were infiltrated and fraudulent documents placed on them in order to compromise him. Instead, as we saw earlier, when questioned over the dodgy documents by the ATO, Wright typically doubled down on their authenticity, only rolling out the hacker theory in 2018 to excuse the avalanche of fraud that Ira Kleiman's team was uncovering. Once he had loosed the story, it grew spectacularly, ballooning to encompass all documents taken from staff laptops, despite Wright initially using these self-same documents in his defence.

During the *COPA v Wright* trial, Wright added some flesh to the bones of his hacking theory:

Some of the staff had made a deal with Ira Kleiman and others and the belief that they had was that if the company goes into liquidation all the intellectual property can be just taken. They didn't understand that even if it goes into liquidation it's still property...They thought they could liquidate the companies by leaking false information about all this to the ATO.

As we have already alluded to, Wright went so far as to claim that Ira Kleiman used his position as a shareholder in Coin-Exch to knowingly file a fraudulent document with the ATO in order to harm Wright's battle with the agency. Ira Kleiman utterly denies this, and, indeed, it isn't clear how a shareholder would be able to obtain the authority to act in this capacity.

Wright has also come up with a reason why the creation dates of so many documents and emails are clustered around specific points in time, such as February and October 2014. This was propounded by Kurt Wuckert Jr, a self-titled 'Bitcoin historian' for *CoinGeek* and noted mouthpiece of the pro-Wright movement, in December 2021:

> In 2014 among the ATO investigation, it looks like employees of [Craig's] company basically...colluded with the Australian tax authority and his servers had to be rebuilt from scratch. So that was a major point where there was document loss and all metadata is basically updated to 2014, making it very difficult to prove time and place of files that happen before that point.

During the *COPA v Wright* trial, Wright was challenged over his suggestion that these server rebuilds affected the creation date of documents; Wright responded by doubling down on his theory in the face of expert testimony to the contrary. As with the hack story, Wright would have mentioned to the ATO that his server rebuilds pushed the creation date of multiple documents and emails to the date of the rebuild, especially those on which he was relying to prove his claims. Instead, he either reinforced their authenticity or offered up the various excuses we have already covered, only to roll out the server rebuild and hack stories years later as a blanket excuse that even covered the fake documents he had hired experts to verify as legitimate years earlier.

Wright's rationale for delaying the attribution of the forgeries to hackers and server rebuilds is that he wasn't aware of their full impact until 2016. By this time, the ATO had already handed down final decisions and penalty notices to some of his companies, suggesting that Wright had missed the chance to exonerate himself. However, much of the investigative work was done in 2015, when Wright could easily have said that he suspected something, and the appeals process would have allowed him to include this crucial information. There is no publicly available evidence to suggest that Wright ever mentioned the hacker theory to the ATO in any context, though, with the first private discussions of it coming in the wake of the 2015 'doxxings'.

When it comes to important details such as how the hacks were allegedly carried out and who was behind them, Wright kept largely quiet on this until his April 2019 deposition for the *Kleiman v Wright* case:

>   COUNSEL: *What are the names of the staff that stole information?*
>
>   WRIGHT: *I would need to double-check that. I do not want to go on record defaming someone who has not been formally charged or anything like this...I am trying to remember his name. There were two people in particular. Both of them were systems engineers. I really do not remember their names.*

Wright's desire to tread carefully around potential defamation of innocent parties lasted less than three months when, in a July 2019 blog post, he named longtime nemesis Greg Maxwell as the perpetrator:

> *Greg Maxwell was involved in AntiSec, and helped with the theft of thousands of copyrighted documents and other intellectual property. He broke into computer systems, altered records, and released such stolen information to the world. Yet he calls for me to be imprisoned as he claims I altered records.*

Maxwell remained the prime candidate until March 2020 when, in another deposition for the *Kleiman v Wright* case, Wright expanded his suspect pool. When questioned whether he had any idea who had tampered with an email between himself and Dave Kleiman which Wright didn't recognise, Wright suggested that a collection of IT workers at Hotwire could have 'formed into a group' with the aim of compromising his position with the ATO. Potential candidates included one Phillip Montecillo, a Hotwire business analyst who Wright said was 'in communications with a French bank to sell things', and also pointed the finger, again, at Jamie Wilson. In addition, Wright had no compunction in throwing Uyen Nguyen under the bus, saying that she had 'raised external capital and loans personally in America' which Wright said she did by forging his signature. This was a fine way to repay someone who had been more malleable than a plasticine doll for his benefit and had filled in as director and CEO of many of his companies whenever he needed (aside from the times when her appointments were backdated forgeries). Incidentally, Andrew O'Hagan was never able to get the full story of how the then-eighteen-year-old Nguyen was able to propel herself so rapidly through Wright's companies, mentioning only that by early 2016, Wright had begun to 'seem worried' about her and adding that he felt Wright was 'in the middle of a very complicated lie' when he talked about her. In return, Wright described Nguyen as being 'volatile, capricious and beyond control', adding that 'she wants to help and this always leads to trouble.'

Nguyen's role in Wright's ecosystem was brought up during the *COPA v Wright* trial, where an email to her from 'Satoshi Nakamoto' was pleaded by COPA to be a forgery. After this was confirmed, Wright massively played down Nguyen's role in his life and work, saying that she was merely 'an intern at my companies that I was training'. This paints a vastly different picture of Uyen Nguyen compared to the one painted by history and by Wright himself; not only did she take up multiple senior positions within his companies and look after his Twitter account for a spell, but Wright even credits her with penning what was effectively a love letter to an associate in 2015, which we will discuss in Volume II.

Wright's expanded suspect pool in that March 2020 deposition featured another notable addition, bringing in a by-now-familiar foe:

> *I believe that Ira Kleiman worked with other people who were fired from my organisation to fabricate this and many other documents. I believe that he knew that the document dates that were changed in 2014 would have been changed...that the administration I told you about where people are talking about e-mail headers and things like that changing on that date and being forensically differed, that was because we had gone through an administration and had to rebuild all the servers and import e-mails to a new domain...I believe that the only reason all of those documents purporting to be my forged documents that can be demonstrated to be involved with the administration and the changes of re-scanning are all because Mr. Kleiman and other people that used to work for me worked basically to take money. That he is a con man, a fraud and he is making up things for this court in order to steal or attempt to steal funds. That is my testimony.*

In an attempt to corroborate his claims, Wright's lawyers demanded all communications between Ira Kleiman and Blockstream so he could, in the words of Samson Mow, then Chief Strategy Officer of Blockstream, 'check if we were involved in hacking him and making all the Satoshi forgeries.' This search for evidence that Wright claimed to already possess unsurprisingly came to nought, with Mow adding, 'I couldn't make this up if I tried.'

Wright's mind was seemingly made up on the matter of the identity of the hacker-in-chief in November 2021 after Jamie Wilson's deposition was played in front of the jury and Wright himself during the *Kleiman v Wright* trial. As we've alluded to, the cross-examination of Wilson was tame in the extreme, with even *CoinGeek* saying that 'other than entering into the record an opinion of Dr Wright's fashion habits, it didn't appear to achieve all that much...' Indeed, the only discussion on the subject of hacking came through a generic discussion of email hacking, with Wilson saying that Wright had never discussed any such hacks with him and that he had no idea that the systems had been compromised prior to his departure in October 2013. This timeframe is backed up by Wright and Ramona Watts, who both testified that they didn't know until 2014 that the systems had been compromised. Five days after this, perhaps following a word from Wright to *CoinGeek* proprietor Calvin Ayre, it changed its mind:

> *Wilson also had more opportunity than anyone to plant damning and convincing forgeries in a way that would implicate Dr Wright. He had been working in Wright's companies since 2012, well after Bitcoin had been released to the world, so he would have had a front-row seat to the inner workings of the Wright machine during the elusive time period which is the focus of the Kleiman lawsuit.*

As we know, of course, the forgeries were far from convincing, as *CoinGeek* itself pointed out on numerous occasions throughout the trial. Wright's perception of Wilson may have been coloured by the fact that Wilson emailed Ira Kleiman's legal team to congratulate them on the lawsuit against Wright in 2018, but we invite anyone to look through Wilson's testimony and come to anything resembling *CoinGeek's* second conclusion.

At this point, we have to consider what evidence Wright has produced to back up his claims against these individuals. In a deposition for the *Kleiman v Wright* case in 2020, it looked like the world was finally going to see it:

I have things that I have discussed with my solicitors, I have the fact that I was not available or sending e-mails on that day, I have the evidence that my machines were compromised, I have the evidence that the machines were shut down and rebuilt, I have the public records to do with the administration of the companies, I have testimony of other people, I have forensic analysis of some of the signatures proving that it was not me who signed them but other people, I have other documents.

For all Wright's talk of public and private records, forensic analysis and documents galore, not so much as a Post-It note containing proof of a hack was examined during the *Kleiman v Wright* case. Nevertheless, Wright perpetuated the story in future cases, saying during the *COPA v Wright* trial that he became aware of the infiltration after analysing documents and data on a company laptop (the only evidence Wright has ever produced from company laptops and used in his defence has been found to be fraudulent). Nevertheless, Wright continues to talk about the hacking conspiracy as if it is an established fact. Greg Maxwell, meanwhile, wholeheartedly denies Wright's allegations:

Wright's allegations of criminal conduct on my behalf are false and completely baseless, but more significantly they're just absurd. In his blog posts he's also falsely accused me of a variety of other wide-ranging crimes without ever giving a word of substantiation. As a respected and financially successful open-source developer with a spotless record, I had no interest in hacking anyone and nothing to gain from doing so.

What cannot be ignored, of course, is the suggestion that there was no hack and that Wright was behind the forged documents. These were the findings of Judge Reinhart in the *Kleiman v Wright* case and Justice Mellor in the *COPA v Wright* case, and, indeed, we can turn to Justice Mellor for a summary of Wright's position on the matter:

If Dr Wright's evidence was true, he would be a uniquely unfortunate individual, the victim of a very large number of unfortunate coincidences, all of which went against him, and/or the victim of a number of conspiracies against him.

The scale of these coincidences and conspiracies bears repeating in order to bring home their unlikelihood. As we have noted, Wright's attempts to extricate himself from a sticky situation with the ATO typically involved a sudden change in narrative in order to explain an unfavourable finding. These were often accompanied by documents or other information to back up his new story, sometimes on the same day, and yet each time, the hackers managed to create a document that implicated Wright and swap it for the real one right before it was sent over, hoping he wouldn't notice. When the ATO came back to Wright to point out the flaws in the new story, rather than questioning the errata, Wright either doubled down on the fake document or changed his story again to fit the narrative spun by the fabrication, seemingly playing right into the hackers' hands. The level of knowledge and effort required to maintain this on the hackers' part, not to mention the questionable motives, make it impossible to comprehend. Wright's inexplicable behaviour also works against his theory that he was being compromised by outside sources and, as we have already stated, calls into question all his computer security qualifications.

In June 2018, Wright's *Kleiman v Wright* team took what they would later call the 'stinking heap' of fraudulent documents that had been pulled from Wright's systems and used it in a motion to dismiss the case, arguing that Ira Kleiman's pleading was 'replete with cribbing from unreliable internet sources, stolen Australian government transcripts, pilfered hard drives, and hacked emails.' Again, this was asserted with no corroborating evidence, with Wright's legal team only able to call on the 'public knowledge' of the hack, based purely on the *WIRED* and *Gizmodo* articles, evidence they did a good job of undermining themselves:

> There is no way to determine whether documents obtained from an internet hack job are authentic—we don't even know where they came from.

In his summation of Wright's hack theory and the arguments put forward to support it, Judge Reinhart was unequivocal:

> When confronted with evidence indicating that certain documents had been fabricated or altered, [Wright] became extremely defensive, tried to sidestep questioning, and ultimately made vague comments about his systems being hacked and others having access to his computers. None of these excuses were corroborated by other evidence.

As a result of this, Wright was sanctioned and given a stern rebuke by Judge Reinhart, who ruled that Wright 'intentionally submitted fraudulent documents to the Court, obstructed a judicial proceeding, and gave perjurious testimony.' Wright's long-time associate, Jimmy Nguyen, attempted to corroborate the hacking theory in his deposition for the *Kleiman v Wright* case but admitted that he was relying solely on the word of Craig Wright and Ramona Watts that it had happened. Nguyen also testified that he only heard about the hacks in February 2018, despite having worked for Wright since 2015.

Characteristically, Wright has not let this lack of evidence or his judicial dressing downs deter him from his hack theory, as he demonstrated in a filing for the *Tulip Trading Ltd v Bitcoin Association for BSV & Ors* case in 2021:

> It is also alleged...that I used hacking as a convenient excuse...to explain an apparently forged document. As I have explained, I have never forged documents and therefore, in the Florida Proceedings...I was speculating as to how the document was on my computer system. I am regularly subject to hacking attempts and I stand by the possibility that a forged document may have been put on my computer by a hacker or through other unauthorised access.

Wright was back to his old tricks three years later for the *COPA v Wright* trial, where he blamed everyone from COPA's law firm to Arthur van Pelt for being complicit in a campaign against him, which involved Wright's house being bugged and hackers watching his every move online. Perhaps unsurprisingly, Justice Mellor found these claims to be 'absurd and without any support in evidence'. Some of this evidence, Wright said, was out there simply waiting to be collected, such as unreleased private messages between Satoshi Nakamoto and Gavin Andresen regarding early hacks:

> WRIGHT: *Only Satoshi and Gavin knew the full extent of those communications. They have never been released by Gavin and are not in the evidence pile you have here.*
>
> COUNSEL: *Not released by you either?*
>
> WRIGHT: *Er... I've got them on a piece of paper... like... I've written them all down and the lawyers have them...*

The fact that Wright's lawyers didn't enter his notes into evidence or try to solicit the messages from Andresen speaks volumes about their evidentiary potential.

With regard to Wright's claims of compromised systems and mass document manipulation, we could dig deeper if we wanted. We could ask, for example, why world-renowned IT security consultant Craig Wright didn't apparently back up his files and didn't know that there was a risk that the dates on the files might be altered when the servers were rebuilt. We could ask why Wright has never gone to the police with his evidence, given the damage supposedly done to him by the 'hackers'. We could ask how legitimate emails between Wright and the ATO referenced details from earlier emails supposedly not sent by him. We could ask why Wright has never produced more documents affected by the server reboots for corroboration. We could ask why Wright never warned his legal teams that documents from staff laptops were all compromised until they were found to be fraudulent. We could ask why the manipulated documents almost always linked back to Craig Wright's systems and no one else's.

We *could* ask these questions and many more, but they answer themselves at this point.

Chapter 17 – The ATO Strikes Back

Valentine's Day 2014 should have been a day of joy for Craig Wright, marking the first time that he and Ramona Watts could celebrate it as a married couple. The ATO was in no mood to allow him this pleasure, however. The audit of Hotwire, and by extension the entire stable of companies under its umbrella, had been going for just four months, but this was long enough for it to issue Coin-Exch and its related entities, DeMorgan (in its capacity as trustee for the Wright Family Trust) and Cloudcroft, with interim findings. The report alleged that Coin-Exch hadn't properly accounted for the bitcoins it had supposedly spent on the IP from W&K through DeMorgan, also noting that the deal itself was invalid because, at the time it was signed, the IP was still four months away from being awarded to Wright:

> *DeMorgan purports to have acquired the software (which it licenced to you) from Craig Wright, pursuant to a contract dated 15 July 2013, which predates its existence and establishment as a trust. DeMorgan cannot have licenced to you something which it did not validly own. Craig Wright, in acting on your behalf, would have known this as he created documents relating to the sales and licencing of the software, such as invoices and contracts; many of which are signed or dated before any valid transaction could have occurred.*

This report led to the already cited interviews between Wright, his advisors and the ATO, which took place in the days following its issuance. These interviews carried on later into the year as Wright's stories changed and the flow of 'evidence' increased. As we have explored, Wright's aim throughout these interviews was to get the GST rebates released and sent to the relevant companies, but the ATO was understandably reluctant to hand anything back. By April 2014, however, the withholding of the $3.1 million tax rebate proved terminal for Hotwire; on the 28th, it announced that, due to cash flow issues, it was broke. Wright explained during the *Kleiman v Wright* trial how he had tried to save the company:

> *I had a shareholders' meeting and a staff meeting. And I said to everyone: "If you don't force me to put the company into administration, if you allow me to trade through this, I will pay you a certain amount per month, and I will give you eight Bitcoin each person, per month."*

Given that there are no records of Wright's companies ever legitimately owning any bitcoins, it was probably a wise move for the creditors to reject this offer.

The news of Hotwire's financial problems came two months to the day after MtGox announced its own bankruptcy following the loss of 850,000 bitcoins, and Wright told liquidators McGrath Nicol that it was the combination of the withheld rebate and the collapse of MtGox that killed the company, given the 'significant exposure' Hotwire allegedly had to the defunct exchange. This loss of its funds meant Wright could 'no longer provide financial accommodation' to Hotwire, but a liquidators report the following June made no mention of MtGox, laying the blame squarely at the feet of the ATO:

> *As a result of a Goods and Services Tax ('GST') refund claim of circa $3.1 million relating to the September 2013 quarter being withheld by the Australian Taxation Office, the Company was unable to meet its trading liabilities from around February 2014. Following continued efforts to secure the GST refund and attempts to raise funding from other sources (which were ultimately unsuccessful), the Directors resolved that the Company was insolvent and appointed Administrators on 28 April 2014.*

This lack of a reference to MtGox isn't surprising given that its records showed Wright's 'significant exposure' to be just 14.6 bitcoins, worth some $9,000 at the time of the exchange's collapse. Wright would later claim that Hotwire held some $4 million worth of bitcoins on MtGox and complained to the ATO that 'The little buggers won't release my fucking money.' We have confirmed that neither Craig Wright nor any of his companies ever filed a claim with the MtGox trustee over his missing coins, however, so it's unclear how he thought he was going to get his 'fucking money' back if he never asked for it. Wright's timing over his MtGox claim is also suspect, given that he had been informed of the halted $3.1 million refund the prior October. This gave Hotwire seven months to obtain other sources of funding, such as launching products and offering the services it had promised, but it was clearly unable to do this. Wright has never stated why he didn't use the $30 million he had supposedly taken to Singapore just three months before Hotwire's collapse, or indeed any of the hundreds of millions of dollars worth of bitcoins he would later tell the ATO his companies could call on, to save it. The reason, of course, should, by now, be obvious.

To outsiders, it must have appeared that the collapse of Hotwire came out of the blue, given that just two weeks before the fall of MtGox, Hotwire was tweeting about its upcoming product launch and even featured in an article for *Business Insider Australia*. In the piece, which painted a very rosy picture of what was, in truth, a dire situation, Wright proclaimed the imminent launch of Denariuz, which he said would offer Bitcoin-based equivalents of conventional savings accounts, term deposits, credit and debit cards and loans. Denariuz, Wright said, would kick off with a global pool of more than 100,000 bitcoins, worth some $71 million at the time, from its backers. This was news to the ATO, which knew, as Wright most certainly did, that rather than sitting on tens of millions of dollars in backing, Hotwire was on the brink of collapse due to a lack of funds. However, as late as May 2021, Wright was still trying to make out that Hotwire had been going strong prior to its collapse:

> *I had around fifty staff earning an average of 124,000 dollars per year. On top of that, we had offices, computers, network systems and contracts and licensing agreements with banking software firms.*

Wright also claimed in a 2018 blog post that Hotwire had been 'going well until the 2014 Bitcoin crash', but this is nonsense; Hotwire was going nowhere at the time the Bitcoin market began to reverse in early 2014, and, given that all its claimed bitcoin holdings actually belonged to other entities, it certainly didn't suffer from a loss of dollar value in this respect.

The launch of Hotwire and the publication of its multifaceted Bitcoin plans also helped Wright seek another kind of tax rebate alongside GST. In the late 1990s, the ATO launched a number of tax concessions for eligible research and development (R&D) programs operated by taxpaying companies. Deductions for R&D could be claimed against taxable income, with the scheme intended to encourage growth in the tech sector. In 2011, they were amalgamated into the Research and Development Tax Incentive scheme, operated by AusIndustry. Wright was familiar with the process, having tried and failed to claim R&D tax rebates through Ridges Estate between 2001 and 2004, and he picked up the baton again through Hotwire, lodging millions in R&D rebates alongside GST claims in 2013.

Wright may have been trying to hype Denariuz to the public, but to the ATO, he was issuing a very different message. Just two weeks before telling *Business Insider* that Denariuz was about to revolutionise the banking world, Wright appealed to ATO Assistant Commissioner Michael Hardy (described by Wright's accountant John Chesher as 'one of those dandies in a pink striped shirt and a bow tie') over its treatment of him and the potential ramifications:

> *Right now, it seems to me that there is a game at the ATO designed to drive me out. If a company I am involved with but not director of lodges a claim, it is withheld. If I lodge a claim, it is withheld. It does not make any difference that the times have been exceeded. I am treated differently from all the other BTC companies. There are several filing BAS returns and not a one has been audited or made to pay GST on Bitcoin.*

Wright added that 'The Bitcoin I control was mined in the US for a foreign trust and [a] company that was setup following the Information Defense incident', a claim of which the ATO was already sceptical. Wright signed off by saying, 'What I see resulting is a legal battle where the ATO will end up having to pay me but where I [move] everything overseas losing jobs and revenue for the country.' If this was a threat, it would turn out to be an idle one.

The interim audit issued to C01N Pty in March 2014 following the February 2014 interviews has never been made public, but in report issued on Coin-Exch at the same time, the ATO highlighted something Wright had told them, which showed that he wasn't helping his chances:

> *Fiat is not true money. Bitcoin and Gold are ... If a value added tax is applied, we will create a system that undermines this through the use of legal avenues. We will create financial instruments based on the item we wish to promote, but as a derivative that undermines the effect of the tax.*

This mantra, the ATO opined in a later report, 'shows a level of indifference to the law', which Wright illustrated to a spectacular degree through the use of his businesses. As we know, more meetings with the ATO took place throughout 2014, when Wright and his financial representatives argued why his companies shouldn't have their rebates frozen. During an 18 August interview that year, Wright was challenged over his story regarding Hotwire's funding, with the ATO accusing him of 'double-dipping', where a company seeks to benefit from accounting for the same sum of money twice, for example, by claiming expenses on two different purchases using the same funds. Wright asserted that he wasn't double-dipping despite using the same Bitcoin addresses for multiple payments, an assertion that led the ATO to ask how he could be so sure, given that he hadn't been able to 'paint a global picture of his companies'. In that interview, Wright was asked to state how much his companies had to spend overall. Wright put the figure at a staggering $650 million, a $571.5 million increase from the year before, despite Hotwire having gone into administration just four months previously, mainly due to $3.1 million being withheld by the ATO.

Andrew Sommer wrote to the ATO in May 2104 to argue Wright's case, citing 'a number of factual and legal errors' in its methodology, although Sommer did note that the relationship between Wright, Hotwire and some of the suppliers, such as Al Baraka, was 'complicated'. Sommer's appeal fell on deaf ears, however, with the ATO unimpressed by Wright's efforts to prove his claims using documents he would later disown; in October 2014, the agency sent Coin-Exch its final audit report, candidly summing up its view of what the company and its related entities were really up to:

> *Although you have explained that there is an intention that the entities will promote bitcoin and establish a platform for, among other things, trading and loaning bitcoin, you have not demonstrated that the related entities are conducting an enterprise. It is our position that in the absence of ATO refunds, the companies would likely be insolvent – this relevantly indicates that the companies are not operated in a business-like manner, nor is there an intention to make a profit.*

The only business taking place within the companies, the ATO said, was the business of achieving tax rebates through inter-company transactions, noting, 'Your activities and those of your related entities during the relevant period consisted entirely of related party transactions and there [are] no records of commercial sales of product that have or are reasonably likely to occur in future.'

Clearly, the ATO was not confident in Wright's ability, or even his desire, to actually build anything, despite his public claims to the contrary. Wright didn't help matters when he said during those August 2014 interviews that he didn't anticipate Coin-Exch to be profitable for some time while splashing out hundreds of millions of dollars on software and IP, which, of course, he was claiming back the tax on. This finding rather put into perspective Wright's argument in that January 2014 email to Michael Hardy, where he claimed that he was 'trying to work to build a business and create employment in Australia'. While Wright was indeed employing staff, any work they were doing was merely a front for the real activity of collecting tax rebates.

Wright's two August 2014 interviews also threw up some new complications over the transfer of $120 million worth of intellectual property between his companies, including that from W&K, Professor Rees, Siemens and Al Baraka, all of which had supposedly been farmed out in early July 2013. Wright told the ATO that the IP had been sold to DeMorgan before being split up and sent to his various companies, but the ATO soon found out that De Morgan hadn't been registered until 26 August 2013, meaning it couldn't possibly have received the IP from Wright the previous month. Wright's response was to invent the DeMorgan Trust, which he said had been the actual recipient and which he had asked Dianne Pinder of Lloyds Solicitors to establish, the same lawyer who, ten years later, he would say set up the Tulip Trust for him in 2011. Wright said he asked Pinder to do this in June 2013, adding that he, Ramona Watts and Jamie Wilson were all also involved in its creation, which, he told the ATO, was a case of too many cooks:

> WRIGHT: *The first iteration was in July; the second iteration, and that was the crap document—*
>
> ATO: *Which document is that?*
>
> WRIGHT: *It was a trust deed that was wrong, all the names were wrong, everything else [was] wrong. It came back in August.*

And who was responsible for this mess? Dianne Pinder, for one, whom Wright claimed 'did a crap job' setting up the trust, as well as – wouldn't you know it – Jamie Wilson:

> *Jamie was useless. I left Jamie in charge to do some things and Jamie, God knows what the fuck he did.*

Some of the many things Wilson got wrong, according to Wright, were all those invoices between DeMorgan and the companies in the Hotwire stable concerning the $120 million worth of IP. These, Wright told the ATO, 'needed quite a bit of fixing', which Wright took care of personally. What exactly was wrong with them, Wright didn't say, but the result was a bunch of fresh invoices all backdated to 1 July 2013. Wright, however, didn't see a problem with these forgeries:

> *I don't see why it's such a big issue because July, August, September, it's the same GST reporting quarter.*

Wright's only evidence of his request to set up the DeMorgan Trust was a series of emails to Wilson 'bitching about the fact that it wasn't set up correctly,' citing no correspondence with Lloyds over the matter.

This dismantling of Wright's scheme led to the ATO conspiring with Ira Kleiman, disgruntled Hotwire employees and the cabal of Bitcoin developers to bring Wright down and steal his IP. This is the view propounded by Wright and his acolytes, with Kurt Wuckert Jr laying out the campaign in *Hero / Villain*:

> *My theory is that, when the ATO were looking into Craig's tax stuff in 2013 and 2014, there were people inside of Craig's organization who were working with the ATO, and by extension, also working with Ira Kleiman...I think people wanted to either blackmail Craig or leak his information.*

The reason for this, Wuckert Jr says, was because it was 'highly likely that Craig had done work for the CIA and/or Homeland Security at some point', and when the ATO contacted these agencies for information on Wright for its investigations, they hired 'a skilled engineer to unwind it all'. This story is typical of the 'deep state' conspiracy theories that sprang up around Wright in the late 2010s, with his acolytes advocating him as a Donald Trump-esque saviour of Bitcoin in the same way Trump was lauded by his supporters for a supposed campaign against the tyranny of an overbearing government. Like all good conspiracy theories, there is no evidence whatsoever to back up Wuckert Jr's claims, with some advocates reduced to numerology and the sovereign citizen movement to prove the supposed campaign to silence Craig Wright.

The event that gave birth to this conspiracy theory took place on 15 April 2014 when auditors within the ATO who were investigating Wright's $57 million IP grab contacted Ira Kleiman to ask what he, as heir to W&K, knew about the deal Wright had pulled off through the Supreme Court of New South Wales. This contact came a month after the agency had sent Wright five pages' worth of questions regarding W&K, including details of its ownership and activities, alerting him to their continued interest in the company. The auditors sent Kleiman copies of the documentation Wright had used to secure the legal victory, and it didn't take Kleiman long to see what the Supreme Court registrar hadn't:

> *I don't understand why Dave would make that agreement with you for a business divorce. Why would a successful partnership suddenly seperate and leave one partner with everything of accountable value and the other (Dave) with only 10% in a future venture and a[n] undisclosed amount of Bitcoins? And the contract...is signed the same month of his death and without his real signature. Nor do I believe it to be a digital signature. It doesn't even come close to his handwriting That is obviously a females signature. Things just don't make sense.*

In reply, Wright stated that the transfer had been above board and that he had carried it out because 'accountants etc advised it was necessary', something Jamie Wilson would have no doubt had an opinion on. Wright added, ironically, that the ATO's intentions were to 'mislead you as to what this is about', adding that the agency was unhappy because it was not able to levy GST on the $57 million worth of IP, and so it was trying to claw back money through other means. This, as Wright was to find out, would prove to be an inaccurate assumption and, ultimately, an expensive one. Ira Kleiman's trust in Wright seems to have irrevocably broken down from this point, and although the pair continued emailing on and off for another three years, the feeling that Wright had tried to cheat Dave Kleiman's estate out of millions of dollars led to an irreconcilable deterioration in their relationship and, eventually, a lawsuit.

While Wright was trying and failing to convince Ira Kleiman that the IP grab had been legally sound, he was fighting the same battle with the ATO. Wright had tried to convince the agency that he had always owned the IP due to the agreements struck with Dave Kleiman and that his two lawsuits in Australia were merely him formally bringing the IP into the country. This, as we know, was one of many GST and R&D tax breaks he was seeking, including for the Siemens and Al Baraka software. The ATO had asked to see evidence of the W&K software during its April 2014 visit to Clayton Utz, with agent Stuart Coulson reporting that he saw 'folders of what appeared to be software that [Wright] said was W&K's'. Coulson also saw code that Wright said belonged to W&K but which 'could have just as easily been anyone's software', although he did add that he was confident that the code would have resulted in a functional system if run. During the *Kleiman v Wright* trial, it was put to Wright that he had transferred W&K's IP to his various companies following the award, something Wright denied, bringing Greyfog into the mix:

> *The information that I created an Australian company -- venture funded one called Greyfog, that was copied into W&K -- I retained. And that was transferred. The rights to W&K's software and any copies they had were never moved. So sorry. You're mischaracterizing that completely.*

This, of course, was undermined by Andrew Sommer's statement to the ATO that the IP had been 'broken up and transferred to other group entities', with Wright falling back on the argument that the ATO transcripts were false, and so Sommer had never said that. As part of the ATO's assessment of the IP, project manager Alan Pedersen was commissioned to compile a report calculating its value. Pedersen arrived at the remarkable figure of $303.8 million, an increase of 431% in the six months since Hotwire had acquired it. It was later established that the data for this calculation had come from a single source: Craig Wright.

During questioning over the deal to bring W&K's IP into Coin-Exch, the ATO quizzed Wright over another important anomaly: the deal was dated 22 August 2013, more than two months before the Supreme Court of New South Wales awarded Wright the IP. This led to a back-and-forth which saw Wright at his petulant worst:

> WRIGHT: We thought it would happen earlier and the judgment said to be applied as of 30 September, so —

ATO:	*But the judgment doesn't exist as at the date of this licence agreement.*
WRIGHT:	*Well, you tell the Supreme Court that they can't say 30 September.*
ATO:	*No. I understand that —*
WRIGHT:	*The Supreme Court gave me a judgment that said I had to apply it by 30 September.*
ATO:	*But the relevant judgment was dated 6 November 2013.*
WRIGHT:	*That judgment on that date said I had to apply it as of 30 September.*

Wright's eventual excuse was that he dated the transfers against a completely fictional timeline he anticipated the court to work to rather than waiting for the ruling, saying, 'As far as I was concerned, it was mine, the judgment was there to finalise and make sure that there was nothing wrong,' adding that 'ended up being bloody messy.'

The ATO delivered its verdict on the legitimacy of Wright's companies in a series of lengthy Reasons for Decision reports in October 2014, covering several entities formerly under the Hotwire umbrella. These reports would have made grim reading for Wright and would have afforded him a very clear idea of what was coming down the pipeline. The report into Coin-Exch saw the ATO list twelve factors which precluded the company from being awarded deductions and collecting tax rebates on $120 million worth of deals between it and Wright's other companies. The list also laid out the manifold issues the ATO had found with many of these inter-company dealings, including a hammer blow for Wright over his $57 million W&K IP grab:

> *...we do not accept that the NSWSC court proceedings resulted in any acquisition by you of software and or IP from W&K, or any acquisition by you of software and or IP from W&K for the value asserted. The NSWC did not consider any evidence or make any findings of fact as to the existence or value of the software you purportedly acquired from W&K as a result of the proceedings.*

Wright's grand plan – hatched some eighteen months previously – looked to be in tatters; the ATO had been utterly unconvinced by the evidence it had seen (and more importantly when it came to Wright's lofty claims of what W&K had been doing, what it *hadn't* seen) and wasn't giving him a penny. Worse, it would inevitably be issuing demands for back taxes and likely penalties. The report also criticised Wright for doing what he said he wouldn't with regard to his accounting records:

> *The NSW SC settlement agreement appears to be back-dated to 9 July 2013 in order to come within this period, despite the fact that the decision in these matters was handed down in November 2013. This appears to be a deliberate attempt to ensure that the acquisition of the legal title to the W&K software was recorded at a time which enabled you to transfer those rights to DeMorgan and for DeMorgan to supply that software before 30 September 2013.*

The ATO added that, given Wright's version of how the W&K deal supposedly went down, some of the software – had it existed – would have been related to the four DHS contracts which Wright had claimed were awarded when they were not. It also found that the court documents underpinning the W&K proceedings focused primarily on the repayment of the bitcoin loans and gold bonds Wright had allegedly provided, bonds that he later denied sending and loans that he could not verify. It also had trouble believing that software transferred for $5,000 in 2010 was worth $57 million three years later, given that W&K had conducted no actual work in the interim.

When considering Coin-Exch itself, the ATO took issue with the price tag Wright had put on a properly functioning platform:

> *You have noted that in order to do what you want to do, you would need to spend approximately $500 million developing the relevant banking platform. This appears to be an extraordinarily expensive way of developing bespoke software compared to, for example, hiring programmers to develop the software for you.*

To back up its point, the ATO noted that other Bitcoin companies, such as Bitcoin exchanges and even Bitcoin ATM machine makers, had been able to 'adapt current systems to enable the use of bitcoin without the extraordinary level of capital which you have sought to expend.' It was almost like Wright wasn't trying. The ATO also rejected Wright's defence that the losses for Coin-Exch were factored into his financial planning, pointing out that his unprofessional business dealings and massive expenditure were out of the ordinary for such an operation and noted the 'unnecessarily complex' way in which Wright had distributed the software from W&K.

If Wright hadn't been aware by this point that his plan to engineer a seven-figure tax rebate had been rumbled, the ATO disabused him of this notion:

> *In your case we consider there was a scheme which involved you acquiring software from MJF and W&K in order for it to be on supplied to your related entities so as to generate GST refunds in Coin-Exch, Hotwire and Cloudcroft. You had initially planned to use bitcoin to fund these transactions in such a way that you would never lose control or access to those bitcoins. However, on receipt of the private binding ruling advising you that the supply of bitcoin in consideration for an acquisition would be a taxable supply, you altered the scheme to insert the Seychelles trust to which you transferred the bitcoin.*

The ATO then laid out, in step-by-step order, exactly how Coin-Exch, Cloudcoft, DeMorgan and Craig Wright had gone about trying to deceive it:

1. Wright established the Seychelles trust.
2. Wright acquired software from MJF at a purported cost of $38.4 million in order to generate a GST credit with a corresponding GST liability by MJF Mining, which would never be paid.
3. Wright initiated a court action to confirm legal title to W&K software at an inflated value of $58.7 million (including other taxes).
4. Wright entered into a Deed of Loan with the trustee of the Seychelles trust in order to access 650,000 bitcoins.
5. Wright assigned the right to call for the bitcoins under the Deed of Loan to his related entities.
6. Wright sold the intellectual property and software to DeMorgan and Cloudcroft at a price reflecting the purported cost bases.
7. DeMorgan licensed the software and IP to entities related to Wright. The licences were paid for by rights to call for bitcoin provided to those entities by him.

8. The related entities claimed input tax for the acquisition of the licenced software, resulting in significant refunds.

In summary, the ATO alleged that Wright's companies were created and operated with the 'principle effort' of carrying out a 'scheme [to attain] GST benefits'. It then revealed a startling statistic that shone a million-watt torchlight on Wright's business activities:

> For the past 2 years, based on information available from your bank accounts and accounts of entities you control, 94% of your income or money to which you have access is comprised of GST or income tax refunds.

This statistic, more than any other, puts Wright's activities between 2012 and 2014 into sharp relief. For all the blog posts, press releases and fancy websites promoting a financial revolution, the ATO boiled Wright's operation down to nothing more than a multi-million-dollar tax racket, totally undermining the sanctimonious complaints of illegal Bitcoin usage that would issue from Wright's lips in the years to come. Wright was presented with this document during the *Kleiman v Wright* trial, where, perhaps unsurprisingly, he denounced it, noting that it was 'not headed with the official logo of the tax office' and, therefore, 'I don't recognize this as an Australian Taxation Office document.'

The ATO's takedown of Coin-Exch was the beginning of the end for Wright's multifaceted tax rebate 'scheme', as the agency framed it. It confirmed that none of the evidence provided by Wright for the W&K IP grab was ever examined by the Supreme Court of New South Wales, largely because all sides had, apparently, signed off on the deal. We already know that the emails appointing Uyen Nguyen as director of W&K were forged, but there is still the question of why Jamie Wilson accepted the role as temporary director of W&K's affairs in Australia, which allowed him to sign off on the deal. This was answered in June 2020 when his testimony for the *Kleiman v Wright* case was made public, where Wilson spoke for the first time about the alleged 16 August 2013 meeting that saw him take a post as temporary director of W&K. Wilson acknowledged that a meeting had taken place that day but denied that there were any discussions of him taking a position within W&K either during or after it, saying, 'This is my first knowledge that I was acting as a director of [W&K].' Wilson's argument, then, was that Wright had fraudulently appointed him to the role in order to smooth the passage of the IP, something that Wilson alleged Wright had also done with another of his companies, Interconnected Research Pty Ltd. The situation is eerily reminiscent of Wright's actions in 2003 when he claimed during the *Ryan v Wright* case that he and Lynn Wright had been reappointed as directors of DeMorgan in an extraordinary general meeting, a meeting for which there were no minutes and which the judge ruled had not taken place.

As for why Wright had used Wilson in this manner, the answer may be rooted in the Cryptoloc affair, but there is every chance that Wright simply abused Wilson's position as CFO for his own ends. Wilson was also caught up in the document-forging aspect of the *Kleiman v Wright* case when Wright's counsel found that an IP address of the servers connected to the forged emails between Dave Kleiman and Uyen Nguyen was, in the words of *CoinGeek*, an '11-minute stone's throw' from the Cryptoloc offices. *CoinGeek*'s insinuation was clear: Jamie Wilson was behind the forgeries, cooking them up in his Sydney office, which was just five miles away from the physical location of the IP address from which the emails were sent. However, among the litany of questions and considerations raised by such a theory is one particularly pressing one: if your story hinges on a five-mile-long stone throw, it is already in serious trouble.

During his closing arguments for the *Kleiman v Wright* trial, Ira Kleiman's lead counsel, Vel Freedman, summed up his opinion on Wright's activities regarding the W&K IP grab:

> So [Wright] files sham lawsuits against W&K to steal its intellectual property and he forges Dave's signature on a contract...that is dated weeks before Dave dies, which says that Dave gives Craig 570,000, half of the 1.1 million bitcoin to Craig, gives Craig all of W&K's shares and all of W&K's intellectual property, all in exchange for a minority stake in a company that doesn't even exist yet and a company that amounted to nothing called Coin-Exch.

The jury in the *Kleiman v Wright* case eventually ruled that Wright was liable for the conversion of the IP supposedly held in W&K and was ordered to pay US$100 million, later increased to more than US$145 million with post- and pre-judgment interest. At the time of publication, Wright has not paid a penny of this.

The ATO's destruction of Wright's plans must have shocked him to the core: not only had the seven-figure windfall he had been banking on been stripped away from him, but he was, in fact, facing the prospect of shelling out millions in back taxes and penalties. If the ATO decided his actions had been criminal in nature, things might be much worse. It is likely that this set of reports was what spurred Wright to take his Seychelles trust gambit to the next level; while some of the reports are not dated, we can peg them to October 2014 through references to other dates and talk of a Seychelles trust rather than the Tulip Trust, which was birthed in the middle of that month. As we have explored, the Tulip Trust was supported by dozens of documents and communications concerning both the trust itself and the bitcoins supposedly tied up in it, most of which were produced in the last two weeks of October 2014. Wright, of course, blames this catalogue of forgeries on hackers and the need to rebuild his servers as a result of their actions. However, the timing of these acts would have to be one of the many improbable coincidences required to make the story true.

In his April 2019 deposition for the *Kleiman v Wright* case, Wright commented on his battles with the ATO, where he painted himself as the victor and the ATO as nothing but underhanded cheats concerned for their jobs:

> ...*they have taken me to court multiple times, and multiple times they have been forced basically to apologise. Multiple times they have doctored records. They have constructed records. They have done anything possible, since the time I told them about Bitcoin, before it was called Bitcoin, to basically find something to get me on. Because little things like where I said Bitcoin means we do not need as many auditors because it gets rid of fraud, means that they do not like what it is.*

It goes without saying that Wright has never produced these apologies or any evidence of document doctoring by the ATO, while ATO documents show that Wright failed to mention Bitcoin in any capacity until late 2013. Once more, we see Wright playing the victim and alleging that he is the subject of a huge, illogical conspiracy, all offered without any proof whatsoever. Wright has also never produced any evidence for a claim he made in a July 2020 interview when he alleged that the ATO was fed lies over his activities by his enemies:

> *I was talking to the tax office, and, of course, the tax office decided to verify things, but instead of doing it properly, they talked to people like [Andreas]*

Antonopolous and Greg Maxwell, and they told them, 'No, that's not how Bitcoin works. You can't tax Bitcoin. It's all hidden. And this guy scamming you'...so they made up stories about me, and they've been doing it ever since.

As we have seen, the ATO was perfectly capable of conducting its own investigations into Wright even if it had received a tip-off, which seems highly unlikely, especially from the sources Wright has put forward. It's also worth noting that Wright went off the radar following the failed 2016 signing sessions and brought himself back onto the scene the following year through his support of Bitcoin Cash. Many people, including those he claims have been relentlessly attacking him, would have been far happier if he had stayed away.

In a filing for the *Tulip Trading Ltd v Bitcoin Association for BSV & Ors* case in 2021, Wright reminisced about his battles with the ATO, where he echoed a similar refrain:

I recall attending interviews with the ATO, but most of the documentary material was provided by company staff, internal and external accountants and the companies' lawyers. I was surprised to see various allegations referring to 'Dr Wright' in the ATO Reasons Document for the simple reason that I had very little to do with the provision of documents to the ATO.

This comment comes straight out of the Craig Wright playbook, as it exculpates him from any wrongdoing and fits his narrative that forces both within and outside his companies colluded with the ATO to bring him down. Wright's claim that the fraudulent material was only ever provided to the ATO by third parties represents another catch-all excuse for the reams of forged emails, contracts, deeds and all the other pieces of evidence that would prove to be his undoing. It also handily negates the fact that, as company director for most of the organisations, Wright was ultimately responsible for what was sent out to the ATO.

We should also point out that, in many instances, there was at least a two-year gap between the ATO first telling Wright's companies that rebates were being withheld and final penalty notices being issued. In that time, multiple emails, face-to-face meetings, phone calls and personal visits by the ATO took place, all with a very obvious focus. If Wright really couldn't tell that he himself was under investigation, even when the ATO kept dragging him in for interviews and visiting his offices, then we have to seriously question whether he was fit to run a company in the first place. As well as twisting the facts over the W&K IP grab, Wright misled Ira Kleiman when, in an August 2015 email, he said that the issues with the ATO were down to 'differences of views and interpretation' over his research activities, adding, rather tellingly, that 'there was an error in invoicing, a genuine error, where we have over claimed about $4.9m in Coin-Exch.' This, of course, merely led Kleiman to foster suspicions about all the other 'errors' he was finding through his and the ATO's research into Wright's companies.

Nik Cubrilovic summed up Wright's method of operation succinctly in a 2016 Reddit post, referring to Wright's Bitcoin ownership claims, which the ATO would eventually deduce were as false as the assertions over his IP:

> *Wright's primary MO these past few years...was using various entities to create real-dollar tax refunds out of non-existant Bitcoins. I'm surprised it worked for as long as it did.*

Wright, however, has a different argument, as he espoused to his followers in August 2022:

> *The limit on R&D rebates, where you get money and NOT a tax credit is 20 million in revenue, turn over. So, a spend by a group of over 100 million CANNOT get a tax rebate. Not difficult. It [is] on the ATO Website and any moron can EASILY verify that. I have before. So, to say I have a scheme to get money is showing either...1. You have shit for brains, 2. You are dishonest, or 3. Both.*

This came nine months after Wright had told the court in the *Kleiman v Wright* trial that his disputes with the ATO weren't over tax refunds but were, instead, over 'how much I had to pay them.' Wright also testified in a June 2019 deposition for that case that he was cleared of any wrongdoing:

> *I ended up having to go before the GAAR panel, which is the General Anti-Avoidance Review panel because the tax office argued that the creation of rights to Bitcoin was effectively a tax-avoidance scheme. I won that, even though the tax office didn't agree...*

The results of the GAAR panel have never been made public, so we only have Wright's word that he scored another victory over the ATO here. During the same trial, Wright claimed to have evidence of the ATO's transgressions during his battle with them:

We had a forensic report done. The forensic report demonstrated that the documents were fabricated within the tax office...the ATO then dropped the case against me when it was demonstrated that internal to the government department the document changes were made.

There is no evidence in the public domain to confirm Wright's version of events, the same of which can be said for his next story:

What you're neglecting is that this went to court during the insolvency thing the ATO brought up. The first auditor found no evidence of fraud. The ATO fired and had the Court replace the auditor. The second audit firm found no evidence of fraud. The ATO tried to fire the second and have a third auditor appointed. The Court said: 'You had two bites at the cherry,' and closed the case. That was in 2017. Sorry.

These are even grander claims than Wright's supposed GAAR panel victory, but, again, they come without evidence. It is worth noting, however, that Wright's companies eventually settled all their debts with the agency following to outside investment, much to Wright's chargin. Given that this was what the ATO wanted all along, it is far more likely that a deal was done where it would drop its investigation upon full and prompt payment.

Cubrolivic's summary of Wright's activities came as the final penalty notices for some of Wright's companies were being issued, three years after his alleged effort to defraud the tax office began. As we know, this all began with Wright's $57 million IP grab from W&K, a claim that was underpinned by a very important document that would end up having the opposite effect to the one Wright intended: rather than everything it touched turning to gold, instead, it all turned into a pile of very costly and potentially very damaging ashes.

Chapter 18 – A Wicked Deed

We already know that Craig Wright first introduced the idea of his 650,000-bitcoin loan to the ATO in February 2014, hoping to use it to explain where the bitcoins had come from to pay for a plethora of software, IP and more for his companies. We've also covered some of the issues that the ATO and forensic examiners found with regard to Wright's claim over the haul, but we're yet to explore a crucial element of his attempt that touched almost every aspect of Wright's activities between 2012 and 2014: the Deed of Loan.

The Deed of Loan was first produced by Wright's accountant, John Chesher, to the ATO on 26 February 2014, just days after the ATO's assertions that Wright's companies hadn't properly accounted for the bitcoins they had supposedly spent. The ATO analysed the Deed of Loan, which saw Design by Human looking after the 650,000 bitcoins on behalf of a then-unnamed Seychelles trust and loaning them out where necessary, but it didn't take much thread-pulling for the whole thing to start unravelling. The ATO wrote to Wright on 28 March to inform him of two things we have already discussed: Design by Human, the company supposedly looking after the coins, was still owned by CFS Secretaries at the time the deal was struck, and Uyen Nguyen, who signed the Deed of Loan in her capacity as director of both Design by Human and Permanent Success, never held such positions with either company. These issues, the ATO added, meant that the document had not been signed by an 'authorised person' and, therefore, they would not accept it. Wright responded by backdating multiple corporate appointments at Design by Human (or C01N, as it had since been renamed) to ensure that the individuals and companies in question, including Uyen Nguyen and Dave Kleiman, were in the correct roles on the correct dates to match up with what Wright had stipulated on the Deed of Loan. Wright performed all these actions in mid-April 2014, a fact that was recorded in the British government's public company repository,

Companies House. When the ATO checked Companies House and uncovered these backdated appointments, Wright tried to brush them off:

> *I know that our accounting practices in the group have not been the best. I know that we haven't filed things correctly. I know Dave didn't, I know I haven't, I know Nguyen hasn't. I know we're doing our best to try and fix things.*

Of course, the notion that minor paperwork errors were to blame for the backdating of multiple directorships, which happened to address flaws the ATO had found in Wright's story just days after he had been apprised of them, is hard to parse.

At the same time, Wright also rushed off an undated 'Consent to Act' form in which Nguyen accepted roles with C01N and Denariuz UK, first as Chief Operations Officer from 18 October 2012 and then as director from 30 June 2013, the deadline by which Dave Kleiman was supposed to repay the loan from W&K to Craig Wright R&D. This put her in the perfect position to acquiesce to Wright's demands on the off chance that something should happen to Kleiman which meant he couldn't pay back the $28.8 million loan, which, of course, it did. As we know, however, Dr Edman deduced that the series of emails between Kleiman and Nguyen discussing this arrangement was a forgery, but even before that, the ATO had spotted that W&K hadn't been a going concern ever since Kleiman had let it lapse in September 2012. Wright was informed of this fact on 27 March 2014, and within twenty-four hours, W&K had been reinstated by Uyen Nguyen, with two entities listed as registered agents – herself and, oddly, 'Dr. Coin-Exch Pty Ltd'. When questioned over this reinstatement by the ATO, Wright claimed that it had only been administratively dissolved because Nguyen 'didn't even know she needed to bloody pay things or file anything.'

The Deed of Loan sent to the ATO featured an appendix, which listed twenty-six Bitcoin addresses supposedly belonging to the Tulip Trust and which were held in the UK by Design by Human. These included the 1933p, 1Feex and 16cou addresses, which we already know to have had nothing to do with Wright, and the other addresses fared little better; Kim Nilsson discovered that they belonged to a raft of people and institutions also unrelated to Wright, including random MtGox users, various early Bitcoin miners and several individuals

Nilsson did not name for privacy reasons. This suggested, again, that Wright was simply picking addresses with the requisite number of bitcoins for his needs. If this was his aim, Wright failed: the collated figure of owned bitcoins stated on the deed totalled 655,275, over 5,000 more than the loan provided for, showing either shoddy or rushed calculations. Not that it mattered; blockchain records showed that the true total number of bitcoins held in the addresses on the day the deed was signed was 585,386, so even if Wright's calculation had been correct, it still wouldn't have tallied with reality.

Wright was asked to explain the 650,000-bitcoin loan to the ATO on 11 August 2014, where he doubled down on the suggestion that he had, in the words of ATO agent Greg O'Mahoney, drawn down on 'a pile of Bitcoin or a pool of Bitcoin overseas with a value of approximately $120 million.' The pot, Wright said, had contained 1.1 million bitcoins, solidifying the notion that these were the 1.1 million mined and bought in 2009-2010 and sent off to the Seychelles trust, which was the prevailing theory at the time. It was then made explicitly clear by Wright's tax lawyer, Andrew Sommer, exactly what Wright had received:

There's a deed of loan...by a trustee who holds a number of Bitcoin and that deed of loan document is a loan from that trust deed to Dr Wright of Bitcoin in the sum of 650,000 Bitcoin.

Wright also gave an example of how he used the bitcoins from the trust with his companies:

I have a right to call on Bitcoin that's held overseas. I'm doing a deal where I want software. I basically go to the trust and I...sign over and say please transfer these rights and...if they're called on, the Bitcoin that's held overseas.

Wright was presented with this transcript during the *Kleiman v Wright* trial where, to no one's surprise who was familiar with Wright's antics, he denounced it and blamed the ATO:

...we had a forensic exercise and accountants come in and they discredited the ATO documents. It turned out, and we demonstrated this with forensic accountants, that the tax office had actually fraudulently changed documents. There was actually an investigation, and the tax office was

shown to have altered emails, altered files, and put in false testimony. They wanted to bankrupt me, first of all. They wanted to kill my companies. They wanted to destroy Bitcoin. So this document is a false document.

As he had done previously and would go on to do again in later trials, Wright alleged that transcripts of five ATO meetings entered into evidence were inaccurate, including transcriptions of meetings he did not attend but which featured his name, making ridiculous claims such as one meeting being recorded 'without authorisation [on] a little thing under the table' and that 'every second word in these damn things is false.' Wright claimed that the transcripts were 'junked by the tax office' due to their inaccuracy (not true: the ATO quoted them in judgments years later) and added a memorable comparison of one transcript:

If I randomly picked Scrabble characters and put them on a thing it would be more accurate than this document.

Wright also label*led* one document a 'terrible attempt at a transcription...that does not reflect what actually happened'*, and yet for* all his accusations, *he has* refused to say what he believe*s actually took place at* these meetings. When asked if he believed the inaccuracies were down to sloppy transcribing or malice on the part of the tax office, Wright simply repeated his claim that Des McMaster had been 'sent to a different country as punishment because of all these' but failed to make any more specific allegations. Wright was also asked for evidence that the ATO withdrew the transcripts after he had pointed out the errors, but Wright could provide none, simply saying that his lawyers possessed it all and adding, 'The value of what the ATO say out of court is about zero.'

If we are to believe that a vengeful ATO, hellbent on bankrupting Wright, fabricated transcripts to the extent he alleges, we have to believe that the agency went to the trouble of taking those few hundred correct words from the original transcript and padding them out with tens of thousands more for each meeting. These copious additions, Wright claims, were enough to help bring his companies to their knees – with the help of Ira Kleiman – but this simply isn't true: some of the transcripts contain little but eye-wateringly dull minutiae regarding Wright's businesses and past activities which match up with his own claims from blog posts and court filings, as do the Bitcoin transactions he believed to have been erroneously added. We also know that Wright was given the opportunity to confirm the accuracy of at least one of these contentious ATO transcripts, and he quibbled over just one word, while it's also worth noting that ATO transcripts from around this time were supplied to Andrew O'Hagan for 'The Satoshi Affair' by none other than Craig Wright.

Wright was called back to the ATO office a week later, on 18 August, for further discussions over the matter, where he claimed not to know who the beneficiaries of the Tulip Trust were (apart from, as we have already discussed, the whole world), despite purportedly being a director of the UK company looking after the trust. The ATO's investigation continued into 2015, during which it received confirmation from CFS Secretaries that it had formed Permanent Success, Design by Human and Achieve & Succeed in 2012 as empty shelf companies and that Design by Human had been changed to Moving Forward in Business the following year to make it more attractive to potential buyers, three months before Wright bought it. The UK tax office also confirmed that Wright had had no involvement in any of the companies until January 2014, while CFS Secretaries noted that the directorship appointments had been 'backdated by the client'.

In the face of this overwhelming evidence, Craig Wright did the most Craig Wright thing imaginable; he reaffirmed his story that Dave Kleiman had bought the companies in 2012, adding that he, Wright, had had nothing to do with the paperwork. This didn't explain the fact that Bryan Thornton, the owner of CFS Secretaries, was still listed as a director of Design by Human alongside Panopticrypt in the company's 2012/13 annual company information filing. Wright offered the following explanation of these errors in an email to Ramona Watts and Stefan Matthews in 2016:

> *Brian T. was a person used by CFS. He has no involvement now. CFS are hopeless and we do not have them doing anything. They failed to do anything when we paid them. Basically they still have not updated records even now.*

This, of course, is an outrageous slur with no basis in fact; there is nothing to suggest that CFS Secretaries did anything wrong in their execution of Wright's wishes, while Thornton was only removed in 2014 because that was when

Wright bought the company and removed him. In 2015, Wright tried to offer the ATO more evidence that he and Dave Kleiman had owned the companies in 2012 when he furnished them with emails and the following text message purportedly from Kleiman:

I have used CFS in the UK. I have 2 companies in the UK. Design by Human. Permanent Success. I will handle the details for you. Dave

This text, dated 25 October 2012, suggests that Kleiman had indeed bought the companies at a time that tallies with the dates of their incorporation by CFS. However, it doesn't explain the email that Wright supposedly sent Kleiman two months later, which featured a screenshot containing a list of available shelf companies, with Permanent Success highlighted:

Dave. We have 08248988 [Moving Forward in Business] held and reserved at CFS. Should [we] grab another as a backup, at least hold or reserve one? Craig

This email, which clearly shows Wright eyeing up Permanent Success as a backup, ignores the fact that Kleiman had already supposedly bought Permanent Success and Achieve & Succeed, the latter of which was totally ignored once it had been renamed Denariuz. Something we have already covered but which bears repeating here is that Dr Edman analysed Dave Kleiman's reply to this email for the *Kleiman v Wright* case and found that, rather than being sent in late December 2012, it had been created in a time zone 'associated with Eastern Australia' on 26 March 2014, two days before the ATO wrote to Wright about the discrepancies it had found with his UK companies. Similarly, the PGP key Dave Kleiman used to sign the email had been created on 28 February 2014, two days after John Chesher's meeting with the ATO, where the Deed of Loan was first introduced. Dr Edman also found that a document purporting to show the appointment of Dave Kleiman as director of C01N on 14 October 2012 had been created around 15 April 2014 (the day after Wright's backdating of Kleiman's appointment) and backdated to 2012, also by a computer in an Eastern Australian time zone.

As further evidence, Wright furnished the ATO with a company memorandum dated 7 January 2013, which referred to the company '08248988 (To be C01N)' and included pointed references to Liberty Reserve, trusts and Panama. The intent behind this was to imply that the name change to C01N had already been contemplated at this point in time, but public records prove otherwise. Wright was questioned about C01N during a June 2019 deposition for the *Kleiman v Wright* case, where he dismissed all connection to the ATO investigation:

> COUNSEL: ...as part of that investigation, did the Australian tax office accuse you of purchasing Coin UK, 08248988, after 2014?
>
> WRIGHT: I have no idea. I resigned as a director partway through this...I wasn't there at that stage at the end.

Here, again, we have Wright trying to sweep away all the accusations in one go and failing: he was removed as director of C01N in June 2016, not in 2014 or earlier, meaning that he was most certainly involved during the key period.

In addition to investigating the entities involved in their use and custody, the ATO also wanted to know more about the 650,000 bitcoins themselves. In its October 2014 report on Coin-Exch, the ATO had already concluded that 'The Deed of Loan of itself does not in our view demonstrate the effective establishment of the Seychelles Trust or the holding of 650,000 bitcoin pursuant to its terms,' but Wright wasn't giving up without a fight; he told the ATO in March 2015 that the coins had been locked using the Tulip Trust protocol and that a certain number of key slices would be needed to unlock the coins. This claim, however, fell on deaf ears, and for a good reason, as the ATO reported:

> *We have been provided with a number of differing accounts of the number of segments the private keys were purportedly split into, the minimum number required to recreate the keys, who held them and the number held by each person.*

This is a different story from the one Wright would tell four years later during the *Kleiman v Wright* trial, however, when he said that he simply needed to speak to the un-Googlable Mark at High Secured and the coins would be assigned to him. The ATO wasn't satisfied with Wright's protestations, which it summarised in a March 2016 penalty notice for C01N Pty:

> *...the Deed of Loan states that you received a loan from the trust. However you purportedly assigned your right to draw down on this loan to your related entities in exchange for shares they issued. The related entities are*

then said to have assigned this right in payment to DeMorgan for software and IP. This could not have occurred in our view because the Trust either did not exist, did not in fact have 650,000 bitcoin settled upon it, or, had already advanced you the loan funds under the Deed of Loan.

The ATO reiterated its conclusion when issuing the resultant penalty:

We consider it relevant that not only has the taxpayer not verified its holding of the Bitcoin in the [redacted] address, it has not substantiated its holding of any of the Bitcoin purportedly subject to the deed of loan.

This report had more to say on the idea of the Deed of Loan and Design by Human's involvement, relaying all the issues the ATO had found, including the ownership of the company, the backdating of appointments and the fact that Uyen Nguyen had signed the deed six months after its date of execution in a role she never occupied. The agency then offered a devastating rebuff of Wright's version of events:

Further, doubt is cast on all evidence provided by the taxpayer in light of the other electronic communications and other evidence received from the taxpayer and related entities that have been demonstrated to be fabricated. We therefore do not accept that parties intended the deed of loan to have legal effect.

And that wasn't all. A report the following month on Zuhl went even further:

Further evidence indicates that the arrangement for the purported payment of consideration (the loan of Bitcoin to Dr Wright and the assignment of rights to call on that Bitcoin) is a sham...the purported deed of loan and contentions subsequent to it appear to be a response to the unfavourable GST interim report and private binding ruling the taxpayer's related entities received. The related entities had not mentioned the existence of C01N UK, the Tulip Trust or the deed of loan prior to 26 February 2014.

The illegitimacy of the Deed of Loan spread to other entities, too. Denariuz Pty Ltd, the Australian company behind Wright's Bitcoin bank, had tried to claim a $1.44 million tax deduction based on unrealised losses over equitable interests in 10,000 bitcoins assigned to the deed; because the bitcoins didn't exist, the ATO said, no loss had been suffered.

Given this evisceration of his claims, it's no wonder that Wright was argumentative when the subject came up during his multiple depositions for the *Kleiman v Wright* case in 2019. In them, Wright was evasive and combative when answering questions regarding the 650,000 bitcoins supposedly held in trust for him, with his memory once again failing him on certain key details. Wright claimed that he had instructed someone in the UK to change Design by Human to C01N after Dave Kleiman's death but that this wasn't executed until six months later, adding that he had not chosen the original names. This, of course, only bolstered the true story that CFS Secretaries was in charge of the companies and that Wright and Kleiman had no input in their creation in 2012. The ATO also pointed out that Wright had been incorrect on a critical point – the company was called Moving Forward in Business, not Design by Human, by the time he changed it to C01N. After all, if Wright had bought Design by Human in 2012, he would then have been responsible for the name change to the Alan Partridge-esque Moving Forward in Business a year later, something that would have made little to no sense.

Wright also stated that C01N held 'rights to other assets', but when Ira Kleiman's attorney, Vel Freedman, tried to find out what these assets were, Wright was again uncooperative and belligerent, only admitting that, at some point in its lifetime, C01N held rights to an unspecified number of bitcoins but that he had no memory of exactly what it held, who was in charge or where the records were, despite him being C01N's director and company secretary. He was, however, able to remember one thing very clearly: Dave Kleiman had no relationship with C01N in any capacity. This was important for the purpose of his defence in the *Kleiman v Wright* case, but it was an outright lie, given that Kleiman was one of the directors.

In her testimony for the same case, Ramona Watts seemed to get confused as to what the purpose of C01N had been:

> COUNSEL: ...*this company also had to do with Bitcoin, does it not?*
>
> WATTS: *It does not have to do with Bitcoin. This was a wallet that we were trying to produce.*

COUNSEL:	*'CO1N is offering an online scalable eWallet solution with secure vault technology for the Bitcoin market,'* correct?
WATTS:	*It does not have to do with Bitcoin.*
COUNSEL:	*Okay. [It] Has to do with Bitcoin wallets?*
WATTS:	*It is a wallet. It is a Bitcoin wallet, yes.*

We already know that the ATO wasn't convinced by the legitimacy of the BitMessages or emails Wright had offered to back up his story, but verification was provided during the *Kleiman v Wright* case from a very reliable source: BitMessage creator Jonathan Warren. Warren stated that the version of BitMessage shown in Wright's screenshots hadn't been released by the date the messages had purportedly been sent and that they must, therefore, be fake. Wright's defence team tried to argue that someone could have hacked into Warren's machine and released BitMessage early on the dark web, which was how Wright and Kleiman got hold of a pre-release, a theory which is just as implausible as Wright's plethora of other hacking claims.

If we go with the much more likely scenario that the BitMessages were faked, we get a glimpse of the scale of the fraud that Wright is alleged to have perpetrated on the ATO; pages and pages of messages were recovered from Wright's systems featuring conversations between several parties covering a variety of topics, including Wright and Dave Kleiman discussing bitcoins coming out of the 1933p Bitcoin address, the 2012 purchases of the British companies and the funds held by the pair in Liberty Reserve, as well as conversations between Wright and Mark Ferrier over the Siemens and Al Baraka software, discussions over account management with people from High Secured and much more. Each of these elements of the story has been proven to be fictitious, and yet hundreds of BitMessages pertaining to those deals were presented to back up Wright's version of events, but which are not supported by any other facts. This, when considered alongside the fact that multiple forensics experts across three trials, the ATO and the creator of BitMessage himself all denounced the messages as forgeries, paints the picture of someone digging themselves into such a deep hole that they are forced to go to incredible lengths to try and get themselves out, only to end up even deeper. Assuming, as we surely must, that the BitMessages are indeed fake, as are the hundreds of other documents and correspondence we are yet to come across, it's no surprise that COPA barrister Jonathan Hough accused Wright of forging documents on an 'industrial scale' during his opening remarks in the *COPA v Wright* trial, a trial which saw Wright break records with his level of forgery.

The Deed of Loan was a key piece of evidence in Ira Kleiman's argument against Wright during the *Kleiman v Wright* case, with his legal team using it as proof that, as Wright had been preaching up until the filing of the lawsuit in 2018, he and Dave Kleiman had been involved in Bitcoin together from an early stage. Wright, having used the deed as evidence of a partnership for the ATO, was forced to disavow it for the case, denying that he had taken the full 650,000 bitcoins supposedly set aside for him. Wright was quizzed over the document in his April 2019 deposition, where the subject of the handwritten note on the front page of the deed, 'As agreed, all wallets to be held in UK in trust until all regulatory issues solved and Group Company formed with Dave K and CSW', came up. Under questioning, Wright confirmed that the handwriting 'looks like mine' and the signature accompanying the text was also his. He added, however, that the note may have been totally unrelated to the contents of the document due to his propensity to scribble on any piece of paper he could find:

> ...*I have this habit of writing wherever the hell I feel like it, usually over documents people complain that I write on, because I write notes whenever I feel like writing notes, and saying that they are related.*

Somewhat conversely, despite confirming that the handwriting could be his, Wright then went on to dismiss the document as a fake:

> *And then you want me to talk about incomplete records that have been constructed in bits and chucked together from four different documents as if this is real evidence.*

Wright expanded on this four days later in a blog post:

> *The document is an altered compilation of four other documents (at least). Some parts are real, and others are not. It forms some of the so-called evidence and proof showing that I cannot be Satoshi. Effectively, what we have is a long-term campaign to ensure that I have lots of problems allowing the scammers to keep scamming.*

A year later, in a further deposition, Wright denied that the coins had ever been made available in the first place:

> COUNSEL: Dr. Wright, did there come a time when, pursuant to a deed of loan, 650,000 Bitcoin were transferred to Design By Human to be held in trust for you?
>
> WRIGHT: You mean the document that is not signed by my signature? No.
>
> COUNSEL: I just asked you a question. I did not talk about the document.
>
> WRIGHT: No.
>
> COUNSEL: Dr. Wright, did the 650,000 Bitcoin come from a Seychelles trust?
>
> WRIGHT: No.

In the eighteen months between this deposition and the trial, Wright set about cementing his opinion that the Deed of Loan was false by hiring his own forensic analyst, F. Harley Norwitch, to find fault with the document. Sure enough, Norwitch found that it was, in Wright's words, 'not signed by my signature'. Norwitch's report was the sole crutch on which Wright's change of stance relied, a crutch that was whipped from under him when it was stricken from the record after Judge Beth Bloom, overseeing the *Kleiman v Wright* case, found Norwitch's methodology 'unreliable.' This left Wright scrambling for answers when, on day five of the trial, he was shown the video from April 2019 of him agreeing that the signature and handwriting were his:

> COUNSEL: Dr Wright, is that your handwriting on the side? I believe you just testified: 'No.'
>
> WRIGHT: No. At the time when I first looked at this document, I didn't look at it properly. I was angry. You got me angry and I didn't examine the document correctly. I will say now that 'no'.
>
> COUNSEL: So are you admitting that you previously testified it was your handwriting?

> WRIGHT: *I didn't look at the document properly, and I should have noted a number of irregularities with this document. I didn't. I'm sorry that I was angry at the time and I didn't look at the document properly. I admit that.*

It bears repeating that this handwritten note was on the version Wright sent the ATO as proof of his access to 650,000 bitcoins in 2014, with the audit report into C01N Pty specifically mentioning it. Wright's claim, then, is that he only realised the handwriting wasn't his following his *Kleiman v Wright* deposition in April 2019, five years after he used the document as evidence and had a forensic expert authenticate it. Wright had also claimed in a 2019 blog post that, as a legal scholar, he had determined that the Deed of Loan should be considered hearsay and shouldn't, therefore, be used as evidence in the case against him. The fact that it was shows how his objections fared on that score.

Faced with the debunking of his attempts to support the Tulip Trust timeline through C01N, it was no surprise that Wright's appreciation of this line of questioning worsened as the *Kleiman v Wright* case progressed, particularly the clause that the 650,000 bitcoins were due to be paid back to Design by Human between 2016 and 2020. When asked in his April 2019 deposition whether he had paid the loan back, Wright replied that it was 'None of your God damn business' before airing his forgery theory for the first time. The Deed of Loan has never been forensically analysed in the way that hundreds of Wright's other documents have, but this isn't surprising given that Wright himself dismissed it as a forgery in 2019, so there has been no need. However, the fact that Wright first produced it in March 2014, just as the agency was ramping up its investigation into Wright's Seychelles trust claims, means that we can peg its creation to this period. Wright may have gone to great lengths to disavow its authenticity for the *Kleiman v Wright* case, but such was his faith in the document in 2014 that he used it as primary evidence in a Notice of Objection to the ATO's adverse ruling on C01N Pty, effectively doubling down on his belief in its legitimacy. What, then, changed his mind in the intervening years? The likelihood, once again, is that the Deed of Loan was useful for Wright's case against the ATO, so he went to great lengths to authenticate it, but when it was used against him in the *Kleiman v Wright* case, he was forced to do the opposite.

Craig Wright's creation and use of the Deed of Loan are typical of his activities in early 2014. As the ATO attested, it was supposed to be the legal mechanism underpinning the Tulip Trust, which allowed Wright to spend hundreds of thousands of bitcoins he didn't own on software, IP and other material that he never received, all with the aim of securing millions of dollars in tax relief and rebates. Blessed with hindsight, it is easy to see that the whole thing was created backwards; rather than Wright producing all the documents supporting the Tulip Trust at the outset of the ATO's investigation, including the Deed of Loan, he instead dribbled them out one by one over many months, usually when the prior one was found wanting.

Wright imbued the Deed of Loan with enormous importance during his battle with the ATO, but its obvious flaws killed the story he was using it to tell at birth. The fact that Wright was adamant about the deed's authenticity when he needed to prove his bitcoin haul to the ATO but disavowed it when he needed to prove that Dave Kleiman had no part in the Tulip Trust tells one everything they need to know about how genuine his claim is on this front. The Deed of Loan was like a cancer that infected everything it touched, including the W&K IP grab, the Professor Rees material, the MJF software, Dave Kleiman, Uyen Nguyen and virtually all the companies in the Hotwire group. It is not stretching the truth to suggest that Wright put the fate of some ten million dollars in the hands of a fake document describing a fake loan for a fake trust containing fake bitcoins using fake appointments with companies he didn't own.

Wright's need to explain key aspects of his dealings through the Deed of Loan was a sign that things were not going well. He seems to have heeded this warning because, by the time the document was winging its way to the ATO, he had already settled on a backup plan. Aware that his stories about owning, either through mining or purchasing, over a million bitcoins were hanging by a thread, Wright landed on what he believed was the perfect solution to explain where those bitcoins had originated: he had masterminded the entire system.

Chapter 19 – Call Me Satoshi

Craig Wright says that he never proclaimed himself to be Satoshi Nakamoto and that he was dragged kicking and screaming into the limelight. We have already explored why this is a falsehood, one perpetrated to try and elicit sympathy he does not deserve, and we can trace Wright's desire to be recognised as Bitcoin's creator right back to a very specific point in time. Part of the bundle of 'evidence' sent to *WIRED* and *Gizmodo* included an email sent from Wright to Andrew Sommer on 8 January 2014, referencing Wright's attempt to bring Arthur Sinodinos on board the Bitcoin bandwagon. In the email, Wright asked whether bringing 'our Japanese friend' out of retirement might aid their cause and signed off 'Craig (possibly...)'. In reply, Sommer advised Wright to 'keep Nakamoto-san's involvement in the background for now.' Wright's emails came from a known Satoshi Nakamoto email address, satoshi@vistomail.com, forging a supposedly indelible link between the pair. Wright used the same address twenty days later to email Uyen Nguyen, thanking her for 'being on board', presumably with reference to her non-existent acceptance of the role as director of W&K. Given that all the other evidence surrounding Nguyen's involvement in W&K is likewise fabricated, it is no surprise to know that both of these 'Satoshi' emails were found to be forgeries by the experts in the *COPA v Wright* and *Kleiman v Wright* cases; Wright's fingerprints were all over the communications, with various email addresses and Wright-related computer names featuring heavily in the metadata.

When the emails between Wright and Sommer were published by *WIRED* and *Gizmodo* in 2015, Ira Kleiman queried Wright about his supposed use of the Vistomail address, given that Wright had told him that only Dave Kleiman had access to the Vistomail account. Wright claimed, predictably, that it was 'not me using it', although he did not elaborate on this latest claim of infiltration of his systems. He also blamed Uyen Nguyen for spoofing the emails between the pair, an allegation he reiterated in the *COPA v Wright* trial without any evidence and without offering any insight into her motive.

On 11 February 2014, the day before the *Business Insider* piece on Hotwire was published, Wright sent an email to Louis Kleiman, the father of Dave Kleiman, to inform him that 'Your son Dave and I are two of the three key people behind Bitcoin', a technology that would, he added, 'revolutionise the world'. Wright advised Louis, to whom he had never spoken, to search Dave's computers for a wallet.dat file but didn't reveal what it contained, simply saying that he wanted to help the Kleimans 'recover what Dave owned'. This email represents a crossing of the Rubicon for Wright; it is the earliest known occasion where we can say, with reliable evidence, that he told someone he was involved in the creation of Bitcoin.

When it comes to the third member of the team Wright referenced, we already know that in August 2018, Wright posted on WeChat that the Satoshi team was himself, Dave Kleiman and Professor Rees. Shortly after this, Wright said in response to an information demand in the *Kleiman v Wright* case that the third individual 'helped me in the very early stages of my research, well before the release of the Bitcoin protocol'. This, again, points to Professor Rees, but Wright then threw in a curveball by adding that he couldn't reveal the name on the grounds of U.S. national security. This eliminated Professor Rees from the equation but brought Gareth Williams into the picture, despite the fact that he was not known to have worked for the U.S. government. Nevertheless, Wright was told by Judge Reinhart that he could and should name the individual, whereupon Wright confirmed that it was Williams. This, though, was problematic, given that Wright had said in his first deposition for the case a year previously that the second member in question might still be alive, which Williams most certainly was not. This was picked up by Jonathan Hough during the *COPA v Wright* trial:

> COUNSEL: That couldn't possibly have been a reference to Gareth Williams, as you later said, could it?
>
> WRIGHT: No, but I was being difficult at the time, so I was trying to waffle as much as possible.

Wright was then given the chance to clear his story up:

COUNSEL: So, who was the person who might be a member of the U.S. government, still alive in 2019 and was at all relevant to this story?

WRIGHT: My uncle, for a start, but other people as well.

COUNSEL: Your uncle might be a member of the U.S. government, for all you knew, and [in 2019] you didn't know if he was alive or not?

WRIGHT: When I said that, I actually didn't because I hadn't spoken to him in a while, but that's me being difficult and silly and pedantic.

This doesn't stand up either, however, as Wright stated in a deposition for the *Kleiman v Wright* case that Don Lynam had been the *second* player in the drama, taking the place of Dave Kleiman, who, as Wright's story for that case demanded, needed to be absent from the trio. The whole thing was now irreparably confused and called into question Wright's claim, made during the *COPA v Wright* trial, that he had reached out to Louis Kleiman because he wanted to make Louis 'proud of his son'. Given that Wright had sworn under oath just over two years earlier that Dave Kleiman had played no part in Bitcoin's creation, Wright had either lied to his deponent or Louis Kleiman, or both. If Wright really were Satoshi, either on his own or as part of a team, naming the other team members would have been a straightforward process, and yet we are faced with the same issue as with his rationale behind the Satoshi name itself: it changes like a chameleon to suit its surroundings.

When it comes to the construction and sending of the Louis Kleiman email, things are just as convoluted. In his April 2019 deposition for the *Kleiman v Wright* case, Wright was asked about it:

COUNSEL: And it says: "Hello Louis, your son Dave and I are two of the three key people behind Bitcoin." Did you write that?

WRIGHT: I typed that.

A year later, however, Wright had changed his mind:

COUNSEL: Do you see where it says "Hello Louis, your son Dave and I are two of the three key people behind Bitcoin"?

WRIGHT:	Yes, I see that.
COUNSEL:	Did you type that?
WRIGHT:	No, I did not.

Wright claimed that he had tasked Uyen Nguyen and his then Executive Assistant, Angela Demitrio, to reach out to Louis Kleiman, and the wording was their idea. When asked why his story had changed, Wright's explanation was beyond unconvincing:

My recollection was completely correct of the first deposition. You asked me, did I type that sentence? That is a question literally meaning, 'have I ever typed that sentence.' In a response to my lawyers where I said in the e-mail sentence…I typed that sentence. So, the correct answer to "did you type that sentence?" is Yes, because "did you type this" is not the e-mail, it is a sentence. You did not say "did you type or did you create or did you produce that e-mail?"

Wright eventually extricated himself from this semantic maze by denying any involvement with the email at all, saying he didn't send it but that 'other people who worked for me may have', adding that he 'did not review what was sent'. He must have been more than a little annoyed, therefore, that the authors chose to praise Dave Kleiman's work on Bitcoin when, as Wright would later claim, he had no part in it. These typing technicalities, incidentally, were behind another of Wright's claims made in his April 2019 deposition that 'I did not tell anyone until this year that I was the creator of Bitcoin.'

Given Louis's advancing years, he handed the responsibility of communications over to Ira Kleiman, and he and Wright began emailing regularly, with Ira trying to get his head around what Wright was telling him concerning the plans that he and his year-dead brother had supposedly hatched back in 2011. These discussions, as we know, eventually led to Ira cottoning onto Wright's scheme and suing him four years later. Wright's email to Louis Kleiman was, in fact, the second he had sent that day concerning Dave Kleiman, having already emailed Dave's long-time associates Patrick Paige and Carter Conrad about their former colleague. In the email to Paige and Conrad, however, Wright was less candid about his Satoshi claim:

> *Dave and I had a project in the US. He ran it there. We kept what we did secret. The company he ran there mined Bitcoin. I do not believe there has been anything of this in the estate, but I also know his father is not IT literate. I would ask that if you know of any of his computers, that you help ensure that any wallet.dat files he has are saved.*

Paige told *Gizmodo* in 2015 that Wright eventually confided to him that Kleiman had created Bitcoin, only to change his mind and say that the two of them had been part of a group. When faced with this story in his March 2020 deposition for the *Kleiman v Wright* case, Wright said that Paige had heard something and misquoted it, blaming leading questions for Paige's initial assertion over Dave Kleiman's role. Paige also said that Kleiman had only mentioned anything resembling Bitcoin once during their entire association and that he couldn't be sure of the date. In neither of these emails did Wright state that the information he was passing across was privileged in any way or was to be kept confidential, despite having supposedly just let slip a six-year secret.

The reason Wright chose to 'break cover' in February 2014 is almost certainly connected to the ATO's investigation into his companies, a rationale that was put to him during the *COPA v Wright* trial; Wright responded by explaining that it took him ten months to track Louis down following Dave's April 2013 death. It must have been a complete coincidence, then, that Wright managed to get hold of Louis's contact details at the very moment he needed corroboration over his Bitcoin mining story, given that his email to Louis came just five days after the ATO first made Wright aware that it was looking into the affairs of W&K. Having already told the ATO and the Supreme Court of New South Wales that Dave Kleiman was instrumental in his early work when trying to secure his tax rebates, Wright had inadvertently presented himself with an opportunity to back up his new story: if he could convince Dave's family and former associates that the pair of them had created Bitcoin, he could use their support in his battle against the ATO in place of his already debunked evidence. Of course, he may have been considering slipping on the Satoshi mask before the ATO started turning the screw in early 2014, at which point it would have been clear to him that the agency wasn't buying his early mining claim. Having seen the evidence he had so far supplied failing miserably, it is likely that Wright landed on the Satoshi cosplay and sought the Kleimans' buy-in as the final throw of the dice to explain his bitcoin haul. However, this gamble backfired spectacularly, and, in a quirk of timing, exactly ten years after launching his Satoshi claim in this manner, Wright was busy precipitating its endgame: the tenth anniversary of Wright's email to Louis Kleiman came in the middle of a seven-day spell in the witness box for the *COPA v Wright* trial, where Wright lied to the Court 'extensively and repeatedly' over his Satoshi claim, according to the presiding judge, Justice Mellor. A decade after formulating it, Wright's performance during this trial not so much brought the curtain down on his Satoshi fraud as pulled it down and set fire to it.

We will likely never know if Craig Wright contacted anyone other than Paige, Conrad and Louis Kleiman in February 2014 as part of his campaign of external recognition, but just a week later, he dropped the following hint to the ATO during an interview:

I did my best to try and hide the fact that I've been running bitcoin since 2009 but...by the end of this I think half the world is going to bloody know.

If Wright had meant mining Bitcoin as opposed to running it, he would have said so, as he did just seconds after this comment, and so it is clear that he was trying to imbue his activities with an elevated importance. Not that it mattered: in March 2020, Wright dismissed the ATO transcript as inauthentic, for obvious reasons.

Given that Wright's story switched from the mining and buying of bitcoins to being the creator of the entire protocol at this time, it's clear that he came up with the idea of pretending to be Satoshi Nakamoto between late 2013 and early 2014. How long he believed he was going to have to keep up his Satoshi façade when he sent that email to Louis Kleiman is unknown, and perhaps Wright didn't even know himself. His behaviour before and since this pivotal moment suggests that he is very much a short-term planner, doing and saying whatever is needed at the time to extricate himself from a difficult position without a thought for the wider context or his own legitimacy. We can be fairly sure, therefore, that Wright never expected his Satoshi gambit to extend beyond the ATO's investigation into his companies and the small group of people he told in mid-February 2014. In this respect, he is right when he says that he never wanted to be outed as Satoshi, but not for the reasons he states. If Wright was expecting to derive an instant benefit from donning the Satoshi mask, he didn't receive it; the discussions with Patrick Paige and Carter Conrad led nowhere, and it took

Ira Kleiman just a few weeks to become sceptical of what Wright was telling him. Equally, Wright's 'admission' to the ATO in February 2014 did nothing to halt its investigations of Hotwire and associated companies, so it can hardly be considered a success on that front.

As Australia said goodbye to the winter of 2014 and welcomed spring, Wright's mood would not have matched the weather. Hotwire had gone bankrupt thanks to that withheld GST rebate, and the ATO was now turning the screw on the companies within its stable, demanding more evidence of Wright's bitcoin holdings and alleged inter-company dealings. As we know, October 2014 saw Wright take things to the next stage by creating and backdating the Tulip Trust as part of his desperate ploy to explain where his bitcoins came from, but his avenues for escape were rapidly disappearing. This period also saw Wright ratchet up his claims about building supercomputers, which themselves formed part of his tax rebate scheme. A 31 October blog post saw Wright proclaim that two of them, Tulip (which Wright sometimes referred to, unhelpfully, as Tulip Trading) and C01N, had been listed in the Top 500 most powerful computers in the world, and Wright added that he hoped to have 'the second fastest supercomputer in Australia' when he had finished his tinkering. However, the ATO would eventually conclude that these supercomputers didn't exist, and Wright suffered the ignominy of having them removed from the Top 500 list when evidence supporting the ATO's assertions came to light.

As 2014 drew to a close, Wright cast his net further afield for support, attempting to leverage the highest Bitcoin authority in the world – The Bitcoin Foundation – to bolster his connection to the cryptocurrency. Wright, a former paid-up member of the Foundation, emailed the recruitment address on 21 November, introducing himself through the LinkedIn profile he never looked at and asking for an unspecified collaboration:

> I do not want to be paid. I have not been since I left normal employment in late 2008 and do not see it now. I have a team already dedicated to Bitcoin. No begging. I will talk soon.

The foundation was in the throes of a civil war at the time of Wright's approach following the appointment to the board of Brock Pierce, a controversial figure beset by allegations dating from 2000 that he had pressured minors into sex at a company he founded. Gavin Andresen was still with the Foundation following his promotion to Director that May, and, fittingly, it was he who received Wright's missive. Given that Wright had singularly failed to mention that he was the reason for the Foundation's very existence, the Californian understandably ignored the email, thinking that Wright was just a regular Bitcoin supporter submitting his resumé at a time when the Foundation had no vacancies. Wright was faced with another dead end, with the rejection raising the frankly absurd notion that the man who created Bitcoin was refused the opportunity to work with the foundation built to serve its interests. Then again, Charlie Chaplin supposedly finished third in a Charlie Chaplin lookalike contest, so anything is possible.

With his plans for Hotwire down the pan, the Bitcoin Foundation ignoring his entreaties and the ATO closing in on all fronts, Craig Wright ended 2014 in a desperate situation: his companies were facing massive financial penalties and probable closure, while criminal charges were not off the table if the ATO could prove that it was he who had been personally behind the plethora of forgeries. The pressure was mounting, and Wright was beginning to realise that his efforts alone would not be enough to save him. There was one last hope, however: if he could come to a settlement with the ATO, he might be able to at least prevent himself from ending up in a Sydney prison. For that, however, he needed money. Lots of money. With all his companies under audit, with back taxes and fines almost inevitable and possible criminal action against him looming, Wright was not an attractive proposition to an outside investor. He needed a miracle: a rich benefactor who would swallow his Satoshi story and see enough potential in it to erect a wall of money so thick that it might stop the bulldozer heading inexorably toward him. It was a seemingly impossible task, and yet, somehow, in 2015, Wright succeeded to the most extraordinary degree imaginable.

Satoshi was going global.

Acknowledgements

Mark and Arthur would like to express our deepest gratitude to everyone who generously contributed their time, insight, and expertise to help us bring this book to life. Some of these individuals are referenced throughout, while others have chosen to remain anonymous. To all of you – named and unnamed – thank you for your support, your sharp eyes and your dedication to truth and transparency.

This book would not exist without you.

References

Given the nature of the source material, providing a traditionally presented list of references would have resulted in over thirty printed pages consisting of highly impractical and often long-winded web links.

As a result, this web link will take the visitor to the full list of references online, including tweets, blog posts and other internet-specific sources: www.drbitcoinpod.com/vol1-references.

www.ingramcontent.com/pod-product-compliance
Lightning Source LLC
Chambersburg PA
CBHW050327010526
44119CB00050B/706